Praise for
Fight the Good Fight

"Western civilization is at its best when reason and faith are recognized as informing and shaping the other. After all, that unique integration gave rise to the university, provided the roots of the modern sciences, and helped foster limited government constitutionalism, modern economics, and the ideal of ordered liberty. In this book, Jay W. Richards and James Robison show us why the reason-faith integration matters even more for America in our own time."

—**Samuel Gregg**, Ph.D., Distinguished Fellow in Political Economy, American Institute for Economic Research

"A mile wide and an inch deep describes writings that cover a broad span of topics, insufficient to meaningfully inform about any of them. *Fight the Good Fight* is more like a mile wide and a mile deep, but it delivers its truth in a *Reader's Digest* (or CliffsNotes) style of genius that leaves the reader extremely well-informed on the critically important issues of the day."

—**Buddy Pilgrim**, founder, Integrity Leadership, and former president, Pilgrim's Pride Corp.

"There is no better fight than the one for our souls and the soul of our country. So many naysayers claim the culture wars are over and we have lost. Thank goodness Jay Richards and James Robison know better. The fight isn't over until the end of time, and we all have our own part to play until we are called home."

—**Austin Ruse**, president, C-FAM, and author of *Under Siege: No Finer Time to be a Faithful Catholic*

Fight the Good Fight

FIGHT THE GOOD FIGHT

HOW AN ALLIANCE OF
FAITH AND REASON CAN WIN
THE CULTURE WAR

JAY W. RICHARDS and JAMES ROBISON

Regnery Publishing
WASHINGTON, D.C.

Cataloging-in-Publication data on file with the Library of Congress.

ISBN: 978-1-68451-552-3
eISBN: 978-1-68451-578-3

Library of Congress Control Number: 2023943276

Published in the United States by
Regnery Publishing
Washington, D.C.
www.Regnery.com

Manufactured in the United States of America

10 9 8 7 6 5 4 3 2

Books are available in quantity for promotional or premium use. For information on discounts and terms, please visit our website: www.Regnery.com

To Ginny and Betty

CONTENTS

CONTENTS

Open War . . . Whether You Would Risk It or Not

Our country is in serious trouble, and not just from enemies abroad. Leaders in our government, the media, the academy, and many corporations have trashed the American project of ordered liberty. Instead, in the name of "equity," "sustainable development," "public health," "diversity," and "inclusion," these powerful groups attack our history, weaponize ethnic resentments, and alienate children from their parents (and even their own bodies) while denying our God-given rights, reason, and reality itself.

What if we'd told you ten years ago that most states and the federal government would soon close schools, churches, and private businesses and force people to stay in their homes for months during a public health crisis—with no evidence that this would do any good? Would you have believed it? Would you have believed the same government would collude with tech companies to silence and cancel anyone—even experts from Harvard, Yale, and Stanford—who criticized the lockdowns?

Would you have believed that our government would try to squelch any discussion of the fact that the health crisis was most likely coming from a lab in Communist China? Or that it had helped fund the research in that same lab?

Would you have believed that parents around the country would take their young kids to pornographic drag shows? That teachers would teach young kids they might have been born in the wrong body and tempt them to explore dangerous "gender transition" drugs and surgery behind their parents' backs? Or that the U.S. Department of Justice would target parents who complained about any of this at school board meetings as "domestic terrorists"?

Would you have believed that rioters would rampage in a dozen U.S. cities, unpunished, night after night, but citizens who resisted them would be charged with murder? That nonviolent protestors who questioned a fishy presidential election would be treated like terrorists? That the FBI would send two dozen armed SWAT officers to knock down the door and arrest a father because he pushed a man at a pro-life protest—a man who was attacking his young son?[1]

Would you have believed that our nation's law enforcement and intelligence agencies would become so partisan that they would not only defy a sitting president but cooperate in efforts to remove him from office by falsifying documents and lying under oath? Or that media platforms would delete that president's account during a contested election?

Would you have believed the federal government would sit on its collective hands while TikTok—a highly addictive social media platform controlled by the Chinese military—exposed tens of millions of our kids to self-harm, porn, and hatred of their country?

An Elite Betrayal

The people behind all these outrages have rejected America's founding creed for something so alien that it's hard to name. These "elites"—referring to their status rather than competence—have kicked aside our Constitution, reason, and common sense as obstacles to their power. They seek to erase our history, to start from scratch at "Year Zero," as revolutionaries from eighteenth-century France to twentieth-century Cambodia tried to do.

To expand their power, these same people have demonized our historical figures. We shouldn't think of these figures as pioneers, freedom fighters, and profound thinkers, they insist. We should denounce them as slaveowners and racists, religious bigots, or selfish profiteers.

As these dark forces advance, the sources of light—those who love God, family, enterprise, reason, and honest public debate—retreat. All sorts of wedding vendors are driven out of business for declining to participate in same-sex weddings. With the passage of the so-called "Respect for Marriage Act," our federal government now treats defenders of natural (man/woman) marriage as bigots. Already, it's easy to be censored, fired, or "cancelled" for refusing to use fake pronouns or otherwise failing to obey the latest dictates of sexual radicals. Even atheist evolutionary biologists are not safe from the woke mobs.

Families with a married father and mother could soon be the exception rather than the rule.[2] Not only has our country officially kicked marriage to the curb, but it's now dissolving the legal difference between males and females. Male college athletes like "Lia" Thomas compete against female athletes. Doctors sterilize children and call it "gender-affirming care." A Vermont school decides to drop the words "boy" and "girl" and replace them with "person who produces sperm" and "person who produces eggs."[3] All this in the name of gender equity!

And then there are the fiscal troubles. The federal government is now approaching a trillion dollars a year just on interest payments for its mounting debt. If it keeps spending heaps more than it takes in, the debt alone will drown us.[4] Buried in hundreds of trillions of dollars of debt, with a trillion or more added every year, Washington would have to print huge amounts of money or default on its loans. Either way, we would witness a tsunami that no living American has ever experienced if we don't get off the beach and onto much higher ground.

And don't even get us started on the Federal Reserve's money-concocting efforts, which have given us immense inflation in the last few years. The Fed was created to smooth out the booms and busts of business cycles, but in recent years, it's made our fiscal problems worse. In 2021 and 2022 alone, it printed more than 80 percent of all the dollars that existed at the time![5]

The fact that Americans are having ever fewer children makes the debt crisis even more dire. Our population is getting top-heavy, with far too few workers to support ever more retirees.[6] If this continues, Social Security and Medicare entitlements alone will bankrupt us. Most advanced societies, including the United Kingdom, Italy, Spain, and Japan, are in the same, if not a worse, dilemma.

When we published our book *Indivisible* in 2012, we were worried about the rise of the secular left and the prospects for the future if it gained more power. We were also concerned about Christians defending left-wing policies amid calls for Republicans to dump social conservatives. In 2010, Indiana Governor Mitch Daniels proposed a "truce on the social issues" to focus on budget deficits. But a truce requires a cease-fire on both sides of the political aisle. In the thick of a culture war, a one-sided "truce" is surrender.

We thought about updating that book for 2024, but realized we now live in a different world that needs a different book. For one thing, social issues are now the bull's-eye of politics—to the benefit of the right—because the Democratic Party has decided to do the bidding of radical gender ideologues. These people deny the reality of male and female. They replace it with nonsense: "gender identity" and "sex assigned at birth." They insist that kids can be born in the wrong body and need sterilizing drugs and surgery to fix the "problem." Most people know this is crazy and evil. Nevertheless, it's everywhere. Next up: pedophilia, or what activists call "Sexual Attachment to Children."[7] Pedophiles have been rebranded as "Minor Attracted Persons."

Here's the good news: The army forming against this madness is at least as broad as the coalition that beat Soviet Communism during the Cold War. That earlier alliance of libertarians, anti-communists, and social conservatives made up the GOP electoral base. The core of this new army is serious people of faith and social conservatives—those who (on average) get married, have kids, attend worship services at least once a week, and don't conform to the madness around them. Around that core are many blue-collar Americans who rallied to Donald Trump and many ethnic minorities who notice the gap between their religious faith and the Democratic Party platform. It extends to GOP voters who thought that "moderating" on abortion or same-sex marriage would make that "icky sex stuff" go away, and now see that they gave up precious territory and gained nothing in return. It also includes some liberals who are rethinking their former views.

You can also define this army by what it opposes. Draw a circle around conservative Catholics, evangelicals, and Jews who will resist the leftist tide of our culture even if it costs them. Include those who oppose "wokeness" in schools, media, politics, and corporations, and who will risk their jobs and reputations to fight Critical Race Theory and gender ideology. Finally, include everyone who resisted the lockdown fever in 2020 and never wants to see anything like that happen again.

These people form the emerging "alliance of faith and reason."

Woke America

Of course, to defeat a foe, we must first identify it. What do we call the enemy of faith and reason? It showed its face during the COVID-19 lockdowns and so-called Black Lives Matter riots—which left a huge spike in black homicides in their wake.[8] Many old-school liberals who defend reason and freedom of speech found they'd been displaced by fanatics who care not a whit for truth or honest debate. Most refer to the fanatics' view as "woke" ideology—and it ain't pretty.

What is wokeness? We like philosopher Ed Feser's compact definition: "a paranoid delusional hyper-egalitarian mindset that tends to see oppression and injustice where they do not exist or greatly to exaggerate them where they do."[9] The "Great Awokening" is a toxic witch's brew that mixes the worst ideas of the last century:[10]

- Take a half cup of cultural Marxism. Everything is about conflict between some identity group and its oppressors—not just rich vs. poor, owners vs. workers, but men vs. women, black vs. white, gay vs. straight, parent vs. child, "cis" vs. "trans," and so on, forever and ever.

- Whisk in a fistful of postmodern contempt for reason and truth. Reason in this view doesn't help us find the truth; it's just a tool to hide our lust for power. This relativism makes wokeness unstable. That's why it changes constantly.

- Add another half cup of an impulse so totalitarian that its disciples want to control our words—even our pronouns—and our thoughts. Their solution? Something called "equity," which seeks to force the same social and economic outcomes on all of us.

• Now stir briskly and heat the concoction to a raging boil.

That's wokeness.

There are cauldrons of the brew everywhere you look. It's ladled out to the masses in schools, libraries, on social media, in federal agencies, corporate branding agencies and board rooms, Disney movies, children's medicine—even many churches. It induces a zombie-like state in those who drink it and paralyzes those who breathe its fumes. It unites government agencies, private corporations, and international groups from the World Economic Forum to the United Nations.

The wokocracy is far worse than big government. It's a giant conspiratorial blob of governments, nonprofits, and corporations—empowered by technology that the despots of the last century could scarcely have imagined.

The wokocracy is coming for our country, our humanity, and for sex itself. You read that right. For fifty years, the fight against the sexual revolution—a key plank of the leftist agenda—fell mostly to "church ladies" who warned of the evil fruits that would grow if it were left unchecked.[11] Those rotten fruits are now poisoning our children's minds and bodies.

People from all walks of life who are committed to truth—to reality—are wondering how we got here. How did elites across the globe come to believe that chopping off kids' healthy sex organs is good health care? And that only bigots could oppose this quackery? Such ideas are outrageous enough to provoke many "liberals" to rethink their politics, their friends, even their worldview. In 2023, physician Kevin Bass spoke for this group on Twitter. "I am a liberal atheist (voted for Biden)," he wrote, "but the woke Left has me so disturbed about the future of children in this country that I think I am going to start taking my children to Church to help inoculate them against this."[12]

New Cracks on the Right

The looniness on the left helped summon this new alliance. But it's threatened by certain new rifts on the right. We're not talking about the rifts that have opened much needed space. For instance, we *should* squint our eyes at Big Tech's control of the public square, rampant crony capitalism, and the Chinese regime. We're encouraged by elements of National Conservatism, which resists the godless globalists at the United Nations and European Union. Many of the "National Conservatives" are correct: For far too long, the right has not matched the left in vigor. When the left is in power, they pull every lever they can get their hands on to force our courts, agencies, schools, and culture in their direction. When the right wins an election, they may talk tough, but they mostly stand athwart the leftward flood yelling, "Not so fast!" while taking back no ground at all.

Too many self-styled "conservatives" are squeamish about using their legal power. Republican governors wither at the first threat from woke corporations. Christian "influencers" worry about talk of a "culture war." They preach "norms," "civility," and "faithful presence." Two such influencers—Russell Moore, now the editor of *Christianity Today*, and David French—have formed the "After Party." Their tagline is "Towards a Better Christian Politics." What they offer, though, is a smug, we're-better-than-those-Trumpsters surrender as the left seizes new territory.

Our advice is just the opposite. "Open war is upon you," Aragorn advised Théoden in *The Lord of the Rings*, "whether you would risk it or not." We refer, of course, to culture war—a war of ideas, policies, laws, and institutions. For decades, the secular left has been the aggressor. Conservatives and people of faith have been on defense. We've tried to fight the leftist advance on one front while having to debate those in our own ranks who are too fractious, squeamish, or unfocused to press for victory.

Many on the right are fed up with this failure. They know what time it is. They want tough talk backed up by tough action. They want to play offense, not just defense. One shining example: Ron DeSantis legally dissolving Disney's corporate welfare perks after the company opposed Florida's efforts to limit gender propaganda in elementary schools.[13]

More of this, please.

We're not saying we should abandon our principles and do whatever it takes to win. Some on the right are calling for bad policies—from price controls and high tariffs to new welfare programs and an embrace of corrupt labor unions—that ape the left. Some want to retire the word "conservative" and replace it with something else. Others even reject the American Experiment and its legacy of ordered liberty. They dismiss it as misguided "liberalism," see it as doomed to failure, and seek something older and sterner to fight the left.

For the religious, that might be a return to a legally established and intolerant religion. For the irreligious, it might be a return to the "strong gods" and strong men of the pagan, pre-Christian Norse—peppered with quotes from German philosophers like Schopenhauer and Nietzsche.[14] The lust for power for power's sake appeals to young men who find themselves adrift in a culture that despises them. But might does not make right as soon as our people are in charge.

As in *The Lord of the Rings*, in fighting the darkness, we must resist the desire to use it for our own purposes. We must fight, yes. But we must fight the *good* fight. This is a fight not just against bad policies and bad ideas, but against the principalities and powers in the world and in our hearts.

We can't fight the good fight unless we commit ourselves to truth, light, and life. And we can't win if we fragment into tiny warring camps with evangelical "Christian nationalists" in the valley, Catholic integralists in the mountains, and anti-woke liberals tweeting in the clouds. This is what the left wants us to do. Instead, we must build an alliance big and strong enough to resist—and defeat—the global wokocracy.

Hope Remains

Despite the looming darkness, we, and our country, are still here. Yes, the time is short. The stakes are high. The enemies are legion. But this litany of doom hasn't made us gloomy. We recite it here merely to wake you up.

Remember: In the end, reality eats bad ideas for lunch. The ACLU can't reform biology. The public can't rewrite natural law at the ballot box. Solar physics doesn't care if the UN tries to abolish it. And at the heart of reality lies not mere biology, politics, physics, or an erratic pagan god. It is the Logos—the transcendent God of reason, truth, and love, who seeks to forgive and to redeem the penitent sinner.

God is not finished with America. But if we're going to get off our road to ruin, we must do more than slow down and conserve whatever good remains. We must *repent*. That means we need to make a hard, 180-degree turn—and fast.

If we pray, think straight, persuade other lovers of truth to join us, and fight together—wise as serpents and innocent as doves—then there's still hope.

Part I

The Basics

CHAPTER 1

Come, Let Us Reason Together

N ow more than ever, believers need to engage in politics with all the fervor and wisdom we can muster. That doesn't mean we should get riled up for a few months, endorse the right policies, elect politicians who claim to support them, and then return to business as usual. To see our culture restored, we must do far more. We must understand and debunk bad ideas. We must persuade our fellow Americans of the truths we lay out in the following pages. We must live our own lives with integrity. We must build lasting alliances among Christians, Jews, and others who believe in God, and among friends of truth and freedom. We must build our own vibrant institutions that, in turn, shape the culture.

In the pages that follow, we want to help with part of the task: to hack out the weeds and clear the fogs in our thinking that have kept us from succeeding in the past, to explain clearly the issues and policies at stake, to call conservatives to work together, to build an alliance with lovers of truth and reason who don't share our faith, and to offer policy advice to get our country moving in the right direction.

We can't fix our problems if we don't first understand them.

A Party of Death

There has never been a "Christian" party in America. But let's not kid ourselves: There is now an overtly anti-Christian one. Sure, there are well-meaning Democrats on one side and waffling Republicans on the other, but the contrast between the two main parties is stark. Democrats are now captured by a strange alliance of religious skepticism and woke irrationality. Take the 2023 debate in state legislatures over ghoulish "gender transition" surgeries for minors: Almost every Republican who had a chance to restrict those procedures did so. In contrast, almost every single Democrat defended them zealously. And the few Democrats who voted for sanity were viciously attacked by activists in their own party.

"That They May Be One"

Unfortunately, this insanity isn't limited to a few activists. It dominates our culture. So how do we fight it? The first step is to unify the base of opposition. In terms of numbers, that is conservative people of faith—especially Christians. We include conservative and Orthodox Jews as well—there aren't many of them, but they punch above their weight.

Why has this base failed so far to reverse our culture's march to the gallows? One problem is our disunity—especially among Christians. For a thousand years, the Body of Christ was unified. In 1054, however, tensions between the Greek Eastern and Latin Western parts of the former Roman Empire led to a tragic split in Christendom that has never healed. To this day, there's a "Catholic" West and an "Orthodox" East.

Then, in 1517, Martin Luther sparked the Protestant Reformation in the West. For centuries after that, Protestants and Catholics spilled time, energy, and blood fighting each other—to say nothing of how Christians often treated Jews. There are now thousands of Christian denominations worldwide and still counting.[1] But we know the Lord wants us to discover the unity He prayed for on the night He was betrayed. Surely, we can agree that at this moment of great peril, we need to stand together.

With Christians divided, secular leftists have pushed us farther to the margins. What our grandparents saw as common sense—the existence of God, the right to life, the nature of marriage, the difference between boys and girls—is now denounced as bigotry. The moral consensus that sustained our country is gone.

Ironically, secularism's progress has brought believers together over issues such as abortion and marriage. In praying outside Planned Parenthood offices, orthodox Catholics have found they have more in common with faithful Lutherans than with liberal Catholics who think like secularists. While protesting drag queen story hour at the local library, Southern Baptists have joined forces with Pentecostals, whom they used to avoid. At crisis pregnancy centers, staunch Calvinists have learned they have a lot more in common with evangelical Methodists than with liberal Presbyterians.

Sadly, it has taken rabid secularism, abortion on demand, and an assault on the family and human sex itself for Christians to discover what we share. It's a unity based on the principle that "the enemy of my enemy is my friend."

We need to go beyond defensive alliances on public policy, however, and strive for a deeper and more lasting unity grounded in the core beliefs and moral principles we share. If we stand on these, we can partly fulfill Jesus's prayer for our unity, even though we're still divided by institutions and doctrines.

That's only step one. Bluntly, there are no longer enough conservative Catholics, evangelicals, and Jews to form a winning national alliance. We need to bring in many Americans of good will who share our sense that our civilization rests on the edge of a cliff.

Elections are won at the margins: The shift of relatively few votes in the middle can make the difference between victory and defeat. A unified voting bloc of conservative believers is not enough, by itself, to turn the tide. We need to build alliances with those who don't share our faith but prize reason and truth. The sheer insanity on the woke left is a mortal threat to our culture and well-being. It also gives believers a chance to show that, despite media slanders, we're on the side of reason and reality.

That's why, in the chapters that follow, we make arguments that draw on Scripture, the broad traditions that Christians share, and those we share with Jews. But we also make arguments based on natural reason and public evidence. We strive to be as honest as we can be with the facts, even if they gore beloved oxen and winning campaign slogans on the left or the right. We can't, and shouldn't, ignore the facts of history, biology, or economics. If we're going to turn the tide, we need to build an alliance of faith and reason. And to do that, we need to persuade our neighbors who share our concerns about the future but who don't share our faith to join us.

Let's Try Sanctity

Part of building that alliance will require common reasons and a common cause. But it also requires credibility. As believers, we need to deal with our own lack of holiness and virtue. We're concerned about the moral decay of our culture but have not done much to reverse the moral decay in the Church.

We don't mean that Christians should be "nice"—a notion the left has weaponized against us, and which these days is often code for "spineless." To restore our country, our public witness must reflect a growth in holiness, intellectual honesty, and courage.

The British statesman and Christian William Wilberforce linked public witness and personal holiness with two life causes: the abolition of slavery and the "reformation of manners"—that is, moral behavior. Those weren't unrelated interests. Wilberforce discerned the link between policy and personal conduct.

Our public witness is vital. But it's not enough to turn the tide.

Can Politics Change Culture?

The late Andrew Breitbart famously said that politics is downstream from culture. In other words, if we want to make long-term political change, we have to change the culture.

How do we do that? One popular Christian answer is to focus on things of the spirit. "Transformed people," Charles Colson often said, "transform culture." Pope John Paul II said that "if man allows himself to be prompted by God, if he walks together with Him, he is capable of changing the world."[2]

We agree. Our culture needs spiritual renewal. But is that the full story? Not by a long shot, according to Christian sociologist James Davison Hunter. In his book *To Change the World*, he says that idea "is almost wholly mistaken." He argues that even if half of the American population "converted to a deep Christian faith," we would still likely not make a dent in the culture. "Only indirectly," he writes, "do evangelism, politics, and social reform affect language, symbol, narrative, myth, and the institutions of formation that change the DNA of a civilization."[3]

Rather, the main drivers of cultures have always been elites—cultural gatekeepers—and their overlapping networks. Hunter's argument applies even to the way God has worked in history. Sure, God chooses "what is foolish in the world to shame the wise" and "what is weak in the world to shame the strong" (1 Corinthians 1:27). But rather than using a random Joe, God called Moses, who was raised in Pharaoh's household, to deliver His people from slavery in Egypt. Jesus had a ragtag band of apostles, but He also chose Paul—a Roman citizen with a strong grasp of Greek who was taught by the revered Jewish rabbi Gamaliel—to proclaim the Gospel to the Gentiles.

The Church fathers, Augustine, Thomas Aquinas, the founders of Protestantism, the American founders, and the abolitionists were all well-educated, well-connected leaders. While many people supported abolition, the game changers were men like William Wilberforce and his allies in the British Parliament.

Woke Elites

If we want to heal the culture, we can't ignore the role of elite networks. That's especially true now, when networks of woke, godless elites command our culture, even when they're out of step with the public. For instance, in 1973, most Americans thought most abortions should be illegal. As a result, most states had laws prohibiting most abortions. Yet in 1973, seven justices of the U.S. Supreme Court struck down those laws. Even now, with that fraudulent decision overturned, much of our country still has some of most permissive abortion laws in the world.

The average American is center-right, but almost all university faculty and administrators are left-wing. Most Americans believe in God, but almost all our government institutions—education, public museums, the National Science Foundation, etc.—are wedded to materialism. Even when a conservative lives in the White House, almost all career bureaucrats filling scores of agencies under him are committed leftists.

Here's the bitter truth. More than 329 million Americans might have history, reason, and revelation on their side, but the 100,000 with influence can set the cultural agenda. Of course, it's more complicated than that, since tens of millions of Americans absorb the beliefs of those elites and so join the 100,000 rather than the resistance. But that reinforces our point. If elite networks control the culture, then that's going to shape our politics—even if we have a republic rather than a dictatorship.

The Stream Moves in Two Directions

"Once, politics was about only a few things," eminent political scientist James Q. Wilson once observed, "today, it is about nearly everything."[4] Andrew Breitbart's dictum—that politics is downstream from culture—is right. But the stream moves in two directions: Culture is also downstream from politics. As a result, no serious effort to change culture can ignore politics.

This is especially true now because politics is one of the last places where we still have real influence. Even many conservative holdouts in business and the military have now gone woke. In contrast, the U.S. Congress, U.S. Supreme Court, and the federal judiciary, despite their problems, represent our views far more than any elite sphere insulated from voters.

What explains the difference? Political action. If believers had stayed on the sidelines since 1980, do you think the Supreme Court would have included Antonin Scalia, Clarence Thomas, Brett Kavanaugh, Amy Coney Barrett, and Samuel Alito? Would the roughly eight hundred federal judges be far more conservative, on average, than the faculty of Yale Law School? Not a chance. Without conservative victories and years of work from groups like the Federalist Society, the federal bench would be a carbon copy of that law faculty in New Haven.

We're not "politicizing the culture" and inflaming the culture war by calling believers to join the political fray. The left has already politicized everything. As *National Review*'s Jim Geraghty has said, "Everything is the culture war now."[5] The question is, are we going to get real about fighting back? Are we going to devise and follow our own offensive strategy so we're not always on defense? If so, then let's get serious not just about winning elections but also retaking lost territory when we do so. Otherwise, we're just dragging out our inevitable surrender.

What Good Is Liberty?

To craft a winning long-term strategy for political victory, we must think clearly about the leading issues of the day. Let's start with the classic American idea of freedom or liberty. Americans value freedom, but many have a hard time defining it. Ask a teenager who keeps breaking her curfew what freedom means. She'll say something like, "Not having to obey the rules" or "Getting to do whatever you want." If she thinks of a dictionary definition, she might say it is getting to choose between alternatives. If she can decide for herself what time she comes home, she's free. If her parents take her car away for a week if she doesn't get home by midnight, she's not free.

Now apply that to a whole country. If freedom means everyone does whatever he wants, then a country that prizes freedom will have anarchy—with chaos, violence, and debauchery. This would be intolerable and lead to tyranny—where the strongest and meanest person would prevail and then force everyone else to do what he wants.

This sense of the word "freedom" leads many on the "New Right" to avoid it. They associate the word with "Zombie Reaganites"[6] who seemed to prize freedom over justice, truth, reason, and order. This single-minded focus, say these critics, is one reason the right has lost so many culture battles.

This is an important debate to have. But the problem isn't freedom per se, but rather, a modern definition that contradicts what the word used to mean. Freedom does include choice, but even the staunchest libertarians say your freedom to swing your fist ends just short of your neighbor's nose. Something is still missing with this definition, though. It suggests that freedom and law are trade-offs. But in truth, for the American Founders and many classical thinkers, good laws give us more freedom, not less.

Ordered Liberty

The Founders had a much broader idea in mind, called ordered liberty. Katherine Lee Bates captures the idea in her great hymn "America the Beautiful": "Confirm thy soul in self-control/Thy liberty in law." When the Founders defended liberty, that's what they meant.

Liberty in this sense is the power to do what you know you ought to do, to follow your conscience, and not to be unjustly ruled by someone else. That's why, when an addict stops "using," we say he's "freeing" himself. The power of bad habits and base impulses keeps us from living as we know we should—just as other people giving in to their worst selves can lead them to violate our rights or even end our lives. So, laws, ideas, and institutions that empower people to be their best selves without oppressing them enhance freedom. Every good parent knows this.

This thicker view of freedom is what sets the American Revolution apart from its much bloodier and more radical French counterpart.

A few of the Founders, including Thomas Jefferson, saw the French Revolution of 1789 as continuing in the spirit of the Americans. John Adams, however, worried that the French experiment would end in grief—and he was right. While the French radicals toasted liberty, fraternity, and equality, they cut off the roots of those ideals because they were vehemently anti-Christian. At one point, they even dressed up a woman as the goddess "Reason" and placed her on the high altar at the Cathedral of Notre Dame in Paris.

Their view of liberty had more to do with freedom from restraint than with the ordered liberty championed by American patriots. So, it's no surprise that the French Revolution quickly descended into terror. The French started by beheading priests, royalty, and aristocrats, and ended by killing each other by the thousands. They even committed genocide in one region (the Vendée) that resisted those policies. Order was only restored by the military dictatorship of Napoleon Bonaparte in 1799.

In 1823, John Adams described the French Revolution as producing "all the calamities and desolations to the human race."[7] Our War of Independence had a radically different ending because it started with a better view of liberty.

Freedom for Excellence

The right rules allow us to enjoy a much richer freedom. They are the rules that allow us to become what we're supposed to become and to do what we're designed to do.

Years ago, I (Jay) was driving my wife and daughters to church and decided to use the longer route to get a lesson in. "Girls, what do you think eyes are for?" I asked.

"For seeing," they said.

"And what about ears?"

They replied, "For hearing."

"And what about a heart?"

"For pumping blood."

"And feet?"

"For walking."

I did this for a few minutes until I had exhausted their knowledge of anatomy. Then I asked, "Okay, now I want you to think really hard. What are *you* for?" The inside of the car fell silent. They thought it was a trick question and wouldn't venture a guess. I told them to think about it.

After church, our younger daughter, Ellie, said, "Daddy, I'm still thinking about that question, but I'm really stumped." With their interest piqued, I finally said, "Well, if you look at the beginning of the Catholic Catechism, it says that our purpose is to seek, know, and love God. And the very first question of the Westminster Confession, 'What is the chief end of man?' says, 'To glorify God and enjoy him forever.' So, we're supposed to love, seek, know, glorify, and enjoy God forever. That's what we're for."

A free society allows us to love, seek, and enjoy God. It frees us to fulfill our other God-given purposes as free beings made in His image—to love our families and other people and exercise the virtues we need to do that. It lets us be fruitful and multiply and exercise our dominion as God's stewards over His creation.

Jesus said that the greatest commandment is to love God, and the second is to love our neighbor as ourselves. Love that's coerced is not love. To fully obey Christ's commandments, we need freedom. That means not only freedom from unjust coercion but also from the degrading forces of sin and Satan.

CHAPTER 2

The Law Is Written on the Heart, Stone, and Parchment

Where do our laws come from? And how does the law work in a country without an established religion? These questions are pressing for two reasons. First, the courts have, for the most part, abandoned the moral tradition of the founding generation and spent decades sweeping any hints of Christianity from the public square. Both trends reject our constitutional system. And second, in reacting to the overreach of secularism, some conservative Christians now dismiss the American Experiment as a misguided "Enlightenment" project that was always doomed to failure.

We think both sides are wrong. Here's why.

In the last chapter, we said that we all enjoy more freedom in a society based on rules that allow us to become what we are meant to be, and we are all supposed to know, love, and glorify God. But since not everyone knows that his chief end is to love and glorify God and, therefore, to love others, many of our fellow citizens either reject the very concept of a divine Lawgiver or don't give Him much thought.

So how can our country hold together when even believers disagree on central issues? Without one established church as the foundation for our laws, won't we end up in chaos followed by a dictatorship or secular orthodoxy?

That's what some Catholic integralists and Protestant "theonomists" argue. They have a point. Every nation has some institution (not just a text) that sustains an official morality. If it's not a church, it will be something else.

This topic deserves a whole book, but we'll say just two things. First, countries with established churches aren't more faithful to God than others. Indeed, many—such as the United Kingdom with its Church of England—are far more secular than the United States. And when a church is too cozy with the state, it tends to be corrupt. Just look at the mostly empty Catholic and Lutheran churches in Germany. They receive most of their funding through taxes but support every cultural fad from abortion and same-sex marriage to gender ideology and climate hysteria.[1]

Even if it were a good idea to have an established church, the First Amendment prohibits it. And besides, the U.S. is too diverse for that. That would be true even if we focused just on conservative Christians or conservative evangelicals. Does anyone really want the federal government dictating how baptisms should be conducted? Or how God's sovereignty relates to human freedom? Or who can be ordained for ministry?

Fortunately, lacking an orthodoxy enforced by law doesn't mean we're doomed to chaos or arbitrary power. We can still draw on our broadly Christian history and culture, as well as the fact that everyone still has reason and so grasps moral truth even without revelation or a state religion. This might now sound controversial, but it's exactly what the Founders believed. And they were right.

The Laws of Nature and Nature's God

The Founders referred to these moral truths known by reason as "the natural law." That's why Thomas Jefferson appealed to the "laws of nature and nature's God" in the Declaration of Independence. He was talking about moral truths that everyone knows or ought to know. It's natural because it's built into the structure of things and fits our created nature. It's like the instruction manual for how we're supposed to live. Just as we can use our reason to discover physical laws, so too can we use it to discover natural (moral) laws.

This natural law is the basis for our rights and duties (more on those in a later chapter) and stands above even the law of the land. Indeed, it must if our laws are to have a foundation. As Hadley Arkes argues in his masterful book *Mere Natural Law*, we know many basic moral truths as certainly as we know what day it is. Everyone with basic reason knows that murder is wrong. We know parents should care for their children, and husbands should care for their wives. We know bravery is better than cowardice. We know people should not be punished for crimes they did not commit. We know it's wrong to torture children or animals.[2]

Our moral knowledge is reinforced by "witnesses," such as our conscience. We can look at the design of the world and our bodies. We see that children tend to prosper best with a mother and a father, that the male body fits with the female body, that sex outside of marriage causes problems, that gluttony leads to illness, and promiscuity to venereal disease.[3]

In these and thousands of other ways, we learn the basic contours of the natural law. We come to know certain moral truths, just as we know—once we've been taught—that two plus two equals four and that sex in mammals is binary.

Natural Law and Divine Law

In Romans 1, Paul says we can clearly see enough of God's "eternal power and divine nature" through creation to leave us "without excuse" when we violate His laws.[4] Later, Paul writes, "When Gentiles who have not the law [of Moses] do by nature what the law requires they . . . show that what the law requires is written on their hearts" (Romans 2:14–16). If Gentiles knew nothing of this natural law, God would be unfair to hold them accountable. As it is, though, He can hold them to account for their sins.[5]

But if we already know the natural law, why did God bother giving Moses the Ten Commandments? Why give us Scripture or a church? Paul answers these questions, too. He writes that although human beings

> knew God they did not honor him as God or give thanks to Him, but became futile in their thinking and their sense-less minds were darkened. Claiming to be wise, they became fools and exchanged the glory of the immortal God for images resembling mortal man or birds or animals or reptiles. (Romans 1:21–23)

In other words, creation transmits the truth that we can receive with our God-given reason. But we, in our rebellion against God, are often tuned to the wrong frequency. The heavens declare the glory of God always and everywhere (Psalm 19), but sin blurs our eyes, so some only see distant stars and empty space.

Because of sin, Paul says, we do things that are "unnatural"—men lie with men, women with women. Our sin causes us to wage war with our own bodies. We devise clever ways to carve out loopholes in the natural law. For example, rather than defending murder, extremists will try to define those they wish to kill as subhuman or as nonpersons. Few defenders of legal abortion claim murder is okay. Instead, they invoke "reproductive rights" or "choice" while claiming the child growing inside the woman's body is merely a "clump of cells." These word games betray their half-remembered sense of the natural law.

This is why we need God's special revelation. It not only allows us to know Him personally, but to see the natural law far more clearly than we might otherwise. What we know by nature, we see more clearly when it is declared to us, such as through the Ten Commandments written on tablets of stone.

The Founders were so certain about natural law that Thomas Jefferson claimed in the Declaration of Independence that its truths are

> self-evident: that all men are created equal, that they are endowed by their Creator with certain unalienable rights, that among these are life, liberty, and the pursuit of happiness.

Jefferson's words are true but incomplete. He could clearly see the natural law because he grew up in a Christian society that explained it in a thousand ways. Had he grown up on a desert island among pagans (or on Manhattan Island among post-Christians), he would have grasped far less.

So, the Church and special revelation serve to amplify and clarify these truths,[6] and vibrant religious faith reinforces them. Everyone knows these truths by reason, so basing our laws on them isn't "imposing religion" on people. It doesn't violate the Constitution or anyone's liberty.

The Founders wanted a country based on natural law and natural rights (which imply duties). The law would not create rights but rather respect the rights we already have. "The rights essential to happiness . . . are not annexed to us by parchment and seals," said John Dickinson of the Pennsylvania colony in 1776. "They are created in us by the decrees of Providence, which establish the laws of our nature."

The Rule of Law versus the Rule of Man

The Founders had a sober view of human sin—one of the few Christian doctrines that you can prove by reading the headlines. Because of sin, we need institutions that can enforce the rule of law. Otherwise, the strongest and most wicked will oppress and enslave the weak. The main reason Hitler wanted to close or corrupt the churches was that he thought the strong should dominate—even exterminate—the weak, and he knew the Church was an obstacle to that goal. He thought that Charles Darwin had taught us this was the true "law of nature."

When the Apostle Paul talks about the law written on our hearts, he also explains that the state's authority comes from God. He even refers to government as "the servant of God to execute his wrath on the wrongdoer" (Romans 13:1–6). Paul wrote this when Rome was an imperial dictatorship! Even bad government, it seems, is better than no government.

Peter gives the same advice, writing,

> Be subject for the Lord's sake to every human institution,
> whether it be to the emperor as supreme, or to governors
> as sent by him to punish those who do wrong and to praise
> those who do right. (1 Peter 2:13–14)

Does that mean Christians must always obey every dictate of government? No. Tyranny is not government and ought to be resisted.

Might doesn't make right. Short of revolution, we can resist immoral commands. Peter and the other apostles recognized this. When the Jewish authorities forbade them from preaching the Gospel, they replied, "We must obey God rather than men" (Acts 5:29).[7]

As a practical matter, though, societies must have some rule of law that reflects the natural law. Any society that has lasted for long has laws against murder and theft. Every society has rules for marriages, and versions of the Golden Rule can be found in every major religion.[8]

Every culture has a code of laws, written or unwritten. But the American Experiment stood out at its inception because the Founders based our laws on a document that appealed to a transcendent source—natural rights and nature's God—rather than to a person or group. All U.S. government officials and military personnel, as well as new citizens, pledge an oath not to a king or a tribe, but to the Constitution. As Thomas Paine wrote in *Common Sense,* "In America, THE LAW IS KING." Since most countries now have a constitution, it's hard to imagine how odd this was at the time—and given how activist judges revise our Constitution at will, it's nothing to take for granted.

Watching the Watchmen

The Founders saw the paradox that many earlier cultures had failed to grasp: Sin is both why government is needed and why it must be limited. They knew about the failed republics in ancient Greece and Rome, where the line between majority and mob rule was fragile. They had studied biblical and European history. "If men were angels," said James Madison,

> no government would be necessary. If angels were to govern men, neither external nor internal controls on government

would be necessary. In framing a government which is to be administered by men over men, the great difficulty lies in this: You must first enable the government to control the governed; and in the next place oblige it to control itself.[9]

The Founders understood, as Lord Acton would say a hundred years after the American founding, "Power tends to corrupt, and absolute power corrupts absolutely." They wanted to avoid the tyranny of both the one and the many, so they set up a "mixed regime"—a republic that balances the good and bad of different forms of government, from strict monarchy on one end to mob rule on the other. That's why there's a balance among the executive, judicial, and legislative branches of our government. The Founders created a further balance of powers between two chambers of Congress; between the states and the federal government; and among the states themselves.

The Bill of Rights is designed to protect private interests—the press and religious and minority groups—from the tyranny of the government and the mob. The Second Amendment guarantees the right to keep and bear arms. This has nothing to do with hunting and everything to do with counterbalancing the government's power. The Tenth Amendment gives the states and the people all authority not delegated to the federal government in the Constitution.

This system, called *federalism*, was an ingenious way to disperse power and limit the federal government's reach. It's like a maze of booby traps and speed bumps designed to frustrate wannabe tyrants and mobs.

The Founders failed to live out their principles perfectly. (Some of them owned slaves!) But the system they put in place would, over time, come to include former slaves and their descendants as well. That is what Frederick Douglass fought for and Martin Luther King Jr. achieved—not the end of the system, but a fair stake in it.

Just a Few Jobs for the Feds

The Constitution disperses power but gives the federal government "enumerated powers." It should do a few key things well and leave the rest to the states and the people.

The Founders saw human beings as sinners who could be shaped by society but who have a nature that men can't change. The so-called "progressive" philosophy that now dominates our public life rejects this central truth. Socialists and progressives assume that man can be molded and transformed like a soft lump of clay: You just need society to be set up right and run by smart people. But even in an ideal environment, we fall into sin. Even when Adam and Eve were placed in a garden prepared by God, they still managed to get into trouble.

The progressive left, which is now being displaced by woke ideologues, depended on generations of judges and justices to fudge and torture the text of the Constitution to fit their vision of unconstrained state power. They often did this, perversely, in the name of liberty or privacy. This tactic reached its low point when Supreme Court Justice Anthony Kennedy reaffirmed in 1992 the "right" to kill preborn babies. "At the heart of liberty," he proclaimed, "is the right to define one's own concept of existence, of meaning, of the universe, and of the mystery of human life."[10]

This is a terrible defense of liberty. It denies that human nature, and nature itself, has any objective reality that government must respect. It undercuts the constitutional basis on which our liberties are secured. When the Founders defended the "right to life, liberty, and the pursuit of happiness," they meant the right *not* to have your life snuffed out before you are born.

Thankfully, a different Supreme Court majority recognized this howling contradiction in 2022 when it overturned *Roe v. Wade* and *Planned Parenthood v. Casey*. Justice Samuel Alito's opinion shredded the weak, dishonest arguments that had enshrined abortion as a constitutional right. It now allows our states to restrict this ghoulish practice.[11]

Legislating Morality

The purpose of our laws—despite what you may read in countless court cases over the last century—is to legislate our deepest shared moral judgments; to agree on what's fair or unfair, what can and should be coerced, if needed, and what should be left to personal choice. Bumper stickers on Toyota Priuses might say, "You can't legislate morality." But morality is exactly what we legislate. Why do we have laws against wife-beating, dog-fighting, and racial discrimination? Because those practices are wrong.

There is, however, a grain of truth in that cliché. "It may be true that morality cannot be legislated," Martin Luther King Jr. famously said,

> but behavior can be regulated. It may be true that the law cannot change the heart, but it can restrain the heartless. It may be true that the law cannot make a man love me, but it can restrain him from lynching me.[12]

Laws are about behavior, not the state of the heart. That's why we don't have laws against greed, envy, anger, lust, lying (other than fraud or perjury), or private drunkenness. Any state powerful enough to punish such sins would be tyrannical, since it would give vast coercive power to sinful humans.

Even with behavior, we don't make laws against every moral peccadillo because we often would do greater evil by enforcing those laws than by tolerating the behaviors. Because of human sin, we should be slow to give the government power beyond its core competence.

Often, the costs of a law or regulation exceed its benefits. Prohibition is a good example. In the early twentieth century, Congress passed the Eighteenth Amendment, outlawing the sale and consumption of alcohol nationwide, and the states ratified it in 1919. It reduced public drunkenness and probably alcoholism but also spawned organized crime and a sprawling black market. Additionally, it made criminals of millions of citizens who weren't drunkards. The Twenty-First Amendment repealed Prohibition in 1933, and alcohol sales and consumption returned to being local and state concerns. The debacle led millions of evangelicals who had supported Prohibition to drop out of political life for decades afterward.

At the same time, laws shape our morality. Scholars refer to this as the "teaching function" of law. As someone once said,

> It's true that people support the hanging of thieves primarily because they think theft is wrong, not because theft is against the law; however, one of the reasons people think theft is wrong is they see thieves hung.[13]

Did the abolition of slavery and the passage of civil rights laws affect people's views on slavery and race? You bet. Did *Roe v. Wade* shape people's views on abortion? Of course. And since same-sex "marriage" was made the law of the land by a group of judges in 2015, whole Christian denominations have been "adjusting," following the public laws like hungry strays.

What Should We Do?

The American Founders knew that a sound government needs a virtuous people. George Washington insisted that we distinguish "the spirit of liberty from that of licentiousness, cherishing the first, avoiding the last."[14] And Samuel Adams said, "Neither the wisest constitution nor the wisest laws will secure the liberty and happiness of a people whose manners are universally corrupt."[15] Without decent people and politicians, the Constitution is just ink and parchment—like the old constitution of the Soviet Union, which the people knew was written to be ignored.

The rule of law depends on us, too. Adams referred not merely to politicians but to a people. The late Charles Colson often talked about the trade-off between cops and conscience: The more "cops" we have inside, the fewer we need outside.[16] Imagine a country in which every child is born into a loving family headed by a mother and a father, and the adults always do their duty, following their well-formed consciences. As long as the country is sealed from outsiders, it won't need cops and prisons. "Men are qualified for civil liberty," wrote the eighteenth-century Irish statesman Edmund Burke, "in exact proportion to their disposition to put moral chains upon their own appetites."[17]

In contrast, if we can't make our passions submit to our moral reason, they will have to submit to the sword—and that means our government won't stay limited for long. In a sermon in support of the American Revolution, Rev. Samuel West told the Massachusetts Legislature in 1776, "The most perfect freedom consists in obeying the dictates of right reason and submitting to natural law."[18] If we all do whatever we want, we won't stay free to do what we ought.

So where do self-restraint, well-formed consciences, and virtues come from? They come from stable families, real education, robust churches, and vibrant faith. Just as no man can live by bread alone, so no culture can thrive on the natural law alone. That's why we must protect the free exercise of religion. We take that up in the next chapter.

Part II

The Issues

CHAPTER 3

God in Public

At the 2023 Super Bowl, a group of Christians aired an ad depicting Jesus as a refugee, advocate of the poor, and victim of unjust execution. The "He Gets Us" campaign bent over backward to adapt Christian messaging to "woke" concerns about inequity and oppression. The ads didn't make much of sin, Christ's divinity, or even the need for repentance. They were just an attempt to make Jesus appeal to left-wing Americans.

And how did the left respond? Rep. Alexandria Ocasio-Cortez, representing many others, was scathing. "Something tells me Jesus would *not* spend millions of dollars on Super Bowl ads," she wrote on Twitter, "to make fascism look benign."[1]

In response, John Zmirak observed at The Stream: "The poster girl of Woke big government regards Christianity itself, the preaching of Jesus, as 'fascism.' No matter how you dress Him up, she hates Him. And she hates us."[2] Indeed, leftists often demonize and scapegoat faithful Christians, calling us fascists or "Christian nationalists"[3]— even as the number of Christians shrinks. The fastest-growing religious group are people who check the "none" box on polls gauging religious affiliation.

At the same time, paganism is on the rise. Liel Leibovitz recently observed that

> anyone wishing to find his way through the thicket of American public discourse these days should start by embracing one simple and terrifying idea: The barbarians are at the gates. . . . Everywhere you turn these days, pagans are afoot, busily hacking away at the Christian and Jewish foundations of American life.[4]

And always, the Christian-bashers reach back many centuries to faraway countries where vanished institutions (such as the Spanish Inquisition) persecuted people in the name of Christianity. Then these critics pretend that when Christians promote their idea of what's good (which is, you know, the whole point of politics), it portends returning heretics to torture racks in monastery dungeons. We hear cries of "theocracy" and "Christian nationalism." Christians have fast become the one group that our hipster elites think it's okay to scapegoat and hate.

The critics don't seem to know much history. Who stopped the Inquisition? Christians. Who denounced witch trials? Christians. Who decided that governments shouldn't persecute people for following their consciences? Christians. The idea that the government should respect the private beliefs and public faith of every citizen? That's a Christian idea. It arose nowhere else in the world and has spread only as the Church has spread. And as secular regimes have taken over from Christian ones, in country after country, such freedom has vanished. (Try to find it in North Korea.) The very idea of religious liberty emerges from Jesus's words and work. Christians slowly figured this out, long before the rest of the world.

The gnarliest club that Christian-bashers use to pummel believers who vote their consciences is the phrase "separation between church and state." Guess where that appears in the Constitution? Nowhere. Nor is it in the Declaration of Independence or any law ever passed in our history.

It comes from a letter Thomas Jefferson wrote to the Danbury Baptists in 1802. The Baptists were being persecuted by the Congregationalists, who were then the established religion in Connecticut. Jefferson did not object to public religion, but he did object to persecution.[5] He was right, and Christians took action to stop it.

The First Amendment to the Bill of Rights (drafted and ratified mostly by Christians) begins with this: "Congress shall make no law respecting an establishment of religion, or prohibiting the free exercise thereof." Those words are not meant to purge faith from public life, but to protect religion from government overreach. They're also meant to keep the federal government from establishing one official religion.

Secularists now invoke Jefferson's "wall of separation" to shame Christians. But we have the same rights as secular environmentalists, feminists, gender activists, and others who aren't the least bit shy about voting their consciences. If we find that we are, it means we've been gaslighted.

Religious Liberty Is a Christian Idea

Where did the idea of religious liberty come from? Even some Christians think it was made up by secular Enlightenment thinkers. Not true. When Jesus walked the earth, the Jewish homeland was a conquered province of the Roman Empire. In His ministry, Jesus had little to do with politics. He said that His Kingdom was "not of this world" (John 18:3). And during His forty days of fasting in the desert, He rejected the devil's offers of political power.[6] When He met with

Pontius Pilate, Jesus didn't pitch a jobs program. But He did voice a principle that slowly changed how Christians and much of the world now view the proper limits of government and the proper role of the Church.

Matthew, Mark, and Luke describe an event that took place when Jesus entered Jerusalem to celebrate the Passover just before His arrest. While He was teaching in the Temple, the Pharisees tried to trap Him with a trick question: "Teacher," they asked him, "is it lawful to pay taxes to the emperor, or not?"

"Why are you putting me to the test, you hypocrites?" Jesus replied. "Show me the coin used for the tax." When they handed him a denarius, He asked, "Whose head is this, and whose title?"

"The emperor's," they answered.

And to that, Jesus replied, "Give therefore to the emperor the things that are the emperor's, and to God the things that are God's" (Matthew 22:15–22).

Just a few days earlier, Jesus had entered Jerusalem to much fanfare. The crowds cheered Him as the long-awaited Messiah who would deliver them from their Roman oppressors. Such talk of a Jewish deliverer would have worried the Romans. Some Pharisees, who were already plotting to kill Jesus, knew this, and hoped to get Him to say something treasonous so the Romans would do the job for them. Jesus managed to avoid the trap, but He said a lot more than, "Yeah, go ahead and pay your taxes. Not much else you can do."

Notice that Jesus asked His inquisitors for a coin, which they had. That meant they were already involved in Rome's money system. They even carried the coins into the temple, which changed them for ritually pure temple currency. Why the money changing? Because Roman coins not only bore Caesar's image, but also declared his absolute sovereignty, even divinity![7] (By that point, some Romans were worshiping Augustus as one of the gods.)

So, when Jesus says to give to God what is God's and to Caesar what is Caesar's, He's teaching us that Caesar isn't God, and that God's authority is outside Caesar's domain. Caesar has some claim to taxes from those who are part of the Roman system, but not to our worship. God is God. Caesar is not.

By bursting the boundaries of race and nation, Christianity threatened Caesar. So, it's no surprise that Rome persecuted Christians on and off until the emperor Constantine converted to Christianity in the fourth century.[8] The Edict of Milan, which he issued in AD 313, didn't just legalize Christianity: It defended religious freedom for everyone. So far as we know, it was the first government document in history to do so.[9]

Christianity kept growing until it became the official religion of the empire. This was a return to the older way of doing things since, to the Roman mind, one of the main purposes of religion was to unify the empire.

After Constantine, the empire became a complex tangle of church and state. The West slowly became more humane, but a few emperors, some of them heretics, used state coercion to "unify" the Church for the sake of preserving public order.

Christians learned the dangers of fusing church and state the hard way. For centuries, church authorities vied for political power, and politicians vied for religious power. Christians suffered decades of war after the Reformation. Catholics killed Protestants, Protestants killed Catholics, and Protestants killed other Protestants. Christians often treated Jews despicably.

After decades of fighting, many European countries struck a compromise: The local prince would determine the religion of his subjects. If your prince was a Lutheran, then you were Lutheran. If he was a Catholic, then you were Catholic. Of course, this didn't solve the problem. Though it reduced outright warfare, many dissidents were persecuted as before.

The habit was hard to break. Even the early American colonists, who had fled persecution in Europe, set about tormenting other Christian groups. From these bitter trials, though, Christians began to reflect on the nature of faith. They came to see what American Founder George Mason said so well:

> That Religion, or the Duty which we owe to our Creator, and the Manner of discharging it, can be directed only by Reason and Conviction, not by Force or Violence, and therefore all Men have an equal natural and unalienable Right to the free Exercise of Religion, according to the Dictates of Conscience, and that no particular religious Sect or Society ought to be favored or established by Law, in Preference to others.[10]

In other words, as the early Christian martyrs could have taught them, real faith can't be forced. To force a nonbeliever to profess his faith in Jesus is to force him to lie. This is neither a secular argument for tolerance nor an argument based on relativism. Nor is it the absurd argument that government should be neutral on all big questions. It's a *Christian* argument for religious liberty based on our rights and the duty we owe to God! And it's still the best argument for religious liberty.

The Faith of the Founders

Secularists claim that Thomas Jefferson and the other Founders were deists who wanted to keep God and religion on the sidelines. To make their case, they trot out skeptical quotes from Jefferson and talk about the "Jefferson Bible," in which he deleted all references to miracles from the gospels.

To rebut this, some Christians try to prove that most of the Founders were evangelical Christians.[11] But the truth is that the lines separating orthodox Christianity from deism were blurry in eighteenth-century America. We should not try to cram them into tidy modern compartments.[12]

Many of the Founders, such as Patrick Henry, John Jay, John Witherspoon, and Samuel Adams, were serious Christians.[13] None were atheists.

George Washington was Anglican, though he often attended other houses of worship. He believed deeply in God's providence and that religion was essential for morality. In his inaugural address, he said:

> Of all the dispositions and habits which lead to political prosperity, Religion and Morality are indispensable supports. . . . [R]eason and experience both forbid us to expect that National morality can prevail in exclusion of religious principle.[14]

Even Thomas Jefferson and Benjamin Franklin supported public prayer and religious observance.[15] Others, such as Unitarian John Adams, often spoke fondly of the Christian moral system. None were skeptical deists like the French philosopher Voltaire, to whom secularists often try to equate them.

In fact, every one of the Founders would have agreed with today's conservative defenders of religious liberty on each of the following points:

1. The federal government should neither establish nor prohibit the free exercise of religion.

2. The Church has a proper autonomy that the state must respect.
3. Everyone should enjoy religious liberty to the degree that it doesn't violate others' natural rights.
4. Christianity played a key role in the early American colonies.
5. Government need not, and should not, be neutral on the question of God. We know *by reason* that God and a natural law exist.
6. Public, and even official, displays of respect for God and religion, especially Christianity, are right and good.
7. Religion, and especially Christianity, is vital to the survival and prosperity of the American Experiment.

These views allowed the Founders to revere God in public while still opposing a national church. The truths of God's existence and of basic morality, they believed, were public truths, not sectarian doctrines. So, when Congress adopted "In God We Trust" as our national motto in 1956, they weren't imposing religion on the public. They were recognizing God—just as the Founders had. The phrase had appeared on our coins as early as the 1850s.

Remember, it was Jefferson who wrote in the Declaration of Independence, "We hold these truths to be self-evident, that all men are created equal, that they are endowed by their Creator with certain unalienable rights."[16] On this point, the Founders believed, reason and revelation agree.

Faith in Public: Both/And

Think of our most cherished beliefs as Americans—equality and human rights, the value of the individual, limited government, liberty.

These are branches of a tree with Jewish and Christian roots. In nations that persecuted churches, from Revolutionary France to Nazi Germany to Soviet Russia, all the other freedoms soon fell as well.

The Founders held that we can know these same truths by reason. But most of them also believed that knowledge would wither if not buttressed by religious faith. "[W]e have no government armed with power capable of contending with human passions unbridled by morality and religion," said John Adams. "Our constitution was made only for a moral and religious people. It is wholly inadequate to the government of any other."[17]

Because everyone (including believers and pastors) can be corrupted by unchecked power, these men devised a system with no established religion, but broad religious freedom. That way, separate religious groups would hold each other in check, keep each other honest, and even goad each other to work harder by competing. Meanwhile, believers would reinforce the truths they share and on which our nation is founded.

Does that mean we should never quote the Bible or mention God in public debate? Not at all! Christianity is still part of the American vocabulary. Several years ago, a University of Chicago law professor put this point nicely:

> Secularists are wrong when they ask believers to leave their religion at the door before entering . . . the public square. Frederick Douglass, Abraham Lincoln, William Jennings Bryan, Dorothy Day, Martin Luther King—indeed, the majority of great reformers in American history—were not only motivated by faith, but repeatedly used religious language to argue for their cause. So, to say that men and women should not inject their "personal morality" into public policy debates is a practical absurdity. Our law is by

definition a codification of morality, much of it grounded in the Judeo-Christian tradition.[18]

That professor went on to become the forty-fourth president of the United States—Barack Obama.

What Should We Do?

You have every right to apply your faith to every part of your life. That includes your politics. And when government, or a private business, tries to infringe on our religious freedom, we have a duty to fight back in court—not just for ourselves but for those more vulnerable than us. We're grateful for groups such as Alliance Defending Freedom, First Liberty Institute, the Becket Fund, and many others that fight government efforts to purge faith from the public square. Of course, their efforts depend on good courts. That's why we should only support candidates who pledge to appoint judges who will recover the religious liberty envisioned by the Founders, not prop up the cheap counterfeit of recent decades.

At the same time, we must be wise as serpents. Most recent efforts to defend "Christian nationalism" fail this test. Like "nationalism," the term means different things to different people.[19] On one side of the spectrum is *The Case for Christian Nationalism* by Stephen Wolfe.[20] He pines for a Calvinist ethno-confessional state that would punish dissenters. This proposal sounds both unwise and unworkable. Wolfe's orbit of conservative Presbyterian denominations in the U.S. has fewer than a million people. And most of them likely disagree with his views—which are quirky even in his narrow subculture. His view, in other words, is like a tiny island, not a broad landmass fit to build an army that can resist the woke madness overtaking our country and our planet.

The same goes for the handful of Catholics proposing "integralism" or "political Catholicism." This would involve making the U.S. an officially Catholic country that would suppress everyone else's religious liberty. Despite its allure among some Catholics fed up with corruption in the Church and culture, we'd be surprised if even one in a hundred Catholics would rally to such a cause.

Creating a thousand little fractious villages is the perfect plan for losing. We need to get busy forging a broad alliance, not hatching eccentric schemes that pit Presbyterians against Pentecostals, Catholics against Protestants, Christians against Jews, and believers against antiwoke unbelievers. History is rife with such failed efforts; that's partly how we've gotten where we are now.

Of course, some who invoke the term "Christian nationalism" just want their faith to shape the culture. But how does it help that cause to embrace a label the media have spent years using as an insult?

To build an alliance, we need common ground with a committed core in the middle and welcoming gates and bridges on the edges. If you want to get your agnostic neighbor to enter the gate marked, say, "conjugal marriage," then you should appeal to something she already accepts. Your views on marriage may be tied to your faith, but there are also plenty of good arguments for it based on public reason.

You can also make moral arguments without citing Scripture or theology. As we mentioned, atheists know murder is wrong, because, as Paul says, the law is written on their hearts—even when they deny it! Every political debate involves a moral question.

In short, don't let cries of "theocracy!" or "Christian nationalism!" cow you, but don't go out of your way to turn off allies. Faith and morality may be personal. That doesn't mean they are, or should be, private.

CHAPTER 4

Bearing the Sword

A few months after moving into the White House, Joe Biden ordered the sudden withdrawal of all U.S. armed forces from Afghanistan before securing our citizens' safe escape. In the process, our federal government abandoned more than 100,000 Afghans who'd been promised U.S. visas for aiding our frontline troops against the Taliban during the war. The U.S. left behind huge airbases, embassies, consulates, and some ninety billion dollars' worth of military equipment. That's more than the annual individual military budgets of Great Britain, France, India, and even Russia.

The Taliban signed an alliance with Communist China on September 11, 2001.[1] Almost twenty years later to the day, the Taliban waltzed back into Kabul, with all that American loot as an anniversary present.

Biden has worked to purge the military of those who resisted the experimental COVID-19 vaccines.[2] Military brass have been targeting "extremists" in the ranks, which includes conservative evangelicals and Catholics.[3] Now, even *pregnant* women are eligible for combat, and the military foots the bill for costly "transgender" surgeries.[4] It's no surprise that recruitment numbers have plummeted.[5]

Obviously, we can do far better than this. But if we've learned anything in the last twenty years, it's that even the world's sole super-power has limits. When we strain our defense forces, we leave ourselves less prepared to face serious threats, such as that posed by China. And that puts the whole world at risk.

The Problems with Pacifism

Are all wars wrong?

I (Jay) struggled with this question in college and seminary. I knew God commanded warfare in the Old Testament and told the ancient Jews to take an eye for an eye and a tooth for a tooth. Yet the sixth commandment of the Decalogue is, "You shall not kill." The Old Testament also foretold a day when "the wolf shall dwell with the lamb, and the leopard shall lie down with the kid, and the calf and the lion and the fatling together, and a little child shall lead them" (Isaiah 11:6). Isaiah described a time when the nations "shall beat their swords into plowshares, and their spears into pruning hooks; nation shall not lift up sword against nation, neither shall they learn war any more" (Isaiah 2:4).

Was the prophet referring to the coming of Jesus, the Prince of Peace? Didn't Jesus tell us to love our enemies? Didn't He say that if someone strikes you on the cheek, you should turn the other one as well? Didn't He tell Peter in the Garden of Gethsemane to put away his sword, since "whoever lives by the sword will die by the sword"? Didn't Jesus insist that we bear our cross daily (Luke 9:23)? Perhaps He wanted us to resist violence with nonviolence, even if that meant our own deaths.

After college, I attended seminary, where I had a beloved New Testament professor who was a pacifist. I also absorbed the progressive

Christian magazine *Sojourners* and several books by pacifist theologian Stanley Hauerwas.

But on closer inspection, pacifism's appeal withered. Another student asked my professor what he would do if someone tried to rape his wife; he said he might try to stop the rapist by hugging him or sitting on him, but he would not use violence. Another student asked him if it was wrong for the Allies to fight Nazi Germany during World War II. My professor said that if Christians had prayed more before World War II, then God would have prevented Hitler from coming to power.

Of course, God can change the course of history. But this answer seemed like a dodge. Why assume that God would have responded to such prayers that way? Perhaps instead, He used the Allies to bring Hitler to justice.

Frustrated, I studied Scripture and Church history more closely. It became clear that the pacifist view just didn't hold up. The commandment that forbids killing, for instance, uses a Hebrew word, *ratsach*, that's never used to refer to killing in war.[6] The text is better translated into English as, "You shall not murder."

Jesus tells us to turn the other cheek, love our enemies, and pray for our persecutors (Matthew 5). Based on such texts, some New Testament scholars have argued that Christians shouldn't serve in either the military or the police. But Jesus never denies that governments should keep the peace and protect their citizens. In these passages, Jesus isn't talking about the state; He's discussing personal revenge.

This Old Testament policy of taking "an eye for an eye" limited what was common at the time—when whole families or cities could be punished for the crimes of one person. But that policy didn't solve the spiral of revenge.[7] If you kill someone's child because he killed yours, that's not justice, but revenge—and then, like mafiosos, that family retaliates against yours, and on and on. Jesus is telling us how to break this cycle of revenge: by choosing to forgive and absorb the evils done to us. That's why, just before He tells the crowd not to resist the evil person, He says, "You have heard that it was said, 'An eye for an eye and a tooth for a tooth.' But I say to you . . ." (Matthew 5:38).

By contrast, in Romans 13 and 1 Peter 2, Paul and Peter are writing about the proper role of government. Paul tells us that the ruler is "the servant of God to execute his wrath on the wrongdoer" (Romans 13:4). Jesus commands us to absorb and forgive. But the state, as a third party, is supposed to execute justice, not revenge on behalf of the aggrieved party. That's why criminal cases have names like *The United States of America v. Timothy James McVeigh.* It's the state, not the victim, that dispenses justice.[8]

Otherwise, injustice would prevail. We would have a world, in the words of Theodore Dalrymple, in which "the good are afraid of the bad, and the bad are afraid of nothing."[9] It's forgiveness in our hearts plus the state's proper execution of justice that breaks the cycle of vendetta and violence.

The pacifist reading doesn't just make a mess of Scripture; it fails to account for the full picture of Jesus in the gospels. Yes, Jesus tells Peter to put away his sword in the Garden of Gethsemane (John 18:11). But He had earlier told His disciples that the time to buy swords had come (Luke 22).

He could have forbidden police and military service, but He didn't. In Matthew, just after Jesus tells His disciples to absorb evil, He visits the city of Capernaum. While there, a centurion asks Jesus to heal his servant just by saying the word. Does Jesus reply, "You're a Roman soldier. Go and leave your life of sin" as He told a paralytic and the woman caught in adultery (John 5:14 and 8:1–11)? No. Instead, He turned to the crowd and said, "Truly, I say to you, not even in Israel have I found such faith." Then He tells the centurion, "Go. Let it be done to you according to your faith" (Matthew 8:10–13).

In Acts, we meet another Roman centurion named Cornelius, who becomes a Christian, receives the Holy Spirit, and is baptized at Peter's command. There's no hint that Cornelius's work contradicts the Gospel. In fact, he is called "devout."

Self Defense

Pacifism doesn't just make a mess of Scripture and historic Christian teaching on war and the military; it implies that armed protection of the innocent and self-defense are wrong as well. This contradicts the Second Amendment to the U.S. Constitution, which claims we have a God-given right "to keep and bear arms." It also contradicts the moral wisdom of every culture. Imagine an armed rapist who breaks into a family's home in the middle of the night. The father has a loaded gun and gets between his family and the rapist. The rapist then raises his gun to shoot the father.

Would it be a sin for the father to shoot the rapist to protect his wife, daughters, and himself? You can put that question to a six-year-old Methodist girl in Memphis, a Muslim man in Mecca, a young Hindu woman in Mumbai, the guy at the checkout counter at Macy's, or a twenty-five-year-old agnostic medical student from Mali. If they're honest, they'll give you the same answer: Not only should the father be allowed to kill the rapist if necessary; he *ought* to.

This belief about the just use of force is grounded in our basic sense of duty and justice. If you have a working conscience, you know that (1) people have a right to self-defense; (2) the rapist in this situation *deserves* to be shot; and (3) killing the rapist in this situation isn't murder.

Pacifists deny all three claims.

Of course, nonviolent resistance can be a force for good. Think of Gandhi and the Rev. Martin Luther King Jr. Gandhi's methods worked with the British, as did MLK's with Americans. But they were directed not at criminals and moral monsters, but at people who were failing to live up to their own noble ideals. The same strategy on Adolph Hitler or Joseph Stalin would have yielded a different result.

Pacifism as Pretense

We may be taking the arguments for pacifism here more seriously than do many public Christian pacifists themselves. For many left-wing Christians, pacifism is more a pretense than a principle. They oppose military action abroad but support a meddling and coercive state at home.

This is inconsistent. As Old Testament scholar Lawson Stone has observed,

> If one believes in government-provided health care and basic income guarantees, one believes in coercion. Violence and war are just the most conspicuous forms of coercion.[10]

Pacifist logic leads not to a giant entitlement estate, but to anarchy.

Similarly, left-wing pacifism seems to wax and wane depending upon who occupies the White House. Under Ronald Reagan, *Sojourners* often denounced our military but supported the brutal communist Sandinistas in Nicaragua. Years later, when President George W. Bush was leading the wars in Iraq and Afghanistan, *Sojourners* didn't just disagree with his policies; they talked about lies, murder, and war crimes.

When Barack Obama became president and continued the Bush policies in Iraq and Afghanistan, the outrage from *Sojourners* and others softened into tones of regret. We noticed the same unequal treatment of Donald Trump and Joe Biden. Christian pacifists have been mostly silent as the U.S. has supplied tens of billions of dollars' worth of military aid, intelligence, and weaponry to help Ukraine resist Russia.

This is partisan, not principled. Neither the Republican nor Democratic parties are pacifist. When Obama became president, he didn't dismantle the military (though some of his policies weakened it).[11] Biden botched the withdrawal from Afghanistan but hasn't called for the defense budget to drop to zero. It's sheer hypocrisy to invoke pacifism against a Republican but go quiet when a Democrat is in charge.

Politics is about policy that's backed up by the threat of force. The late pacifist theologian John Howard Yoder described Christian ethics as "the politics of Jesus," and called Him a "political figure" and "the model of radical political action."[12] Two other leading pacifist theologians, Stanley Hauerwas and William Willimon, insist that "Christianity is mostly a matter of politics."[13]

Indeed, most leftists have a much more exalted view of the government than conservatives do. After all, they invite it into every nook and cranny of our lives—except, it seems, into the arena of defense, which is one of government's few proper jobs.

Realism and Just War

At the other extreme from pacifism lies so-called realism. The realist argues that since no one can weigh the claims of different nations, the best a nation can do is to act in its own self-interest. The realist says that trying to apply moral rules to our actions while defending ourselves against hostile foreign enemies is to tie our hands behind our back. If we try to avoid enemy civilians, our enemy will just use them as a shield.

If we use our resources to care for prisoners of war, our enemies will get ahead by working to death our captured forces. Realists need not be moral relativists. They may just believe it's better to do what needs to be done to win quickly, even if it means setting aside ethics. We can always pick up our scruples again after we've won.

Between this "realist" view and pacifism lie centuries of Christian wisdom called "just war theory." It tells us when we should go to war, how we should conduct ourselves when we do, and what we should do afterward.

Just war thinking started with Saint Augustine but doesn't depend on Christian doctrine.[14] Just war theorists agree that a nation has a duty to defend its legitimate interests. However, unlike realists, they argue that we can and should use moral judgment in the details of war.

It helps to see the just war criteria in a list:

1. Just cause
2. Right intention
3. Proper authority and a public declaration
4. Last resort
5. Probability of success
6. Proportionality[15]

A just war is pursued publicly, as a last resort but with a good chance for success, by the right authority, for the right reasons, to accomplish a just cause without using more force than necessary, and to win without undue loss of life. For instance, the U.S. government could declare war against another country that has attacked us or one of our allies, or is about to. War should be pursued as a last realistic resort and only if it's more likely to succeed than not. It's wrong to attack an enemy if you know you can't achieve your end. Finally, your response should fit the offense. For example, you don't nuke a small country because of a border skirmish.[16]

"Defensive Imperialism" versus "Defensive Isolationism"

We think Christians and conservatives should embrace just-war thinking. Still, it doesn't solve all the tough questions on which we may disagree. Most conservatives know that in a dangerous world, free nations must have strong militaries. There is, however, one big in-house argument: One camp tends toward "defensive imperialism," the other toward "defensive isolationism."[17]

Defensive imperialists stress the human thirst for freedom and America's power to help spread it. They believe that long-term security and human rights sometimes require us to intervene to reconstruct failed states or to protect free states from tyrants.

Defensive isolationists, on the other hand, resist anything that smacks of nation building. They stress the quirks of history and culture, point out that some cultures are hostile to freedom, and that free societies have been rare in history. They doubt we can plant free markets, religious freedom, and republican virtues in non-Western cultures.

Both views capture part of the truth. Defensive isolationism is rooted in historic American doubt about empire. We like trading partners, strategic military outposts, maybe even a new state from time to time, but not colonies. Meanwhile, defensive isolationists note that some cultures are far less open to freedom and representative government than others. Countries that were once part of the British Empire, for instance, are much more likely to be free and prosperous than ones that were not—though that trend started to change during the COVID lockdowns. Muslim regimes, in contrast, have a dismal record of protecting freedom and human rights.

Still, we shouldn't exaggerate. It's possible to reconstruct some failed states. For example, Japan and Germany were in ruins after World War II. But with a military occupation, a purge of the high Nazi officials in Germany, new political structures and laws, and funds for redevelopment, the Allied victors got both countries moving in the right direction. Germany is now one of the most prosperous countries in Europe. And Japan, despite bad economic policies in the last couple of decades, remains the wealthiest and most advanced country in Asia.

Japan had a different political system, language, history, culture, and religion than ours, and yet Japan and Germany ended up looking a lot like Western Europe and North America. Both remain under the U.S. defense umbrella. These two countries remind us that nation building is not always doomed to failure.

That said, human nature and culture are stubborn things. Sometimes, people long for freedom but vote for bondage.

War and Self-Defense for Christians

We look forward to a time when war and death will end. We still live in a fallen world where evil people and evil regimes prowl about the earth. In the last century, our country won just wars against Nazi Germany and Imperialist Japan, and a just Cold War against the Soviet Union. We now face a new Cold War against Communist China. Winning it will be the work of a generation—even if we have serious leaders. We wish this weren't true. But until God's Kingdom comes in its fullness, we have a duty to protect the weak and defenseless within our care, and to use our God-given reason in deciding when the use of force is not only justified, but just.

CHAPTER 5

Big Government, Bad Government

F retting about big government is as American as baseball and apple pie. For more than a hundred years after our country's founding, most people agreed that the federal government had a few main jobs. For instance, it should maintain the rule of law and protect citizens, but otherwise, it wasn't supposed to be part of our daily lives. Government in those years cost the average American about $35 annually (in today's dollars). Now, it costs each of us on average more than $23,000 per year.[1] If you're forty years old, most of that growth has happened in your lifetime. There are honest debates about the ideal size of government. But no one can seriously claim that ours is still small and unobtrusive.

Government now controls, to some extent, the mortgage market, retirement, education, and health care. It claims to cure poverty and redefine marriage and sex—both here and abroad. It fixes the price floor that employers must pay for labor. It subsidizes some private businesses and punishes a host of others. It buys and sells private companies. It funds and directs scientific research, museums, art, public TV and radio, college student grants and loans, choices of lightbulbs, and billions of dollars in "aid" to foreign governments.

This didn't happen in an instant. The unraveling of limited government began about a hundred years ago with the "progressives." Rather than "promoting the general welfare," as the Constitution put it, progressives saw government as the provider of it. "The object of government is the welfare of the people," said Theodore Roosevelt. "The material progress and prosperity of a nation are desirable chiefly so long as they lead to the moral and material welfare of all good citizens."[2]

That sounds benign, but it has no limit. So, by the 1960s, most elites had come to believe that there was no problem—no matter how large or small—that shouldn't be solved politically. A flood in New Orleans? Call the feds. Poverty in Detroit? Uncle Sam can handle it. Bad seventh-grade math scores in Yuma? Fatty foods in Charleston? Report it to the relevant federal agency. It's no wonder many Americans now look to Washington to wipe every nose and dry every tear.

It's now out of fashion, even in conservative circles, to complain about big government. Even worse, we have a metastasizing administrative state made up of hundreds of agencies and bureaus—and some social conservatives want to expand it even more!

As part of the executive branch, these agencies produce the thousands of regulations that control what we do. Most Americans aren't even aware of them—and yet they're the real policy sausage factories. Worse, these agencies are often joined at the hip with powerful private companies and special interests, from Big Media to Big Tech to Big Pharma to Big Finance to Big Labor. In many sectors, it's not easy to draw the lines between the public and private sector.

As a result, when we talk about big government in the twenty-first century, we're really talking about a tentacled Big Blob that oozes into every sphere of public and private life.

Does God Tell Us How Big Government Should Be?

Believers throughout history have lived and thrived under the shadow of large, unchecked government with little choice but to accept their lot. But we live in a republic, so political choice for us is not just a right but a duty. The Bible, history, and our God-given reason show us that large and unconstrained government undermines the common good and leads, in the end, to bondage.

Turning Good to Evil

One way the Bible warns us about big government is by giving us some terrifying examples.

The last chapters of Genesis tell the story of the sons of Jacob, including Joseph, who was the favorite. Out of jealousy, his brothers sell Joseph into slavery, and he ends up in Egypt. There, his gift at interpreting dreams brings him into the presence of the king, who has had a series of troubling dreams. Joseph explains that the dreams describe seven coming years of bountiful harvests, followed by seven years of famine.

This foresight means Egypt can store grain in the bountiful years so that it can survive the seven years of famine to follow. The famine extends to Canaan, where Jacob and his other sons have settled. In desperation, Joseph's brothers travel to Egypt to buy grain. There they encounter Joseph, who is now a high Egyptian official. Instead of taking revenge, Joseph helps them. The whole family gets reunited in Egypt, where they settle down and begin to multiply. The story is so gripping that it's easy to miss another, more subtle lesson: Joseph helped set up the conditions that, over centuries, led to the Hebrews' enslavement by suggesting that Pharaoh collect "a fifth of the produce of the land" during the seven fat years (Genesis 41:34). No doubt Joseph was well-meaning, but he could have suggested that Pharaoh require the farmers to store a portion for themselves to sell later.

Instead, Joseph assumed for himself the role of "policy czar,"[3] setting off a tragic string of events that would come to fruition centuries later.

The text says, "This proposal seemed good to Pharaoh and to all his servants" (Genesis 41:37). You bet it did! What a perfect plan to consolidate power, since everyone would come to depend on the Pharaoh for survival. He became an absolute monarch in charge of the food supply.

When the story picks up again in the book of Exodus, four hundred years have passed, and a new pharaoh, who did not know Joseph, has risen to power and enslaved the Hebrews. Joseph is so likeable that we often miss this subtle lesson: Consolidating power in the hands of a central power, even when it starts with a good man for good reasons, can lead to tragedy—including slavery.

Give Us a King!

In the book of Judges, another few hundred years have passed. The twelve tribes of Jacob's descendants are now settled in the Promised Land, and have been led, off and on, by judges. The book follows a repeating pattern: The chosen people follow God at first, but then they start to drift off and worship alien gods. God then allows their Philistine neighbors to oppress them. In response, the Hebrews cry out to God, who sends a judge to deliver them. Alas, the people never remember the lesson for very long, so the cycle repeats itself. "In those days there was no king in Israel," Judges concludes. "All the people did what was right in their own eyes" (Judges 17:6).

Samuel is the last judge, a righteous prophet who can speak directly to God. The Bible says he "administered justice" by traveling like an itinerant preacher from town to town, always returning home to Ramah. When he grew old, he appointed his sons to help. Talk about small government!

But all was not well. Near the end of his life, the elders of Israel visited Samuel and said, "Behold, you are old and your sons do not walk in your ways; now appoint for us a king to govern us like all the nations." The Lord told him to grant their request, but to warn them of the results, saying:

> "These will be the ways of the king who will reign over you: he will take your sons and appoint them to his chariots and to be his horsemen, and to run before his chariots; and he will appoint for himself commanders of thousands and commanders of fifties, and some to plow his ground and to reap his harvest, and to make his implements of war and the equipment of his chariots.
>
> "He will take your daughters to be perfumers and cooks and bakers. He will take the best of your fields and vineyards and olive orchards and give them to his servants. He will take the tenth of your grain and of your vineyards and give it to his officers and to his servants. He will take your menservants and maidservants, and the best of your cattle and your asses, and put them to his work. He will take the tenth of your flocks, and you shall be his slaves. And in that day you will cry out because of your king, whom you have chosen for yourselves; but the Lord will not answer you in that day." (1 Samuel 8:11–18)

But the people still demanded a king, so Samuel anointed Saul.

God saw Israel's demand as a rejection of His kingship. The United States is not ancient Israel, but this should still be a warning to us: A centralized power is often a surrogate for God's rule. It comes on slowly and subtly. History teaches us that people will often give up their freedom without a fight. As Benjamin Franklin said, "Anyone who trades liberty for security deserves neither liberty nor security."[4]

The Beast

Finally, let's look at the last book of the Bible. In Revelation 13, the Apostle John describes a great beast, which is given enormous power and authority by a dragon. Most interpret this as a symbol of Satan. The beast's authority extends over every tribe, people, language, and nation. It wages war on believers. It's worshiped by "all the inhabitants of the earth," except those whose names are written in the Lamb's Book of Life.

Since John wrote Revelation as a message to the first-century Church, most biblical scholars think the "beast" refers to the murderous and idolatrous actions of Rome, perhaps under Nero, who viciously persecuted believers. But many suspect this text refers to more than just first-century Rome. Perhaps it describes a series of "evil empires" throughout history. Perhaps it tells us about the end times.

However we interpret it, though, the Bible ends with a horrific portrayal of a state dominating vast multitudes of people. In the twentieth century, more than a hundred million people in communist nations were murdered by their own governments.[5] History and Scripture agree: Because of sin, governments with too much power are the worst propagators of evil known to man.

The Creeping Administrative State

No country's founders have taken these lessons to heart more deeply than ours. The Founders meant for Congress to check the power of the other two branches and vice versa. In the last several decades, however, the checks have unraveled.

First, the Supreme Court has gone far beyond its constitutional mandate. It was designed to interpret laws passed by Congress guided by the clear meaning of the Constitution. Instead, the Court appointed itself the arbiter of right and wrong. For decades, it operated like a perpetual Constitutional convention—rewriting our supreme law to suit the demands of fashion. Recent decisions, such as those to uphold the Second Amendment and overturn the fraudulent *Roe v. Wade* decision, are the fruit of a dogged campaign by conservatives and pro-lifers to elect presidents who'd appoint reliable constitutionalists to courts. In response, our outraged left wants to either expand and "pack" the court or discredit it.

Second, there's the vast administrative state, which has done an end run around our system of checks and balances. "Congress has delegated much of its lawmaking authority to the executive branch since the 1930s," explained Trump's Interior Department Secretary David Bernhardt.

> Federal agencies now issue regulations that have the force and effect of the law. "Administrative judges"—executive-branch employees—routinely preside over trial-like proceedings without juries, letting agencies act as both prosecutor and judge.[6]

The problem has two parts. First is the Supreme Court's "Chevron Doctrine," in which the Court hamstrung itself. That is, lower "courts generally defer to the executive branch's interpretation of the law—both in regulatory and enforcement proceedings. Many of the Constitution's checks and balances, from the separation of powers to the right to a jury trial, have fallen by the wayside."[7] Second is the problem of a permanent government, which stays in place no matter who happens to be in the White House:

The federal government has 2.2 million civilian employees, but only 4,000 of them are political appointees the president can remove at will. Career bureaucrats, who aren't elected by the American people or appointed by the president, therefore make many major policy decisions. Civil-service protections make removing these employees incredibly difficult—and they know it.[8]

Heritage Foundation President Kevin Roberts observes that many federal bureaucrats are "not just unelected but seemingly unfireable."[9] When Donald Trump arrived in Washington, he faced this army of apparatchiks who slow-walked and flat-out defied his policies. And we now know that the FBI and many intelligence and national security officials spun the Russia hoax from thin air. Worse, as the Durham Report shows, they *knew* it was a tissue of lies produced by Hillary Clinton's campaign but pushed it anyway to destroy Trump's presidency.[10]

Through his "Schedule F" executive order, Trump took steps to permanently trim the state. Alas, it was too little, too late.[11] But we should take no candidate for president seriously who doesn't have a concrete plan to dismantle this out-of-control administrative state and ignore fake "conservatives" who want to expand it.

On Autopilot, Flying off a Cliff

At another level, the problem of big bad government is basic math. The growth of government has been fueled not just by overreach, but by borrowing beyond all restraint and wisdom, and by entitlement programs that can't be sustained.

This federal fiscal bender has been going on for years. Here's one scary detail: It took the federal government 215 years to acquire seven trillion dollars of debt, but it managed to add another seven trillion between March 2020 and June 2022—barely more than two years![12]

On top of that, it has made a pile of promises in pensions and entitlements—which voters like—that it can't keep. As of 2021, the federal government's unfunded liabilities (with the bills coming due) amounted to about $30 trillion, which is 128 percent of our gross domestic product.[13] That's $250,000 of debt for every American household.

Before long, those deductions from your paycheck won't cover this. The money we and our employers are paying into Social Security isn't invested, as in a mutual fund; it's spent as in a Ponzi scheme. This was sustainable when the program began in 1935, since the average life expectancy was age sixty-two and people were having lots of babies. As a result, forty-two workers paid in for every retiree who received benefits. But we live much longer and have fewer kids now; our average life expectancy is around seventy-seven. The result is that we now have fewer than three workers for every retiree, and that number is dropping.[14]

Unless we reform Social Security, it will collapse. Ditto for Medicare.

The government's duties mentioned in the Constitution, such as a national defense and a justice system, are deemed "discretionary," and can be cut. In contrast, Congress doesn't even debate entitlements as part of the budget. They're deemed to be mandatory. Their budget is determined by the number of recipients, not by the amount of money collected in taxes. They even have automatic increases every year. Entitlements are on autopilot and flying us straight into a skyscraper.

Let's make this personal: Imagine charging so much on your credit cards that it takes your entire income just to pay the interest on the debt. That leaves you with no money to pay rent, buy groceries, tithe, support worthy charities, get shoes for your kids, pay off the debt itself, or anything else. That's where federal spending is headed. Soon, taxes will get so high that government will consume most of our economy's output but *provide no services*, since all taxes would go to pay interest on previous debts.

Then, the choices will be for the United States to default on its loans, or to print enough money to trigger hyperinflation, so that our debt isn't worth much. Either of these will destroy our society and devastate the world economy.

This has happened elsewhere—such as in Germany after World War I.[15] We saw what came next: The country embraced a dictator who promised that wars of conquest would solve all its problems. In the rubble of Berlin in 1945, Germans had plenty of reason to think back on where they'd gone wrong. Economic foolishness helped pave the way for Hitler and the Holocaust by making everyone desperate.

Tweaking the budget and cutting our waste and fraud won't solve the problem. Slashing spending on defense alone won't do it. And zeroing out foreign aid won't do it. Though these are all problems, the long-term debt crisis is with entitlements—especially the middle-class favorites, Social Security and Medicare.

Recent polls show that most Americans are ignorant or kidding themselves about this. There used to be "budget hawks" in Congress and the public. Now most voters oppose cutting the budget in any major category.[16] Most conservatives say they want smaller budgets and deficits but still oppose fixes to Social Security and Medicare.[17]

If a candidate raises the issue, he can count on the other party to scream that he wants to starve the elderly. If the candidate raises it in a primary, his own party rivals will savage him. This happened in 2023 before the primaries even got started. All politicians in Washington know these programs will collapse if not reformed, but they don't fix them. Why? Because they worry that most voters will punish them for telling the plain truth. Besides, the catastrophe, they assume, is still further away than the next election.

What Should We Do?

As we said earlier, conservatives must get serious about not just slowing down but cutting back the administrative state—especially corrupt entities like the FBI. Look for candidates with concrete plans to do that.

On deficit spending and reform entitlements: If we don't fix these, we will not only harm our children and grandchildren, but people who depend on Social Security and Medicare could get left in the lurch.

We're not running for office, so we can say the uncool thing: Americans can either handle some short-term pain or leave a catastrophe for our children. It's delusional to deny this.

The short-term pain isn't even that painful. We can avoid raising taxes and cutting off services to older Americans. But these programs *must* be reworked for those who have time to adjust. At the least, we need to slowly raise the minimum retirement age, introduce competition into the system—which would improve service and lower costs—and probably change the way they work for those who can do without them. The longer we wait to do this, the more painful it will be to fix. The alternative is not what we have now, but fiscal chaos and millions of Americans left destitute.

If we can't muster the courage to support leaders in both parties who will tell us the truth about government debt and entitlements, and work to fix these programs before it's too late, we will succeed where both the communists and the Islamic militants failed—and destroy ourselves.

These famous words, often attributed to a Scottish statesman, should echo in our minds:

> A democracy cannot exist as a permanent form of government. It can only exist until the voters discover that they can vote themselves largesse from the public treasury. From that moment on, the majority always votes for the candidates promising the most benefits from the public treasury, with the result that a democracy always collapses over loose fiscal policy, always followed by a dictatorship.[18]

We've been warned.

CHAPTER 6

Choose Life

In 1973, the U.S. Supreme Court overturned state laws against abortion in its infamous *Roe v. Wade* decision, which invented a constitutional right to abortion. Since then, there have been more than sixty-four million abortions in this country.[1] That's more than 19 percent of our current population, and far more than the total military deaths (1.35 million) in all our nation's wars since 1776.

The justices voting with the majority thought they were solving a divisive issue. Instead, they helped inflame the culture war, sparking a dogged pro-life movement that has grown in influence each year. The 2022 overturning of *Roe v. Wade* and *Planned Parenthood v. Casey* was a historic victory for that movement. But with the rise of chemical abortions peddled across state lines—with the help of the federal government—there is still vast work to be done.

About one in four American women has had an abortion.[2] Maybe you're one of them. Or maybe you experienced abortion's harms indirectly. If so, you too have been a victim of what Pope John

Paul II called "the culture of death." And in the decades since *Roe*, the culture of death has expanded. Academics such as Princeton's Peter Singer defend the killing of handicapped infants.[3] In countries such as Canada, Belgium, and the Netherlands, euthanasia—even for depressed but nonterminal patients—is becoming a common cause of death.[4] As people lose their Christian reasons for seeing meaning in suffering, they come to see their lives as akin to those of shelter pets whom we humanely put down when their prospects for happiness run out.

No political system can be truly just if it sacrifices the lives of its most vulnerable members. That is the ugly truth of abortion.

Christian History Is Pro-Life

There is no right more basic than the right to life. Without it, you can't enjoy liberty, acquire property, or pursue happiness. The American Founders insisted that we could discover these rights through reason and conscience, and Christians for two thousand years have taught that this fundamental right to life extends to the voiceless unborn.

Killing a helpless, innocent human being on purpose is murder— one of the greatest sins (Exodus 20:13). This applies not only to abortion but to procedures that destroy human embryos for research or drug testing.

The Bible affirms the humanity of unborn children. Through the Old Testament prophet Jeremiah, God says, "Before I formed you in the womb, I knew you, and before you were born I consecrated you; I appointed you a prophet to the nations" (Jeremiah 1:5–6). And the New Testament treats born and preborn babies the same way. Luke uses the same Greek word for "baby" to refer to both John the Baptist before he is born and Christ after He is born (Luke 1:39–45).

The earliest post-biblical records we have show Christians condemning abortion. The *Didache*, for instance, is an early Christian guide written around AD 110, not long after the New Testament was completed, and more than 250 years before it was canonized. It says, without qualification, "Do not murder a child by abortion or kill a newborn infant."[5] Notice the word "murder." This was a rebuke of the common pagan practices of abortion, infanticide, and infant abandonment.

On abortion, Christians—Catholic, Eastern Orthodox, and Protestant—have spoken with one voice almost to the present. We could fill pages with quotes from Church Fathers, councils, and great theologians, all condemning abortion. But none put it better than John Calvin.

> The unborn child, though enclosed in the womb of its mother, is already a human being and should not be robbed of the life which it has not yet begun to enjoy. If it seems more horrible to kill a man in his own house than in a field, because a man's house is his place of most secure refuge, it ought surely to be deemed more atrocious to destroy an unborn child in the womb before it has come to light.[6]

Christians have long understood that life begins at conception. That's why we have celebrated not only Jesus's birth, but also His conception. Many Christians also honor the conception of Mary. Catholic, Orthodox, and Anglican Christians still have feast days celebrating these events.

The greatest thinkers of the two main strands of Western civilization—Greco-Roman and Judeo-Christian—also agreed that abortion is wrong. The Hippocratic Oath dates from the fourth or fifth century BC. Until recently, most physicians recited a version of the oath that said, "I will not give a lethal drug to anyone if I am asked, nor will I advise such a plan; and similarly I will not give a woman a pessary to cause an abortion."[7]

Sadly, Christians no longer speak with one voice on this issue. Some mainline denominations now are openly, even zealously, pro-choice. In 2009, the president of the Episcopal Divinity School even claimed that abortion can be a "blessing."[8] That is not just pro-choice. It's pro-abortion. And it's apostasy.

Despite *Dobbs*, abortion is entrenched in federal policy and the laws of "blue" states. The legacy of *Roe v. Wade* has left Americans with some of the laxest, least protective abortion laws on Earth, apart from China, North Korea, and Canada. France and Germany, both much more secular than the United States, protect the unborn far more than we do.[9]

You wouldn't know it from the news, but most Americans favor major limits on abortions. At the same time, most don't think all that clearly about the issue and don't know what our laws are or how they compare with the rest of the world.[10] With powerful hostile forces of confusion all around, we must always remind ourselves that the fight for life is nowhere near over.

Why Should Abortion Be a Political Issue?

This summary of Christian teaching on abortion might suggest that laws against it are based on religion and therefore violate the First Amendment. "Keep your rosary off my ovaries" is a popular slogan at pro-abortion rallies. Another objection claims it's just a matter of personal preference. "If you don't like abortion," the popular bumper sticker says, "don't have one." (The obvious comeback? "Okay, now try slavery.")

These aren't serious arguments. We don't oppose abortion because it violates some quirky Christian belief, but because it involves killing an innocent human being. If we can't make laws against that, we can't make laws against anything. Moreover, even if we oppose abortion on religious grounds, that doesn't mean there aren't also public reasons to do so. We reject slavery because we believe that every human being is created in God's image and, therefore, should not be owned as property. Does that mean that opposing slavery violates the separation between church and state? Of course not. We could make the same arguments by appealing to the natural law, which everyone knows, at least in part.

Sure, those who trust God's revelation are more likely to stand firm when the culture turns against the moral truth. That's why Christians in the early Church opposed gladiatorial games and, later, slavery. They could see what everyone else ought to have seen. They didn't compromise. They often died for their convictions, and eventually, Rome abandoned the games, and Europe, its colonies, and the United States abolished slavery.

Abortion defenders have spilled a lot of ink trying to show that since a fetus is inside its mother, abortion isn't murder. But these are efforts to obscure the obvious—that the human fetus is a human being. Your right to life, unlike your right to vote, doesn't vary with location.

Other popular arguments are that the fetus is not fully human because it's quite small, or that it depends on another life to survive. Again, these are weak reeds. Newborn babies are small but no less human for it. Is an eight-pound unborn baby a human while a newborn five-pound baby is not? Newborns, the weak, and the elderly all depend on others. Are they nonhuman? A person who crashes on a ski slope and is knocked out cold would freeze to death without help. Is this person now nonhuman because he needs help to survive? We all depend on others to some extent. Does that mean we are not human beings? Of course not.

Erring on the Side of Caution

Of course, many politicians try to bypass all such arguments. For instance, in 2008, Pastor Rick Warren asked then candidate Barack Obama, "At what point do you think a baby gets human rights?" Obama punted.

"Answering that question with specificity is, you know, above my pay grade," he said.[11] In other words, he claimed not to know the answer. We suspect he did know the answer. But even if he were unsure, why would he zealously seek to protect the "right" to kill the unborn? If you don't know if an unborn baby has the right to life, wouldn't you err on the side of caution?

Let's say you live in a neighborhood where the kids often play in cardboard boxes. One day, when you're riding your monster truck near your house, you see a box in the street. Would you plow over it without checking inside first? Of course not. You wouldn't risk killing a child just because you didn't know if there was one in the box. In the same way, if you think the unborn *might* be human beings, then surely the sane policy is to assume they have human rights.

What the Evidence of Science Tells Us

In reality, though, we're not in the dark about the status of the unborn. The key question is simple: Is a preborn human embryo or fetus (fetus means "little one") a human being? To answer, we don't need complex discussions about personhood or doctrines about souls entering bodies. We just need honest biology. And we know that a distinct human life begins at fertilization.[12]

This new life has its own distinct DNA. More to the point, it's an integrated, living, complete being. While dependent on its mother, it directs its own development toward a specific end according to its nature. This marks off an embryo from any of its mother's cells. It also distinguishes it from the father's sperm, from the mother's egg, from the mother, the father, and everything else.

You were once an embryo, then a fetus, then a newborn, an infant, a toddler, a child, a teenager, and so forth. To say that a human embryo or fetus is not a human being, but merely some other thing called a "fetus" or an "embryo," makes no more sense than to say a teenager isn't a human being, but some other thing called a "teenager." These words refer to different stages of development of the same member of the species of *Homo sapiens*. No stage is more—or less—human than any other.

This is the biological truth. The unborn human being is just that. And taking the life of an innocent human on purpose is murder. No one seriously argues that murder should be legal. That's why defenders of abortion do everything they can to avoid talking about it directly.

If You Love Freedom, Be Pro-Life

This is also why appeals to "reproductive freedom" are nonsense. We expect such nonsense from abortion zealots, but now, even many non-zealots still think abortion should be legal in a free country. What they don't realize is that they're striking at the root of their own beliefs.

Those who defend economic freedom almost always make moral appeals. Take the rabidly pro-choice atheist Ayn Rand. "Man—every man—is an end in himself," she insisted, "not the means to the ends of others."[13] Rand's followers make the same argument, as do most libertarians. They're committed to the inherent dignity of every human being—but don't work out the logic of their view. A human being has value because of what he or she *is*, apart from whether he or she is useful to anyone else. That's the foundation of the pro-life position, too.

God created us as free beings, not as robots determined by physics and programming. A society that protects our freedom allows us to exercise our creativity more fully than the alternatives. This idea is so compelling that most Americans take it for granted, even if they don't believe God is the Author of life.

Pro-lifers similarly argue that the state should protect the unborn, the elderly, the infirm, and should prohibit procedures that destroy human embryos. "Human life cannot be measured," noted the late Pennsylvania Governor Robert Casey in a speech at the University of Notre Dame in 1995.

> It is the measure itself. The value of everything else is weighed against it. The abortion debate is not about how we shall live, but who shall live. And more than that, it's about who we are.[14]

Government's central role is to establish justice, which means protecting, under the rule of law, the conditions that allow personal freedoms and private property to prosper. Those conditions do not include the "freedom" for some to kill others.

Should We Be Single-Issue Voters?

Many Republicans complain that pro-lifers overemphasize the issue of abortion. It would be wrong to treat it as the only issue, but it's equally wrong to treat unequal issues the same way. Most political issues involve shades of gray. Should the bottom income tax bracket be 5 percent or 10 percent? Should we have an income tax or a consumption tax? Should we buy thirty more Abrams tanks for the Army, or five more F-22s for the Air Force? These aren't black-and-white issues.

Abortion is different. It deals with the first right, on which all other rights are based. Because it involves a grave evil—intentionally killing innocent human beings—it should be far more central to our voting than other issues. If one candidate in an election wants to protect unborn life and the other does not, then you know who to support.

A Testimony to Life

As important as abortion is in politics, it can also hit close to home. Some years ago, I (James) interviewed a guest on *Life Today* who had become pregnant as the result of rape. At first, she felt as if having the baby would be an ongoing reminder of her experience. But then she heard a song titled "A Baby's Prayer" by Kathy Troccoli and felt the need to pray. She realized that the "little mass of tissue" in her womb was a person with purpose and potential. She was so moved that she decided to keep the baby.

As this young woman told her story on our show, I began to weep because I'm also the product of rape. My mother had no stable income or security and decided to have an abortion. But her doctor said, "I'm not going to abort this baby." My mother told me she went home, sat down, and prayed. *Have this little baby*, she sensed God telling her, *and it will bring joy to the world.* I was born in the charity ward of the Saint Joseph Hospital in Houston, Texas.

Two weeks later, my mother released me to a foster family, who raised me for the first five years of my life. My conception was the result of a crime, and my early years were hard. But God had a plan for this inconvenient child. I've been blessed with sixty years of marriage to Betty, three children, and, as of this writing, twenty-six grandchildren and great-grandchildren who love God.

In fighting abortion, we don't downplay the trauma of unexpected pregnancy—especially by rape or incest. But if we work to protect every life, even in the tough cases, God will honor that and use our choice in ways we can't imagine.

We have both been blessed because a mother in a desperate situation chose life: We both have adopted children and can't imagine life without them.

If you have had or been involved in an abortion, there is forgiveness and a source of healing. God grieves with you over the loss of innocent life, and He can heal your broken heart.

Some of the most faithful women we know made the tragic mistake of aborting their babies earlier in their lives. Yet they will tell you that God's grace covered their sin and removed their shame "as far as the east is from the west."

If you're struggling with an unplanned pregnancy, we encourage you to choose life for your baby and to seek help from a friend, family member, pastor, or pregnancy resource center.

Laws and Policies

What should we do to protect preborn children? The *Dobbs* decision has renewed the fight for life in all fifty states. Even pro-life states are in danger because of chemical abortions available via telemedicine. Planned Parenthood and its allies are now working to make sure abortion pills are widely dispensed online. This allows doctors in blue states like California to dispense these dangerous drugs to women in pro-life states. They even hope to get these pills dispensed over the counter. This fight will keep pro-life warriors busy over the next several years.[15]

Republicans need to drop the talking point that it's now just a state issue. The right to life doesn't end when you cross the Columbia or Mississippi rivers. We need to push for federal safeguards, though we're going to need a new resident in the White House to make much progress there.

For now, much of our work is in the states. And here's the political reality: Most voters want exceptions to allow abortion for rape and incest (about 1 percent of abortions) and will punish politicians who disagree. Such exceptions are morally incoherent: We don't execute innocent children for their fathers' heinous crimes. (Procedures to save the mother's life, as in an ectopic pregnancy, may inadvertently lead to the death of the unborn child. But these aren't abortions, since they aren't performed with the intent to kill the child, and therefore are not "exceptions.")

Still, we should not make the perfect the enemy of the good. We must continue to support the strongest feasible pro-life laws in each state. Some, like Oklahoma, are pro-life enough to protect all unborn human life already. Pro-life, except in the case of rape and incest, might be the best option in other states. And in others, a "heartbeat" law might be doable. (That would protect the unborn after about six weeks of gestation, when the baby's heartbeatbeat can first be detected.) In bluer states, banning abortion when the baby becomes "pain-capable"—which is around the fifteenth week of development—could be the best option. This is weaker than most abortion laws even in Europe, but better than what we had under *Roe*.

Besides pushing for laws to protect life, we must foster a culture of life: praying and protesting peacefully at abortion mills and helping mothers facing tough pregnancies. Adoption, pregnancy resource centers, and homes for poor and homeless mothers are all part of the solution. Let's focus not just on what "society" or government is doing, but on what we can do personally. To truly end the scourge of abortion in this country, we must persuade our fellow Americans that every human life is precious, no matter how small.

CHAPTER 7

A Man Shall Cling to His Wife

Before there were cities or governments, there was marriage. It's the foundation for every other human institution.[1] In Genesis 2, God makes Adam, puts him in the Garden of Eden, and then creates the woman from his rib. On seeing her, Adam says,

> "This at last is bone of my bones and flesh of my flesh; she shall be called Woman, because she was taken out of Man."
> Therefore, a man leaves his father and his mother and cleaves to his wife, and they become one flesh. (Genesis 2:23–24)

Many Old Testament characters, such as Abraham, Jacob, and especially Solomon, didn't follow this ideal of one man and one woman, however. They were polygamists. And though God meant marriage to be permanent, Moses gave the Israelites rules for divorce. When the Pharisees asked Jesus if it was lawful for a man to divorce his wife for any reason, He pointed back to Genesis and explained that Moses acted only because of man's hardness of heart, not because God approved of divorce (Matthew 19:3–12 and Mark 10:2–12).

Christians have always treated marriage as sacred, and almost every known culture has marriage. Sure, there are differences—some cultures have allowed polygamy; others have arranged marriages. But there is a constant, underlying theme: Marriage as a norm is a public joining of one man and one woman for life.

And yet, in 2015, the U.S. Supreme Court issued a social engineering decree as jerry-rigged as *Roe v. Wade*. The *Obergefell v. Hodges* decision waved off vast evidence from history, anthropology, religion, and natural law. It also dismissed state laws and the federal Defense of Marriage Act (DOMA)—which President Bill Clinton had signed with bipartisan support in 1996—and forced every state in the union to recognize same-sex marriage.

To rub it in, in December 2022, Congress repealed DOMA with the "Respect for Marriage Act." Far from simply codifying *Obergefell* into federal law, the measure directly threatens free speech and religious freedom by making it easier to pursue legal action against anyone who opposes same-sex marriage because of their faith.[2] Fixing this error is going to be the work of a generation because most Americans now think it's no big deal. It won't get fixed until Americans witness the full cost of these decisions on our families and our republic.

Where It Started

The problem did not start with same-sex marriage activists. An epidemic of divorce, aided and abetted by the sexual revolution, began chipping away at marriage decades ago. In the early years of the American colonies, very few people got divorced because it was illegal, as in Europe. After the Founding, states established divorce laws that required proof of fault by one of the parties.

Only in the 1960s did states begin enacting "no-fault" divorce laws[3] in the wake of relentless assaults on marriage and chastity from academics such as "sex researcher" Alfred Kinsey and anthropologist Margaret Mead. They misled millions to believe that same-sex relations and promiscuity were normal, common, and healthy. Later we learned that their work was deeply flawed,[4] even fraudulent, but the damage was already done.

Now all fifty states have no-fault divorce laws. Legal marriage is now less binding than a business contract. As marriage expert Maggie Gallagher has written, "Marriage is one of the few contracts in which the law explicitly protects the defaulting party at the expense of his or her partner."[5] Student loan debt is more solemn a covenant than legal marriage.

Along with changing laws has come a changed culture in which divorce carries little stigma. The divorce rate for first marriages—some 40 percent—is about twice what it was in 1960.[6] This trend is even more startling when you realize that divorce rates have gone up while marriage rates have gone down.[7] On average, men and women marry much later than they did just a few decades ago. For a while, divorce was much worse in cities than in the country, but now the countryside is catching up.[8]

Seventy-six percent of Americans in first marriages now live together beforehand.[9] "Cohabiting" is seen as a good trial run that will prevent a divorce later. In fact, people who shack up before marriage are much more likely to divorce than those who keep two addresses until their wedding day.[10]

If the sexual revolution and no-fault divorce were dry twigs and tinder, the birth control pill and legal abortion were a blowtorch and gasoline. Together they destroyed the link binding marriage, sex, and childbearing.[11] Our culture has been stoking these flames for decades, long before talk of same-sex "marriage" arose.

What Good Is Marriage?

Marriage may be personal, but it's not private. Like a rock dropped in a pond, the ripples work their way across the whole surface of our culture. The collapse of marriage since the 1960s has given social scientists heaps of data to study. The results are in: Marriage is good for us, and divorce is not.

Men and women in their first marriages tend to be healthier and happier than their counterparts in every other type of relationship. That includes those who are single, widowed, or divorced. Married couples are also less depressed and anxious,[12] and less likely to abuse drugs and alcohol. "Seventy percent of chronic problem drinkers are divorced or separated," noted marriage experts Glenn Stanton and Bill Maier, while "only 15 percent are married."[13] Married adults have better sex lives. They're better parents and better workers. They're less likely to commit or suffer from domestic violence.[14]

Many men, left to their own fallen instincts, would sleep around. Their sexual energies need to be properly channeled so that they think and act for long-term goals rather than fleeting, short-term thrills. George Gilder argued in the 1970s and '80s that the channeling of male sexuality is one of the key functions of marriage. Marriage helps civilize men.[15] Other scholars have confirmed his point by showing a link between the state of marriage and the historical rise and fall of civilizations.[16]

What Is Marriage?

If marriage is a good thing, why can't men marry men and women marry women? Why can't larger groups (such as "throuples") marry if they love each other?

These questions assume marriage is whatever we decide it is—a way to formalize romantic feelings between two or more people. But if marriage is something else, with a fixed nature and purpose, then calling other arrangements "marriages" doesn't make them so.

By asking "What is marriage?" we're not asking whether people with same-sex attraction should have the same legal rights as everyone else (they should); or whether they should be treated with love and respect (they should). We're also not asking about the origin of same-sex attraction; what consenting adults do in their homes; or even if sex acts outside natural marriage are sinful. We're talking about one thing: the nature of marriage and its role as a public institution.

Of course, it's easy to mix up these issues because of how our language has been hijacked. Note that we're using an awkward phrase, "same-sex attraction." That refers to a tendency some people have. We avoid referring to someone as "a homosexual" or "a heterosexual." We don't concede the false assumptions about identity that have consumed our culture in the last few decades. A sexual tendency is one thing. Acting on that tendency is another. Thanks to the efforts of activist psychologists, everyone now refers to sexual attraction as an "orientation." It was just a short step for everyone to see this as an identity.

Why do these distinctions matter? Well, if one is by nature "a homosexual"—even the word suggests an identity—then it's easy to treat a defense of conjugal marriage as a bigoted attack on those people.

Most people now use these terms because they were slowly coaxed into a whole new thought world of made-up identities—and few noticed what was happening. This made it easy to forget that the word "marriage" refers to a unique relationship. We relate to our coworkers because of our jobs. We relate to our neighbors because of where we live. We relate to our friends because we have common interests. But the way a husband and wife relate in marriage is unique. They unite *comprehensively*, with their whole beings.[17]

We're both body and soul. Bodies can come together in all sorts of ways—dancing, shaking hands, wrestling, playing football, and cramming into a crowded subway car. But the connection of bodies in a true marital union can fulfill a unique purpose—namely, to make babies. The same act that unites the husband and wife can also create new life. Marriage as an institution is thus grounded in biology. It's conjugal—from the Latin word meaning "to unite."

Think about it. Each of our organs has a purpose. The purpose of the heart is to pump blood; of eyes, to see; of lungs, to draw in air and capture oxygen to supply the body. They also have a common purpose: They work together to keep our bodies alive and thriving. Moreover, they're complete in themselves: They don't need another body to fulfill their function.

Every healthy adult in his or her reproductive years, however, has one bodily function that requires someone of the other sex to complete: reproduction.[18] Male and female are "made to fit." Until recently, no one thought to deny this.

Sex within marriage is a good thing even if a baby doesn't result because it involves the organic bodily union of husband and wife. The act still naturally tends toward reproduction.

The sex act is the consummation—the seal—of marriage. Thus, no relationship between two or more men or two or more women can qualify as marriage. Why? Because same-sex pairing cannot "achieve organic bodily union since there is no bodily good or function toward which their bodies can coordinate, reproduction being the only candidate."[19] Eating Styrofoam isn't really eating, and same-sex "mating" isn't really mating.

An infertile man and woman can still marry, since they still bring together complementary organs and body systems. An analogy would be baseball: Winning a game is the proper end of forming a team and playing a game. But the team that doesn't win a game is still participating in the proper end of the game. It is still playing baseball.

Let's boil this down to one paragraph. Marriage is a comprehensive union of two bodies, minds, sets of emotions, and souls. Its unique and proper end is children. Ideally, it should also be permanent, exclusive, and monogamous. Marriage is a public commitment, an act of free will, not a fleeting emotion. Romantic love can be a wonderful blessing, but romantic feelings come and go. Marriage, if it is anything, must be more than feelings.[20]

What Harm Is There in Redefining Marriage?

Does it harm natural marriage for two men to "marry" each other? This is like asking if the value of a real dollar in Texas would be harmed by flooding the market with counterfeits in New York.[21] Counterfeits degrade the value of real dollars and the economy. As economists say, bad money chases out good money.

Likewise, enshrining a false definition of marriage in our laws has harmed all marriages and society. It does not expand the meaning of marriage but replaces its historical meaning with a counterfeit. The effects may lag behind the cause and be hard to connect at first. But we're already seeing the corrosive effects of *Obergefell*. In 2015, the Supreme Court denied that the distinction between male and female has anything to do with marriage, and almost overnight, that distinction itself came under attack. Now we need documentaries that ask baffled intellectuals, "What Is a Woman?"[22]

Laws teach and shape behavior. When we say in both law and culture that people of the same sex can "marry" each other, we lose the rational basis for barring polygamy, polyamory (group marriage), and incest. We also lose the grounding for encouraging marriage to be exclusive and permanent. We even lose its connection to sex. ("Asexual" is now a supposed "gender identity.")

Why restrict marriage to *one* man and *one* woman? Because that's what it takes to make a complete pair—to mate. But that logic of completion evaporates if people of the same sex can marry. The arguments used to defend same-sex marriage work just as well for defending any voluntary relationship. Because our culture no longer legally recognizes true marriage, fewer and fewer people will know what it is.

We're not fearmongering. The jump from same-sex marriage to polygamy, group marriage, and open marriage has already happened. It won't stop there. The campaigns for sex with children and animals are already underway.

Chief Justice John Roberts, in his ringing dissent from *Obergefell*, warned that the ruling also posed a grave threat to religious freedom. What was once prohibited is first tolerated and then required. With same-sex marriage defined as a basic human right, no one will be free to safely defend real marriage. Government has already begun to treat our views as bigotry. And don't expect the logical train of the sexual revolution to stop here. Parents who complain about their kids being forced to read explicit sexual content in school are now targeted by the U.S. Department of Justice as "domestic extremists."

If we don't reverse the trend, criticizing same-sex relations could soon be illegal. That has already happened in Canada, where "antigay" speech is now a crime punishable by up to two years in jail![23] We're seeing an equally chilling trend in punishment (legal and social) of those who won't play along with the charade of gender ideology (more on that later).

Why Is Government Meddling in the Marriage Business?

Marriage is a public institution. If it weren't, the Supreme Court wouldn't have ruled on the issue. It's about public recognition and approval, not private feelings, vows, or tax benefits. That's why same-sex marriage activists wouldn't settle for civil unions: They insisted that the law treat a "marriage" between two men or two women as *identical to* (real) marriage. The new definition thus enshrined the falsehood that there is no relevant difference between a marriage of one man and one woman and any other coupling.

A limited government doesn't try to redefine reality as the Orwellian governments of the twentieth century did. Nor does it bestow our natural rights on us. We get our rights from God. A limited government recognizes and secures key social realities outside its jurisdiction. It protects what already exists. That includes marriage—which predates every government on Earth.

The state has no just authority to redefine our rights or to redefine marriage because it has no authority to redefine reality.

What Can We Do?

To reverse marriage's march toward the gallows, we need to play the long game—and we need a lot of repentance and healing. We should not stoop to hateful attacks on our critics. Even when we're attacked as bigots or "homophobes," we need to pray for the strength to offer love and compassion in return. Our critics need Christ's love, not our anger.

If your marriage is in trouble, we hope you'll do whatever it takes to save it. Even if you've suffered severe hurt or infidelity, your marriage can be restored and become even stronger if both parties are willing.

Early in His ministry, Jesus traveled through the land of Samaria. The Jews thought of Samaritans as half-breed idolaters and did their best to avoid them. When our Lord encountered a Samaritan woman at a well, however, He asked her for a drink. Astonished, she asked,

"How is it that you, a Jew, ask a drink of me, a woman of Samaria?" In reply, Jesus revealed that He was the Living Water that could give eternal life.

He then told her to call her husband. She admitted that she did not have one, but Jesus knew the whole truth. "You are right in saying, 'I have no husband,'" He said, "for you have had five husbands, and he whom you now have is not your husband; this you said truly." What did Jesus do? He did not justify her sin; he *named and exposed* it, but still offered her His love (John 4:3–42).

This woman cast off her shame, then went out to invite everyone to meet the man who knew all her sins. If Jesus could offer grace to the Samaritan woman, He can do the same for anyone else.

All of us who are married need to model what marriage is supposed to look like and stop surfing the wave of no-fault divorce.[24] As believers, we also need to repent from what *we* have done. Divorce is almost as common among professing Christians as among the general population, but the stats improve among those who attend worship at least once a week and who pray together daily.[25] And for some reason, couples who practice "natural family planning"—whether Catholic, Protestant, or Jewish—have very low divorce rates.[26]

Paul's advice to the church at Ephesus is still timely:

> Be subject to one another out of reverence for Christ. Wives, be subject to your husbands, as to the Lord. . . . Husbands, love your wives, as Christ loved the church and gave himself up for her, that he might sanctify her. . . . Even so husbands should love their wives as their own bodies. (Ephesians 5:21–28)

Paul's command to wives rubs some people the wrong way, but his command to husbands is even more bracing. And he also tells husbands and wives to be subject to each other. Remember, this was written in the first century when women were considered property, and their legal testimony counted for nothing. And still, we husbands are told to love our wives as "Christ loved the church and gave himself up for her."

What if every married person reading this book resolved to put Paul's words into practice? This we know: We'd all have a lot more credibility when defending marriage.

CHAPTER 8

Male and Female He Created Them

When God created the heavens and the earth, He ended Day Six by speaking to Himself:

> "Let us make man in our image, after our likeness; and let them have dominion over the fish of the sea, and over the birds of the air, and over the cattle, and over all the earth, and over every creeping thing that creeps upon the earth." So God created man in his own image, in the image of God he created him; male and female he created them. And God blessed them, and God said to them, "Be fruitful and multiply, and fill the earth and subdue it; and have dominion over the fish of the sea and over the birds of the air and over every living thing that moves upon the earth." (Genesis 1:26–28)

God creates each of us in His image. Yet we can't fulfill His command to multiply and fill the earth without the difference of male and female. Why? Because it takes one fertile male and one fertile female to reproduce after our kind. It's not just that males and females are different; it's that we're *complements*. When we come together in the right way, we're much greater than the sum of our parts. One man and one woman can give rise to the entire human race.

Even without special revelation, everyone knows the following:

1. There are men and women.
2. Men aren't women.
3. Women aren't men.
4. Men can't become women.
5. Women can't become men.
6. It's not possible to be a man but have a woman's body or to be a woman with a man's body.

Until recently, these six claims would have seemed trite. But we live at the shocking moment when our cultural elites deny them all and seek to silence those who resist. In what seems like a flash, "gender ideology" has overrun our schools, our media, our laws, the HR and C-suites of most corporations, the United Nations, and even many churches and synagogues. This ideology has deep roots going back centuries, but it has really picked up steam in the academy in the last few decades.

In 2015, so-called transgender people, such as Caitlyn (formerly the Olympic decathlete known as Bruce) Jenner, suddenly appeared on dozens of magazine covers. A few years later, a collegiate male swimmer, "Lia" Thomas—a male who "identifies" as a woman—won the women's 500-yard freestyle in the NCAA Division I national championship. A twenty-six-year-old man, Dylan Mulvaney, started acting like a parody of a 1950s teenage girl and instantly rose to fame with his picture emblazoned on cans of Bud Light. A male sex offender "identifying as a woman" was sent to a women's prison, where he then raped a female prisoner.[1] Meanwhile, the acronyms kept growing: LBGT morphed into LBGTQIA with a + added to keep the options open.

What produced the backlash from normal people was the assault on kids: Children have been bombarded with sexual content. Schools stock shelves with explicit porn, such as the notorious *Gender Queer.* Activists are teaching young kids to "queer" (that is, blur the boundaries of) reality at drag queen story hours at libraries nationwide. The popular Twitter feed, Libs of TikTok, contains videos of young children twerking and gyrating at drag shows in ways once reserved for dark adult bars.

And amidst it all, teachers and social media influencers are telling children they might have been born in the wrong body. Doctors are "treating" troubled minors with sterilizing drugs and surgeries. When word of this first got out, activists tried to pretend it wasn't really happening. When that became implausible, they pivoted. Sure, it's happening, they conceded. In fact, it's great, and how dare you object, bigot!

Twenty years ago, everyone—left, right, and center—would have denounced such scenes. But overnight, approval became the litmus test for tolerance and taste.

These are the worst ideas of our time—the mutant spawn of some nameless demon set free to roam the earth and devour our children.

"Gender-Affirming Care"

Let's look at just the gender quackery. Here's how fast it spread. In 2007—the year the first iPhone was released—there was one pediatric gender clinic in the U.S. By 2022, there were about eighty. And that doesn't include hundreds of the Planned Parenthood "clinics" that dispense cross-sex hormones like candy to minors.[2] These places are where thousands of minors who struggle with their sexed bodies go to receive "gender-affirming care"—the euphemism for what is, in effect, a school-to-sterilization pipeline.

It starts with "social transition," usually in school and often behind parents' backs, such as a troubled boy who "identifies" as a girl assuming a new name, as well as using the pronouns and bathrooms of his new identity. No student or teacher is exempt from playing along, and punishment is swift for any who dare to resist.

Social transition fast-tracks the child to puberty-blocking drugs if he or she is still early in puberty, and then to cross-sex hormones—estrogen for boys and testosterone for girls. Next will come surgery to remove healthy breasts, penises, testicles, uteri, and ovaries. The details, of course, depend upon the sex of the child.

Finally, this pathway leads to surgery to fashion faux penises for the girls, vaginas for the boys, and other options for those who identify as, say, nonbinary—that is, neither male nor female, or both, or somewhere in between. And don't forget lifelong cross-sex hormones and complications that are as common as they are unadvertised.[3]

California teen Chloe Cole is one such victim of this protocol. She started suffering from gender dysphoria (the current term for distress over one's sexed body) when she was twelve. Through social media, she came to believe she was really a boy. California mandates that parents, teachers, and therapists "affirm" a child's "gender identity." As a result, Chloe was soon taking puberty-blocking drugs and testosterone. When she was fifteen, she received a double mastectomy (that is, "top surgery").

At age eighteen, she joined the brave band of "detransitioners" who speak out against this medical travesty. In her testimony before California's Senate Judiciary Committee in September 2022, she referred to herself as the "canary in the coal mine."[4] Yet Chloe is one of the lucky ones: She got off the train before it reached its destination. She did not have a hysterectomy and may still be able to bear children, which she now wants.[5]

This sort of thing has been happening for more than a decade across Europe and North America. According to one report, the number of teens reporting to the main gender clinic for kids in the United Kingdom rose by 4,400 percent in the ten years from 2009 to 2019![6] In the U.S., surgeries to remove breasts for adolescent girls increased nearly 500 percent between 2016 and 2019.[7]

Until recently, gender dysphoria (previously called "gender identity disorder") in children was extremely rare. It occurred mostly in prepubertal boys, with most cases resolving after puberty. But it's now common among girls and can crop up in friend groups. In 2017, this crisis led researcher Lisa Littman to coin the term "rapid onset gender dysphoria."[8] Littman was careful how she described this—but that didn't save her from suffering a devastating professional attack by critics.

This gender quackery has overtaken not just schools and social media, but even groups claiming to speak for medicine. This includes the American Medical Association, the American Academy of Pediatrics, and, under sweeping orders from Joe Biden, the U.S. Department of Health and Human Services.[9]

What It Is and Where It Came From

If sterilizing kids is where the gender mind virus ends, where did it start? Its intellectual roots are complex.[10] But as it has erupted in our culture, it comes down to this. Gender ideology displaces the sexual binary of male and female—which describes all mammals, including humans—with a state of mind and a social construct. The state of mind is called a "gender identity," which is distinct from—even in conflict with—the body. The social construct is called "sex assigned at birth."

Hence, the gender groupies avoid references to sex when defining their terms. "Gender identity," explains the Ontario Human Rights Commission,

> is each person's internal and individual experience of gender. It is a person's sense of being a woman, a man, both, neither, or anywhere along the gender spectrum.[11]

Note that "gender" appears in both the definition and the word being defined. Yes, that's circular, but it can't be helped since gender identity is supposedly distinct from sex.

You might think the "trans issue" involves, say, a man (referring to biological "sex") identifying as a woman ("gender"), which means he's "transgender." But what we're talking about here is more radical than that. Consider the popular book for kindergarteners *It Feels Good to Be Yourself.* "Some people are boys," it explains. "Some people are girls. Some people are both, neither, or somewhere in between."[12] Sex as a biological truth has been displaced by an internal self-perception—gender identity—and by the mere choice of the doctor attending one's birth. "Trans" is only one of the options. There's also nonbinary, asexual, two-spirit, eunuch, and dozens of others of very recent vintage.[13]

Gender ideology is a deadly toxin. To resist it, we, and especially our children, need to build up antibodies in our minds. And once inoculated, we must fight it wherever it appears—in our schools, our churches, medicine, media, corporate advertising, and more.

Let's start with the immunotherapy: a clear definition of sex and a clear grasp of what it means to be human.

Defining Male and Female

An idea that denies basic biology could only gain ground through a campaign of confusion. In this case, gender activists have confused the public by falsely claiming that disorders of sexual development, often mislabeled "intersex" conditions, prove that there are more than two sexes—or that the sexes are fluid or mere endpoints on a spectrum.[14]

Such disorders do occur—in 0.018 percent of the population.[15] In some such cases, newborns are born with ambiguous genitalia, which makes it harder to determine their sex. But appealing to these disorders to justify gender ideology is a diversion. First, none of these disorders produces other sexes or "genders." Second, gender ideology provides no new insights into them. Third, people who identify as transgender or nonbinary almost never have one of these disorders. And fourth, no such disorders correspond to the growing list of "gender identities."

Alas, many who want to defend the reality of sex don't get the details right. People often claim, for instance, that a male is anyone with an XY chromosome, and a female is anyone with an XX chromosome. But there are rare conditions where this doesn't hold. That would mean some people are neither male nor female—hardly the intended outcome.

We see the same problem with some common ways of defining the two sexes. Someone might say, for instance, that "a woman can have babies. A man can't." That's true, but it's not a definition of "man" or "woman." After all, what about women who have hysterectomies, or who have gone through menopause? Do these people not count as women? Of course they do. So that definition doesn't hold up.

We all know that men differ from women. And if you remember high school biology, you know that childbearing, XX and XY chromosomes, and the like, have something to do with sex. But biology is

complex, and definitions are hard to get just right. Vague legal definitions create openings for gender ideology to gain a toehold.

Any good definition of "male" and "female" will refer to what
happens under normal development while accounting for disorders.
It will also account for the fact that organisms have and do different
things at different stages of development.

These definitions will seem technical if you haven't studied this
before. But if we want to beat gender insanity, we must think and speak
clearly about sex and avoid the traps the activists have set for us.

The most straightforward way to define the sexes is in terms of
their gametes. A "gamete" is a reproductive cell in a plant or animal.
A human male is a member of the human species that, under normal
development, produces the smaller, mobile gametes—sperm—at some
point in his life cycle, and has a reproductive and endocrine system
oriented around the production of that gamete. A human female is a
member of the human species that, under normal development, produces the larger, relatively immobile gametes—ova—at some point
in her life cycle, and has a reproductive and endocrine system oriented
around the production of that gamete.

That is the bare-bones definition of male and female.

Of course, we can say more. Under normal development, males
have XY chromosomes, testes, and a penis. Females, under normal
development, have XX chromosomes, a uterus, ovaries, a cervix, and
a vagina. Under normal development, females can carry, give birth
to, and nurse offspring at some point in their life cycles. Males can't.
Males and females also differ in the prevalence of hormones such as
testosterone and estrogen, respectively. And they develop distinct
secondary differences in their bodies under the influence of these
hormones, especially during puberty.

To see why sex is binary, though, we should focus on the gametes.
There are exactly two—sperm and eggs—with two corresponding

body plans, and so only two sexes. There are no erms or speggs, or bodies that produce them.

What's more, there's no gamete or body plan that corresponds to a "gender identity"—a made-up concept from gender and queer theory. It has nothing to do with disorders of sexual development—none of which negate the reality of sex. In fact, we only know they're disorders because we know *what normally happens*.

Yet this made-up term from a crazy ideology is now official in American medicine, the federal government, and among global elites. The U.S. Department of Health and Human Services now defines "gender-affirming care" for adolescents not as helping children adjust to their sexed bodies, but as refashioning the body with drugs and surgery to better conform to the child's reported "gender identity."

Evidence for the benefits of this "treatment" is in very short supply, and the harms are obvious.[16] As a result, several countries that started down this path before the U.S. did, such as the United Kingdom, Finland, Sweden, and Norway, have now stepped back. The U.K.'s National Health Service now concedes that many teens reporting gender dysphoria should receive therapy in the hope that they will do what almost all such teens did before this craze: grow out of it.[17]

How did such ghoulish myths take over our culture? The backstory reads like a bad James Bond script. Billionaires, some of them men posing as women, funded activists who pushed it into schools, law, medicine, and politics.[18] Drug companies that stood to profit from lifelong patients got in on the act, even funding groups to push the ideas in schools.[19] The media, acting as ventriloquists' dummies for the activists, amplified their message through Instagram, TikTok, and so forth.

But the idea itself is the fruit of a false view of human nature. It fails to grasp that human beings are both spiritual and material.

Christians say Jesus is fully human and fully divine. Man, we might say, is fully material and fully spiritual—not merely one or the other. Not half one and half the other. Both—at one and the same time.

Genesis 2 says that, in creating us, God took the dust of the earth and breathed into it the breath of life. We're neither upright apes nor ghosts in meat suits. We're embodied persons—*Homo sapiens*, mammals, with bodies made of cells and chemicals. Christians confess not just eternal life, but the resurrection of the body. (Our survival between death and resurrection is an incomplete, temporary state.)

Beyond that, we're sexually complementary creatures, not androgynous drones. To fulfill God's command to our first parents—to be fruitful and multiply—it takes exactly one male and one female coming together. This gives rise to children. Thus, the institutions of marriage and family, in which children are best raised, are the guardrails of biological reality.

Notice that we just ran together the biblical view of the human person and family with biology. We meant to do that. If the biblical view is true, then reason reflecting on human nature can't escape its basic outline. And that's what we find: Even honest materialists and Marxists assume they have free will, can tell boys from girls, and can't help but find that intact marriages are better for raising kids than the alternatives.

Because of sin, though, we tend to distort the truth—especially those truths that keep us from pursuing short-term pleasure. So, following the iron logic of the sexual revolution, many pretend that sex, marriage, and reproduction need not go together. And when it comes to the nature of human beings as both matter and spirit, people tend to lurch from one side of this compound truth to the other, rather than embracing the complex whole. Even many Christians talk as if we're really just souls trapped in bodies.

Many others are in worse shape. They waver between contrary opinions: Are we just bags of chemicals? Or are we really some dis-embodied entity that will soon be upgraded with more durable hard-ware, as the transhumanists claim?

Gender junkies check the second box. They treat a person's identity as a merely "psychological self"—as theologian Carl Trueman puts it[20]—independent of the body. This self is somehow "gendered"—whatever that means—but not "sexed." It's immaterial and yet in need of a body refashioned with the latest drugs and scalpels to match what it believes itself to be.

What Can We Do?

To escape this freak show, Christians, Jews, and everyone else on #TeamReality need to offer a better view of the human person—one that captures human beings in their fullness, body and soul. That means that, among other things, we must also defend basic biology.

This battle will define our politics for the next decade at least. As we write this, one political party fully promotes gender ideology, while the other, with fits and starts, opposes it. The Biden administration has turned the federal government into the globe's most powerful mission effort of the gender cult. Until that changes, we'll play defense in Washington.

The red states can be safe zones, but we must fight in every nook and cranny—at school board meetings, in the workplace, with our investments and shopping choices. Every red state should protect kids from these medical procedures. They should also define "male" and "female" in state law,[21] prohibit secret social transitioning in schools, purge gender ideology from school curricula, protect teachers and others from being forced to use fake names and pronouns, and reverse laws that allow people to change the sex on their birth certificate based simply on how they "identify." Well-crafted parents' rights bills can help here, and red states have passed several in the last few years.

We suspect the gender clinics will be sued into oblivion as more of their young victims come of age. But we can't wait for that to happen. We need to fight gender madness as if our children's lives depend on it. And even when the clinics close their doors, that will be but one victory in a larger battle to defeat a fanatical force that makes twentieth-century communism look tame.

Gender ideology attacks who and what we are. But it also marks an inflection point. We're being offered a glimpse of the deadly path ahead. Either our culture will see it for what it is and reverse course—or it will suffer costs we can't begin to imagine.

CHAPTER 9

Multiply and Fill the Earth

The book of Genesis is a family history. It starts with Adam and Eve and their sons Cain, Abel, and Seth. One man and one woman give rise to a family, which gives rise to a larger family, which over time gives rise to a group of tribes, which over time become a nation. At the root, trunk, and branches of it all, there is a family.

The family is not just a human institution. The Bible describes Israel as the children—the family—of God. Later, Paul tells us that the Church has been adopted into this family. He also describes the Church as the Bride of Christ. What's more, Jesus taught us to call God "Father." And in reflecting on God's nature, the Church learned to refer to the Father, the Son, and the Holy Spirit as the three persons of the one God. So, the concept of family allows us to better see ourselves, our relationship to God, and even His nature.

"The future of humanity," said Pope John Paul II, "passes by way of the family."

Intact Families Are Better for Kids

We know from both revelation and reason that families matter. The natural result of sex between a man and a woman is children, and children are best raised in a family headed by a married father and mother. As Maggie Gallagher put it, "Sex makes babies. Society needs babies. Children need mothers and fathers."[1] Being raised by their mother and father matters more to children's well-being than their race, their parents' education, or even their neighborhood.[2] In school—from test scores and GPA to expectations of attending college—kids raised by both their mother and their father together are better off than their peers from divorced, cohabiting, or single-parent homes. Children in such intact families commit less crime, have less sex outside of marriage, and have fewer children out of wedlock than others.[3]

Children of divorce are far more likely to get expelled from school and, later, end up unemployed.[4] For decades, poverty in the United States has had much less to do with jobs than with divorce. According to one Harvard professor writing in the 1980s, "The vast majority of children who are raised entirely in a home where parents are married will never be poor during childhood. By contrast, the vast majority of children who spend time in a fatherless home will experience poverty."[5]

In the U.S. and other developed countries, the best antipoverty program for women and children is for the woman to be married to the father of her children. According to a study from the Institute of Family Studies, childhood poverty would be 17 percent lower if marriage rates were still as high as they were even in the 1980s.[6]

Heroic single parents and their kids can overcome the odds. But in general, children of divorce are more likely to abuse substances and develop health problems that linger even after they become adults. And as tough as having only one parent in the home can be, stepparents may not improve things. Kids living with adults who are not their biological parents are much more likely to die of maltreatment and to suffer physical and sexual abuse.[7] God can heal many traumas, of course; but on average, divorce is bad for kids.

Not Just Two Parents: A Mom and a Dad

In recent years, activist journals have published articles claiming (but never proving) that kids are as well or better off in homes headed by a same-sex couple or other "sexual minorities." This contradicts everything we know.[8] What matters most is not two (or more) "parents" but the presence of a married mother and father. Moms and dads aren't interchangeable Lego pieces. "A father is not a male mother," says family expert Glenn T. Stanton. "Fathers are categorically different kinds of parents than mothers, and this is good for children."[9] Mothers and fathers bring unique and irreplaceable assets to parenting.

Social science confirms this: In general, dads and moms interact differently with their children. Dads tend to tickle and roughhouse; moms tend to cuddle and comfort. Dads challenge; moms encourage. Dads stupidly throw their toddlers in the air. Moms gasp when dads stupidly throw their toddlers in the air.

We also tend to communicate and discipline differently. "Dads tend to see their children in relation to the rest of the world," note Stanton and Maier. "Mothers tend to see the rest of the world in relation to their children."[10]

Two sociologists summed up the evidence this way: "If we were asked to design a system for making sure that children's basic needs were met, we would probably come up with something quite similar to the two-parent ideal."[11] A healthy culture requires a healthy marriage culture, which encourages "adults to arrange their lives so that as many children as possible are raised and nurtured by their biological parents in a common household."[12] It's cruel to strive for anything less.

The Family Limits Government

Some fiscal conservatives talk up smaller government, free markets, and individual rights, but treat the family as a private matter that has no bearing on public policy. Without strong families, however, we won't have freedom and limited government for long.

First, if the state ignores the family, it undermines the logic by which it protects individual rights. The American republic was founded in part to secure the rights of individuals. The state does not create but rather recognizes what already exists—namely, people with "prepolitical" rights. These limit the state. The family is another prepolitical reality. A just and limited state does not invent the family but rather recognizes the nature of the family in its laws. If the state won't grant something as basic as the family—which every culture in history has recognized—why should we think it will continue to respect individual rights, which are a much more recent idea?

Second, destroying families leads to a larger, more intrusive nanny state. Research shows a link between the breakdown of marriage and the growth in government spending in Scandinavia.[13] The family is a huge check on government power. As Mike Huckabee has said, "The most important form of government is the family."[14] The better a family functions, the less you need from the state.

The family exists, in large part, to protect and bring up children. Each of us is born helpless, clueless, and selfish. Humans are more helpless early in our lives than almost any animal. Some animals, such as horses and elephants, can stand hours after birth. Within a few months after birth, kittens and puppies are potty trained, eating from a dish, and attacking your ankles. Newborn children, in contrast, won't raise their heads or use their hands for many weeks; they seldom walk before they're a year old and may still be wearing diapers on their third birthday.

Ideally, in their families, children learn to love and be loved; how to eat properly and feed, bathe, dress, and clean up after themselves; to brush their teeth, treat others kindly, speak clearly, share, negotiate, sit still, study hard and do their homework, follow the law, pray to God, and control their tongues and their vices.

Though they may delegate some of their children's education to schools and churches, parents should still oversee the process. If all goes well, parents will teach their kids to internalize the rule of law that a free society depends on, and the discipline and knowledge that allow them to create wealth and value, rather than merely consume it.

The Fiscal Fruits of Families

Little of the work that parents do at home ever shows up in economic stats, and yet that work may create more long-term value than the work that gets counted as part of the Gross Domestic Product. Take, for instance, two couples: the Smiths and the Joneses. The Smiths work hard raising four kids, who grow up to be successful parents and workers. Two parents have given society four productive citizens. The Joneses, in contrast, neglect their four kids, who grow up to be idle hoodlums. They'll be supported with tax money taken from the Smiths.

An intact family uses fewer resources, such as food, shelter, and health care, than it would if it were split into more than one household.

The intact family can save more and invest more because it's much more efficient than either single life or a broken family. Anyone who has been single knows how hard it is to cook and save leftovers for one person. Those big bundles of ruby red grapefruit and hearts of romaine at Costco aren't that useful until you have several people under one roof. According to family scholar Pat Fagan, intact families "work, earn, and save at significantly higher rates than other family households as well as pay the lion's share of all income taxes collected by the government."[15]

Families also give to "charity and volunteer at significantly higher rates, even when controlling for income, than do single or divorced households."[16] After looking at American patterns of giving, economist Arthur Brooks concluded that "single parenthood is a disaster for charity."[17]

Someone has to raise children; in the modern world, when families break down or don't form at all, the government steps in. If parents divorce, a family court will decide who has custody of the kids, when and on what days the parents get to see their children, how much the parents spend, and on what. It will garnish the wages of parents who fail to comply. Mom and Dad may both have to submit to psychological tests. The most intimate details of family life can become a part of the public court records.

Though most kids of divorce survive, and some prosper, on average they're much more likely to become wards of the state and later to give birth to wards of the state. A Brookings Institution study attributes $229 billion in welfare expenses from 1970 to 1996 to the breakdown of marriage and the social problems produced in its wake.[18] And that's just a tiny slice of the total costs to society.

This scenario gets even scarier when parents abuse or abandon their children. Then the state must put the kids in either orphanages or foster care, making the state the distant, all-powerful nanny.

How the Great Society Wrecked the Family

As divorce laws became ever more lax and divorce ever more common in the 1960s, the federal government launched "Great Society" welfare programs. President Lyndon Johnson labeled these programs the "War on Poverty." Rather than curing poverty, however, the war encouraged out-of-wedlock births and generational cycles of poverty. "When the federal government's War on Poverty began in 1964, only 6.3 percent of children in the U.S. were born out of wedlock. . . . By 2008, four out of 10 births occurred outside of marriage."[19] That figure remained the same in 2022.

These trends have gutted the black family in many urban areas—around seven in ten black children are born out of wedlock[20]—and harmed all families, but especially the poor. The sexual revolution and the welfare state have conspired to create a vicious cycle: Family breakdown leads to a bigger, more meddlesome government, which leads to even more family breakdown, and so on.

Marriage, children, and divorce also shape people's political views. Single women tend to support bigger government and higher taxes than married women, and divorced women with children are much more likely to vote for progressive tickets than married mothers of children. "Generally, as divorce rates have increased," John Lott notes, "women voters have become more liberal."[21] Getting and staying married, and then having kids, makes people more conservative.[22] But by striking at the family—the cell of the body of society—the sexual revolution could end up destroying society as we know it.[23]

What Should We Do?

It's easier for the modern state to disrupt family life than to improve it. Politicians try to connect every policy to "the children." But if we really care, we must think past the rhetoric to the reality.

To know what any policy will do, we must figure out the incentives it sets up. Does it encourage the mothers and fathers of children not to marry, not to stay married, or not to stay in the home with their children? Does it raise the net cost of having kids for the parents or society as a whole? If so, we can safely say it will not be "good for the children."

Still, there's one policy we should all get behind: ending the "marriage penalty."[24] For decades, conservatives have complained that our tax code and welfare system is set up so that it may cost a couple more to get married than if they have kids out of wedlock. Before we get behind complex policies to try to coax people to have more kids, let's demand that politicians fix this problem.

Part of the Problem, or the Solution?

Too many of us have taken our cues from enemies of the family. Divorce rates are only slightly better for professing Christians than for the general public. Our views on childbirth aren't much different, either. Did you know that before the 1930s, all Christians believed that sex and childbearing should go together? While few thought they had to have as many kids as possible, all Christians took God's commandment to be fruitful and multiply literally.

This has radically changed, and yet few Christians ever give it much thought. You can see the effects on fertility rates. The "total fertility rate" refers to the average number of children born to a woman in her lifetime. To keep its population steady, a country needs a fertility rate of 2.1. In 1800, the fertility rate in the United States was 7.04 for white people and 7.9 for black people (statistics were kept separately).

Except for a brief uptick after World War II, called the Baby Boom, America's fertility rate has been dropping since the Founding.

It dropped by half from 1960 to 1980, then took a nosedive after the 2008 financial crisis and hasn't recovered.[25] Today, the fertility rate in the U.S. is 1.64. Take away the effects of immigration, and our native-born birth rate is in the same pickle that sent countries like Hungary into desperation moves to pay people to have children.

For decades, "world opinion" claimed we were running out of food and needed to prune the human swarm to survive. As recently as 1979, the worldwide fertility rate was 6.0. Now the worldwide rate is 2.3 and dropping.[26]

Even the UN, which has been pushing population control for decades, concedes the point. It now predicts that the world population will level off around 2050—while developing countries are still growing—and then start to drop. This worldwide trend masks the trends in developed countries, most of which are committing "demographic suicide." No European country is at replacement rate. Many Asian countries are in even worse shape. Japan has a fertility rate of 1.34 and South Korea is at 0.78! Many experts think countries can't recover from such low fertility rates. Time will tell.

Many Christians have been part of the trend. Did God send a new revelation telling us to stop being fruitful and multiplying? We say "many" because not everyone has swallowed this propaganda. Religious people have more children on average than nonreligious people. And the more devout (Catholic, Protestant, Jewish, and others) tend to have more kids than do the lukewarm. They also have fewer of their children out of wedlock.[27] And one study reveals that the more siblings people have, the less likely they are to divorce as adults.[28]

A strong religious faith may be the main reason people have children.[29] If you're married, have faith, and see children as a duty and a blessing, then you'll *try* to have kids—by birth and/or adoption. But what if you fear the future and view human beings as wasteful carbon footprints, or a drag on your hip lifestyle—or hips? Then you might think you should not have children, should abort the ones you carry, or at least should have no more than one. Take a walk through the secular urban areas of Manhattan, San Francisco, and Seattle. You'll see lots of dogs on leashes but not many babies in strollers. In 2020, some 34.5 percent of preborn babies in New York City were aborted.[30]

Restoring the Culture One Baby at a Time

Some people are single, either by calling or happenstance. And some couples can't have kids, or not as many as they would like. But if believers have more kids (on average) than others and transmit their faith to their children, over time there will be far more believers than unbelievers as a percentage of the population.

This has some atheists worried. "It is a great irony but evolution appears to discriminate against atheists and favour those with religious beliefs," said researcher Michael Blume of the University of Jena in Germany. "Most societies or communities that have espoused atheistic beliefs have not survived more than a century."[31]

Having a big family and passing on your faith and ideas to your children, then, may be one of the most concrete ways to renew our culture.

CHAPTER 10

Train Up a Child

The main way most of us contribute to the future is by having children. But we must do what we can to keep them from becoming part of the problem of our rapidly declining culture.

"Train up a child in the way he should go," Proverbs says, "and when he is old he will not depart from it" (Proverbs 22:6). This is a rule of thumb rather than an ironclad law. We all know faithful parents who raised their children in the faith—only to see those children leave the faith as soon as they leave home. According to the Barna Group, 64 percent of those raised as evangelicals drift off in early adulthood.[1] About half of Americans raised Catholic leave the faith, according to Pew. Some return later, but many do not.[2] Orthodox Jews—perhaps because they're so countercultural—do better. According to Pew, around 67 percent stay observant as adults. And the more orthodox, the better.[3]

Since children have free will, parents can't guarantee what their kids will do once they leave the nest. But the proverb suggests parents can do a lot to improve the odds of a good outcome. Much of that has to do with education.

The End of Education

A proper education will impart knowledge: multiplication tables, the periodic table of the elements, history, grammar, and literature. It will teach kids how to weigh arguments and think clearly. Still, the purpose of education is not just to teach, in some neutral way, "reading, writing, and 'rithmetic." After all, kids must read *something*. Education should guide them to the Good, the True, and the Beautiful. It should enlarge their minds and their souls. It should provide them not only with knowledge, but with wisdom and virtue. It should civilize. It should help them find not just their calling, but their purpose.

Alas, cultural decay, government's near-monopoly over education, and crackpot theories have conspired to make a mess of education from kindergarten through college. The best single way to improve American education is to foster real choice for parents and real competition with the government and its schools.

The Root Cause

To understand our current plight, though, we need to know how we got here. The first proto-public school law in the nation was called the "Old Deluder Satan Act of 1647." (Really.) It required towns with "fifty or more families" in Puritan Massachusetts to teach children to read so they could read the Bible and avoid being tricked into sinning by "that Old Deluder, Satan."[4]

Fast-forward two centuries. In 1837, Horace Mann set up state-sponsored schools in Boston, taking his cues from the Prussian military. He, more than anyone else, set our country on the course toward secular, bureaucratic, government-controlled education.[5] The goal was to homogenize students and "cure" them of their parents' "backward" religious beliefs.

You may have heard of the noxious influence of the early twentieth-century thinker John Dewey of Columbia University's Teachers College, who dismissed old-fashioned questions like, "What is true?" He insisted, instead, that students ask, "Does it work?" or "Does it work for me?" Public schools, for Dewey, were not about imparting truth but making practical citizens.

But our problems with public schools really started with enmity among Christians. The early American colonies had established churches, and education reflected that. In response to immigration in the early 1800s, though, legislators in New York and elsewhere got worried. With waves of immigrants coming from Ireland, Italy, and Germany, many feared Catholic kids would go to Catholic schools and become secret agents of the Pope. Lawmakers reasoned that if "Protestant schools could be made less expensive through government subsidies . . . some Catholics would transfer their children there."[6]

This led to the infamous Philadelphia "Bible riots" in 1844, when Irish Catholics were attacked for objecting to the sole use of Protestant Bibles in public schools.[7] In the 1850s, an anti-Catholic group called the "Know-Nothings" (because they would say "I know nothing" if asked what they were up to) emerged. Members pushed anti-Catholic policies such as requiring public school teachers to be Protestant and read only from Protestant Bibles.[8] This, of course, encouraged Catholics to set up more Catholic schools.

Meanwhile, the many Protestant schools that enjoyed government subsidies competed to attract Catholic students, watering down their religious instruction. (By this time, school for kids between certain ages was pretty much compulsory.) In response, lawmakers started limiting subsidies only "to the approved Protestant school nearest to a student's home," to keep them from competing with each other. This set the precedent of government control and geographical restrictions on schools.

Here's what happened next, according to education expert John Lott Jr.:

> As government programs tend to do, over time the subsidy scheme grew until it began eliciting complaints that the subsidized schools were getting most of their money from the government while being protected from competition. With the Free Schools Act of 1867, the state simply took over the subsidized schools, which then became public institutions.[9]

We'll never know what would have happened if believers had fought the forces of statism and secularism that were then gathering strength instead of using the state as a weapon against each other.

You know the rest of the story. Public schools became secular and centralized. The Supreme Court later declared that even generic prayer and talk of God violate the First Amendment. Untethered from God, education has gotten worse and worse.

Of course, it's still supposed to inculcate virtue. So these days, public (and some private) schools use tools like "Social Emotional Learning" (SEL) to teach the "whole child." This sounds nice but it ends up training kids to swallow woke pieties—to "empathize" with "oppressed" groups rather than to act justly. Moral training is reduced to lessons on how to get informed consent before performing a sex act—followed by a demo on how do it "safely."[10] And in case that doesn't work, there's even a movement to transform schools into health clinics: "Community schools" will provide birth control, abortions, and gender medicine for students.[11]

Freedom on the Fringes

Despite these problems, local school districts and states still mostly run the show. That's why you should be involved in your local elections—maybe even run for school board. These boards control hundreds of billions of dollars and much of what's done in public schools. There are still some good public schools and many good teachers. But they are good despite the system, not because of it. Many districts have been hijacked by radicals, while the U.S. Department of Justice tars as "domestic extremists" sane parents who try to push back.

This drives many people away from public schools. That movement creates demand, which is met by thousands of good private schools. There are also about 3.1 million homeschooled students nationwide.[12] (Compare that to "tolerant" countries such as Sweden, where you can go to prison for homeschooling your kids.)[13]

The freedom to educate has been hard won, though. Oregon's 1922 "Compulsory Education Act" was sponsored by the Freemasons, the Ku Klux Klan, and the state's Democratic governor to keep Catholics from sending their kids to Catholic schools. It would have forced all students to attend government schools, but the U.S. Supreme Court struck it down in 1925. "The child is not the mere creature of the state," the justices wrote. "Those who nurture him and direct his destiny have the right, coupled with the high duty, to recognize and prepare him for additional obligations."[14]

In recent years, through the tireless efforts of parents and groups like the Home School Legal Defense Association, well-off parents have lots of educational choices for their kids.

Why Haven't We Fixed This?

Imagine if we all had to pay into a general government food fund instead of buying our own groceries. The government then opened cafeterias in our neighborhoods, forbade us from eating at those across town, and hassled anyone who tried to cook at home. It would make no sense. And yet that's pretty much the current situation with public schools.

When private businesses fail, they go bankrupt. When public schools fail, or commit fraud or gross negligence,[15] they often get more funding. Clearly, choice and competition would drive down costs and improve education across the board.[16]

Why do we tolerate this quasi-monopoly on something as personal as a child's mind? Two reasons: teachers' unions and public apathy fueled by what we might call It's-Different-in-My-District syndrome.

The teachers' unions—the National Education Association and the American Federation of Teachers—hate reform. Combined, they are the largest political campaign contributors in the country, and 94 percent of that money goes to Democrats in national elections.[17] (They manage to recruit some Republican politicians, too.)

The other reason we haven't replaced this creaky system is that, until COVID, affluent Americans didn't feel the urgency of the problem. Parents who can afford to live in nice neighborhoods can challenge their public schools. If things don't improve, they can lobby (or run for) school board, move elsewhere, or remove their kids from the system. That freedom functions as a release valve. These parents don't suffer enough from the system to fix it.

The poor, in contrast, remain trapped in failing schools, where they become victims of every silly educational fad and social dysfunction. Those who have choices must summon the courage to make educational freedom a priority for everyone.

Real Choice

The U.S. spends more on average per student than any country in the world.[18] Yet our public schools rank lower than you'd expect: "The U.S. placed 11th out of 79 countries in science when [the Program for International Student Assessment] was last administered in 2018. It did much worse in math, ranking thirtieth." That's well behind leaders Singapore, Macao, Hong Kong, Taiwan, and Japan.[19]

For years, polls have shown that most Americans across the political spectrum support "school choice" in theory.[20] The silver lining of the gender and COVID craziness is that they're now starting to support it in practice.

Thirty-three states plus the District of Columbia have policies that allow funding to follow at least some children to whatever learning environment their parents choose. Most programs are limited to children from low-income families or students with special needs. But six states—Arizona, Arkansas, Florida, Iowa, Utah, and West Virginia—offer education savings accounts (ESAs) or similar policies to all K-12 students.[21] These policies connect funds to kids rather than systems and let parents decide how to spend the money.

ESAs turn parents into free, discerning, focused consumers, rather than passive victims of a lumbering bureaucracy. Right now, only a fraction of parents has this choice, but it's a start.

Wait. Won't government shekels come with government shackles? That's a fair worry. But remember: The government already can (and often tries to) regulate private and home schools. So, we are not losing any ground with this. Besides, this is public, not government, money. Right now, the government taxes the public and uses it to prop up a bad monopoly. ESAs help break that up. And parents who don't want them should be free to decline the money. The good news is that states with the best school choice policies also have the least burdensome regulations on private and home schools.[22]

Bad Philosophy

College is a different ball of wax. Despite a costly "education bubble" that has been pumped up by government but is starting to deflate,[23] the U.S. has some of the most sought-after colleges and universities on the planet. This includes a few dozen excellent Catholic and evangelical colleges.

Still, most colleges and universities are left-wing brothels of bad ideas that can poison minds and spirits.[24] So, unless your kids attend one of the few exceptions,[25] you can expect them to be exposed to the entire political spectrum from left to far left. They'll be told that America and free markets are bad for the poor, bad for their health, and bad for the environment. They'll be told that faith is at odds with reason, and that America started as a conspiracy of slaveholders trying to stop King George III from emancipating millions. Ideas so absurd that only an academic could defend them—like Marxism and gender ideology—will be treated kindly or as gospel truth.

The left-wing politics are easy to spot. In the sprawling zoo of bad ideas, though, the hidden threats are relativism, materialism, and hysterical woke pseudo-moralism.[26] Sending your kids to college unarmed against these hazards is like pushing them into a jungle river filled with piranhas and expecting the experience to toughen them up. No one should be surprised if they get eaten alive.

Relativism is the idea that our knowledge, religious beliefs, and/or moral judgments are just "social constructions" we've picked up from our parents or culture that have no more claim to the truth (whatever that is) than other, equally narrow beliefs of other cultures.

Relativism is itself a truth claim, and so refutes itself. But professors often use relativist mantras to break down the ideas that students arrive with to replace them with the ideas professors favor.

Add to this mix hysterical woke moralism, which is now the loudest voice. It demands that we tear down statues, rename buildings, and deep-six the works of Shakespeare and Jane Austen—or worse, prostitute those great works by using them to table-thump about the latest political fetish, such as queer theory, systemic racism, or transphobia.

You've been warned. If we want to restore our culture, though, we must excel in academia, despite the obstacles.

Where Should We Send Our Kids?

No one type of schooling fits every child or family. Through prayer and counsel, seek out what works best for you. Just don't tell yourself that the easiest choice happens to be the best one. All parents have the same duty until our kids leave home: We must try to give them what they need to grow in character and faithfulness, a broad knowledge of the world that prepares them for adulthood, and a way for them to develop marketable skills and find their calling. Many people are on tight budgets; that's why we need educational freedom.

If you can homeschool, hire the best private tutors you can, customize a curriculum to fit your children's interests, strengths, and weaknesses, and be thankful.

The classical school movement is a bright light in the darkness. Different kinds of classical schools are now popping up in almost every city.[27] If you have school-aged kids, you should consider them; just don't assume that just any private school will be safe. Many prep schools are as woke and toxic as the average public school.

If you send your kids to a public school, watch out! No matter how rigorous, you *must* supplement their schooling, or they'll come out as good secularists.[28] Help your kids connect the worldview dots during their school years. Think about giving them a "thirteenth year" after they graduate from high school, in which you devise a curriculum to prepare them for life and college. We'd suggest that they study critical thinking and logic, apologetics, Scripture, theology, Christian and American history (if they don't know it), speed-reading, memory techniques, and some classic books they may not read in college.

If they haven't formed spiritual disciplines—prayer, Scripture and devotion reading, etc. —focus on that. You might include some seminars and retreats in the mix. There are many quality resources to help with all these subjects. Finally, encourage them to plug into a serious accountability group in college. Be nosy. Don't leave it to chance.

Inoculate, Inoculate, Inoculate

When it comes to bad ideas, you should avoid two extremes: quarantining your kids on the one hand or overexposing them on the other. Instead, work to *inoculate* them.

Millions of parents, including Christian ones, assume that an hour or two of church a week plus some short chats at dinner should be enough to counteract thirty-five hours of schooling in which God is "He-Who-Must-Not-Be-Named," plus another thirty-five hours of TV and porn-saturated and addictive social media per week. This defies common sense. Scads of data show the harm done to kids from too much screen time. Don't delegate your parenting to these blind guides.[29]

At the other end of the spectrum are the parents who quarantine their kids from the world—or think they do. They homeschool them or send them to Christian schools and tell them what they are supposed to believe, but never give them strong reasons to think these things are true. As a result, the education doesn't take. The kids read a book by a smart skeptic and realize their parents have fed them caricatures of "worldly ideas."

In some cases, these parents think they are inoculating their kids but are teaching things about science or history that wither when exposed to bright light. In other cases, the parents spend so much energy helping their kids see the flaws in other Christian traditions that they fail to teach them the glories of Christian history and the fatal flaws in secularism and atheism. The ranks of atheists are filled with people who were raised in sheltered homes.

Inoculation means that we expose our children to the strongest ideas the world has to offer but in a way that allows them to build up intellectual antibodies. We must acquaint them with the best arguments on opposing sides of each issue and teach them to evaluate the arguments critically. Obviously, that's easier said than done; see the endnote for some resources.[30]

Preparing our children for the world isn't all about inoculating them from bad ideas, of course. We must also insulate them with attention, love, truth, wisdom, and virtue. We want to help our children become strong in mind, body, and spirit. That's real education.

CHAPTER 11

All Men Are Created Equal

No idea in the modern world has gone farther off the rails than "equality." Of course, one of the bedrocks of the American experiment is the truth that all of us are created equal. What this meant to the Founders is that no one is, merely by birth, specially fit to rule over others. It also meant that we all have basic rights to life, liberty, and the pursuit of happiness, with corresponding duties. That is, your right to life corresponds to our duty not to murder you. Our right to liberty corresponds to your duty not to enslave us. Because of these rights, the law should treat us as equals. No one should get special favors just because he's rich or well-connected, or poor and marginalized.

Detached from its source, however, the related concepts of rights and equality become deadly toxins. "Rights" come to mean little more than "stuff we'd like everyone to have." And in recent years, the left has abandoned even the word "equality"—to sever it from its historical source—and replaced it with the word "equity." Equity means equal outcomes, no matter the details. Equity logic turns statistical differences between groups of people into proof of "systemic" racism or oppression. This way of thinking is central to wokeness—which casts the lens of conflict upon every social fact, no matter how benign.

The wokerati claim, for instance, that if there are proportionately more Jewish than black physics doctoral students at MIT, that's proof of "systemic" racism. Male soccer pros make more money than female soccer pros?[1] Sexism! More men than women win Nobel Prizes in science? Sexism again![2] The wokerati don't bother to account for age, effort, skill, value to others, personal and cultural preferences, or anything else. After all, that would take work and intellectual honesty. (And for some reason, they never denounce the imbalance between males and females among, say, trash collectors, workplace injuries, or war casualties.)

We know from the twentieth century what happens when equity is applied in the real world: It leads to widespread poverty, atrocities, and death. The reason is simple: People differ in all sorts of ways, and only a police state could level those differences—and even then, very poorly. Some equity warriors are honest about this. In 2020, Washington State assembled an Equity Task Force. Here's how they defined equity: "Equity = Disrupt and Dismantle."[3]

Give them points for honesty. Imagine a law that required the surgeon who operates on your brain and the person who invests your retirement funds to have the same wage as the kid who serves you waffle fries at Chick-Fil-A. Would it be just? No. But it would "disrupt and dismantle" civilization in service of an imaginary utopia of equity unsuited to real human beings.

Such a society would be sheer madness—which is why no one tries to apply equity logic consistently. In any case, it has no basis in Scripture or morality. Jesus tells His apostles that they will sit on twelve thrones (Matthew 19:28) in the Kingdom of God. So far as we know, nobody else will get those thrones. While rain falls on both the just and the unjust (Matthew 5:45), God does not disperse His gifts uniformly to His creatures; He gives them in various ways. Some folks are strong; some are weak. Some are smart; some are dimwitted. Some can pitch a ball as if they got throwing lessons in the womb; others throw so poorly that it's painful to watch. God has given blessings to all, but our gifts differ both in degree and in kind.

In Jesus's parable of the talents, a rich man gave his slaves different amounts of money. One gets five talents, another two, and another one. There is no equality of gifts there. The rich man then leaves to go on a long trip. When he returns, he judges his servants based on what they've done with what they each were given (Matthew 25:14–30). They get different amounts; the one who earned nothing is even called a "wicked servant."

Likewise, in the parable of the landowner, all the workers should have been glad that they got what they were promised, and that they were better off than when they started. Instead, the workers who came early were grumpy because of what *other* workers received. If none of the workers had known about the workers hired at other times, though, they would not have felt cheated; their attitude was wholly the result of knowing what others had received. That is envy masquerading as justice.

That is "equity."

Our culture was bound to reach this point. For a hundred years, the left has been feeding us the lie that justice means sameness in everything. But this just reinforces the deadly sin of envy.

If we want to think clearly about these matters, we must purge our notion of justice of any hints of envy.

Some Perspective

It helps to keep a wide perspective. People in Western societies have far more choices than most people throughout history. A society in which people seek out jobs that provide goods and services others want is surely better than one in which John is forced to pay James a certain amount no matter what James wants. That's reverse slavery. It's not only immoral; it's a lousy way to get what people want and need. People often think inequality is unjust because they aren't thinking correctly about value. Without realizing it, they're thinking like Marxists—those architects of fabulously wealthy economies in places like Cuba and Venezuela.

For instance, many think the high salary of a business owner, entrepreneur, or a corporate CEO is unjust. But in a market economy, wages and salaries tend to reflect the economic value of their roles. Business owners bear the risk for their venture, and CEOs make decisions that can make or break a company. The skills of a good executive are extremely rare. Bad executives bankrupt companies and put thousands of people out of work.

Disparity of wages is not proof of injustice. In a just society, we have a right to the fruits of our labor. We can exchange labor—our time, knowledge, skill, willingness to risk, and effort—for other things we value. Your own labor varies by time and place. Why assume that the value of everyone else's labor should be equal to yours?

Justice requires equal treatment for equal cases and unequal treatment for unequal cases. The logic of equity, in contrast, requires treating unequal cases the same.

Spreading the Wealth Around

A free economy works by letting the free choices of consumers "nudge" wealth toward people who do a good job of meeting others' needs. That's how the world went from donkey carts to jumbo jets. Chick-Fil-A became a success story by serving others, as did Costco.

The founders of both companies became billionaires for their service. They created jobs and wealth that didn't exist before.

Where does such wealth come from? Is it in a pot or a safe somewhere in Washington, D.C., where Treasury officials can scoop it up and spread it around like hot tar on a flat roof? Of course not. The government must first tax it from private citizens before it can spread it around.

Many such efforts to spread wealth do more harm than good. Take minimum wage laws. What if the federal government decided everyone should be paid $100 an hour? Then everyone would be rich, right? No. The law would help some people in the short term—namely, those doing unique, indispensable work who were getting paid almost $100 an hour already. But what about everyone else? If your labor was worth less than $100 an hour, your employer couldn't afford to keep you, and you'd be laid off while most new hiring would grind to a halt. The law would create massive unemployment and black markets for labor. As Henry Hazlitt wrote, "You cannot make a man worth a given amount by making it illegal for anyone to offer him anything less."[4]

Labor is a cost of doing business, and wage laws are price controls on labor. These price controls harm the poorest of the poor: the untrained, unlucky, inexperienced, and handicapped. No matter what the minimum wage is, the labor value of these workers will be the farthest below it. These are the people who most need to grab the bottom rung of the economic ladder. If you raise it too high, they can't reach the bottom rung.

Here's what we mean by a "ladder." Few Americans stick with low-wage jobs for their whole career. In a diverse and competitive economy, low-paying jobs are entry-level jobs that tend to improve the value of one's labor over time. This is just what the poor need to improve their lot. Some people need entry-level jobs very close to the ground floor. Minimum-wage laws eliminate those jobs. Such laws favor the politically powerful and lucky, who retain their jobs over the vulnerable workers who most need them.

Forget the Gap. Focus on Poverty.

As it happens, much of our thinking about income inequality is based on confusion. We often speak, for instance, as if the wealth of some causes the poverty of others. But the wealth in our economy isn't a fixed pie, in which Peter getting a bigger slice causes Paul to get a smaller one. The late Steve Jobs and his many well-paid employees didn't get rich by stealing iPhones from homeless people! Thinking of total wealth in terms of "gaps" and slices of pie is as misleading as saying the health of some causes the illness of others, or the intelligence of some leads to the ignorance of others.

Focusing on income gaps distracts us from the real problem—poverty. Imagine you earn $100,000 one year, while some big investor earns $100 million during the same year. In absolute dollars, the gap is $99.9 million. As a ratio, the investor earns a thousand times more than you.

Now imagine a fruit picker in Costa Rica with a wife and four kids who is earning $1,000 a year. The gap between his income and yours is $99,000. Your income is a hundred times greater than his. So, the gap between you and the fruit picker is much smaller than the gap between you and the investor, and yet the latter case should trouble us far more. Why? It can't be the size or the magnitude of income gaps. If it were, we should be ten times more troubled by the gap between you and the investor. So why are we much more troubled by the gap between you and the fruit picker? Because we assume that if the picker is only bringing in $1,000 a year, then he's dirt poor. The fact that someone somewhere is making more just isn't the issue.

Here's another problem with defining poverty in relative terms: The bottom 15 percent of income earners could be much better off than the bottom 15 percent were forty years ago, but they would still be labeled "poor." With this logic, if you make $100,000 a year (with the purchasing power of 2023 dollars), but 90 percent of the public makes at least $1 million a year, you'd be defined as poor. This is absurd. Rather than helping us grasp a complex reality, our statistical method blinds us to it.

Gaps, then, aren't the problem; absolute poverty is. Alleviating such poverty should be our goal; getting rid of gaps should not be.

What is absolute poverty? The UN and World Bank often define it as living on less than one or two dollars a day.[5] A better definition focuses on basic needs—calories, basic nutrients, clean water, shelter, basic health care, and so on. If you can meet these basic needs, you may be poor, but you don't suffer from absolute poverty.

In our work at LIFE Outreach International, we often send our supporters pictures of our work in impoverished nations. Since we provide basic nourishment and clean water, these may be pictures of young African children with little or no clothing drinking out of dirty puddles of water or foraging for scraps of food. These children are often emaciated. They have skinny arms and legs and distended stomachs—the telltale signs of extreme malnutrition. You know absolute poverty when you see it.

In the U.S., however, the Census Bureau draws a line in the income scale and defines everyone who falls below it as "poor." The number varies by year and family size. For example, in 2023, the poverty threshold was $35,140 for a family of five.[6] Based on this way of dividing up the population, 11.6 percent of Americans are defined as poor—and so qualify for all manner of means-tested welfare programs.

This measure doesn't tell us who suffers from extreme poverty, though, or even how the lot of those defined as "poor" changes over time. For instance, the average poor American child consumes the same nutrients as upper middle-class kids. (That's not to say that any of them are eating as nutritiously as they should be.) A big problem with today's poor is obesity. Just getting enough calories is no longer an issue.

These are averages, of course. Millions of Americans experience periods without enough to eat and without adequate shelter, health care, and clothing. To help them, though, we need a clear picture of American poverty.

Start with the Right Questions

Again, the right questions focus not on gaps or inequality but on poverty and improvement over time. This helps us compare what's happening right now with longer trends.

Here are three key questions:

1. Can people at the bottom of the economic ladder create more wealth for themselves and their families? Do virtue, study, and hard work tend to pay off?
2. Are the rich getting richer by making the poor poorer?
3. Do the people at the bottom do better over time?

The first question is easy to answer. Hard work still pays off. If you graduate from high school, find a full-time job, and wait until you're married to have kids, you're very likely to be at least middle class.[7] That's not everything, of course, but it's something. Yes, our current policies make this much harder than it should be—especially for people without college degrees. (More on that later.)

The answers to the other two questions are "no" and "yes," respectively. If you look at the Census Bureau stats, you don't find that the top 20 percent are getting ever richer, and the bottom 20 percent are getting poorer and poorer. Despite our recent problems with wage stagnation, COVID policies, and inflation, all income groups have improved their lot over the last four generations. Since 1947, average total family income (in inflation-adjusted dollars) has gone up by 85 percent.[8]

From 1970 to 2018, the median middle-class income rose by 49 percent. But then things get complicated. As the Pew Research Center notes, "the median income of middle-class households in 2020 was 50 percent higher than in 1970."[9] The median income for upper-tier households, though, grew 64 percent over those same years.[10] In other words, both middle- and upper-class household incomes went up, but upper incomes increased faster.

This doesn't mean large groups of people in the middle got poorer; it means the distribution of incomes has changed over time. If we divide the population into three income groups, then, as a percentage, the shares in the upper and lower tiers have gone up compared to the middle. As the Pew survey explains, "The shrinking of the middle class has been accompanied by an increase in the share of adults in the upper-income tier—from 14 percent in 1971 to 21 percent in 2021—as well as an increase in the share who are in the lower-income tier, from 25 percent to 29 percent."[11]

Now, remember, we're talking about income groups. Even if 15 percent of the population lives below the ever-rising poverty line at any one time, that segment doesn't always contain the same people, and the state of that group could still have improved. Don't confuse an abstract distribution of incomes with individual people. Except for those who inherit a fortune, most of us move up and down the income ladder over our lifetimes.[12]

Jesus's statement that we will always have the poor with us is a logical truth; there will always be someone in the lowest income group—even if the members of the group change over time. But He wasn't saying our efforts to overcome (absolute) poverty are fruitless. In fact, that's our calling!

Moreover, income doesn't provide a complete economic picture. As technology improves, most goods and services cost less—even accounting for inflation. Take food, for instance. For most of history, people spent much, if not most, of their labor on getting enough to eat. As recently as 1930, Americans spent about a quarter of their income on food.[13]

It's good to keep this long view in mind. But that doesn't mean everything is now great. For instance, the long-term trend in food prices has reversed in the last couple of years. Because of government-induced inflation, food prices went up 11.4 percent from 2021 to 2022! Americans have not experienced such high inflation since the 1970s.[14]

It's a similar story with incomes. Everyone is much better off (in economic terms) than they were a century ago. In the last few decades, though, certain kinds of jobs in the middle have dwindled.

We should support policies that allow all Americans, wherever they start, to overcome poverty by virtue and hard work, and create value for themselves and for others. We should not pursue equity, however; that would not heal the Golden Goose but poison it.

Of course, there's still the question of what we should do with the genuinely poor among us. We'll take that up in the next chapter.

CHAPTER 12

Am I My Brother's Keeper?

In the early chapters of Genesis, we read the story of Cain and Abel—the first two sons of Adam and Eve—each presenting an offering to God. God accepts Abel's offering but rejects Cain's. Out of jealousy, Cain kills his brother. God, of course, knew what had happened to Abel, but rather than accusing Cain, He asks, "Where is your brother Abel?" Cain replies, "I do not know; am I my brother's keeper?" (Genesis 4).

Most readers suspect the answer is "yes." Throughout Scripture, God shows His care for the poor, orphans, and widows, and He expects His people to share that concern. The Psalms are filled with references to God as a deliverer of the oppressed and needy. Alongside His command to treat the poor justly, God commanded ancient Israel to make provisions to alleviate poverty by leaving some grain in their fields after the harvest—"gleanings"—so that poor sojourners might have something to eat.

In His parable of the sheep and the goats, Jesus describes a time when the "Son of Man comes in His glory" (Matthew 25:35–40). The sheep are invited into God's rest; the goats are not. The King (representing God) tells the sheep:

> "Come, you that are blessed by my Father, inherit the kingdom prepared for you from the foundation of the world; for I was hungry and you gave me food, I was thirsty and you gave me something to drink, I was a stranger and you welcomed me, I was naked and you gave me clothing, I was sick and you took care of me, I was in prison and you visited me."

Jesus cares so much about the poor that He identifies with them. Few people doubt that we should care for the poor. The pressing question is how best to do so.

Can the Government Eliminate Poverty?

In well over a hundred biblical passages about the poor, not one mentions the government. Yet almost everyone assumes the state can and should eliminate poverty through welfare programs.

Why think that's even possible? Jesus said, "The poor you will always have with you" (Matthew 26:11). This is not a counsel of despair, but it should temper our hopes. Perhaps poverty is part of the fallen human state—like sin, death, and disease. If so, then it would be presumptuous to think that anyone can eliminate it this side of eternity.

Even if poverty could be wiped out, why think a government program should or could do it? After all, the vast reduction in poverty worldwide over the last several decades had nothing to do with government welfare programs. If we really want to reduce poverty, then we should focus on how that happens in the world as it is, rather than as we'd like it to be.

How did we come to think that government could do the job? In the early twentieth century, hundreds of private charities fought poverty. Then, along came progressivism, which inspired the attitude that politics could fix everything, including poverty, if only the right experts were put in charge. These efforts started crowding out many private efforts.

A few government programs got their start in the 1930s under President Franklin D. Roosevelt. These were supposed to end the Great Depression, but likely worsened it and made it last longer than it might have otherwise.[1] Most programs that we identify with the welfare state, though, started in the mid-1960s with President Lyndon Johnson's War on Poverty, as part of his Great Society agenda.

Since 1965, the United States has spent at least $25 trillion on welfare. According to the U.S. House Republicans,

> In fiscal year 2022, the federal government spent $1.19 trillion on more than eighty different "means-tested" welfare programs. That represents almost 20 percent of total federal spending and a quarter of tax revenues in 2022 or $9,000 spent per American household.[2]

That's more than we spent on national defense during that time.

This huge price was not a short-term surge: It follows a steady five-decade growth in spending. At first, most of the expense went to the poor directly, but now most of it goes to the Welfare State bureaucracy.[3] We now spend about thirteen times more on welfare than we did in the mid-1960s. The Welfare Reform Act of 1996 helped a bit, but it reformed only one of more than seventy programs.[4] So welfare costs have kept growing.

This might have been worth the price if poverty had been wiped out or even reduced. The poverty rate, alas, has stayed about the same, in contrast to the down before we declared war on it. From 1959 to 1965, the poverty rate dropped from 22 to 15 percent. In 1965, it started to level off and now stays in the 12 to 15 percent range.[5] It stood at 14.4 percent in 2022.[6] Worse, these programs have created social problems like rampant out-of-wedlock births and cycles of dependency that didn't exist before. Our government-run welfare is well-meaning, but it hasn't worked.

Foreign Aid

Ditto for government attempts to solve global poverty. For half a century, our weapon of choice against this enemy has been foreign aid—loans and grants given either directly to other governments or through the UN, the World Bank, or the International Monetary Fund.

Scholars have criticized foreign aid for decades. They tell a sad story of bureaucrats and corrupt dictators using the money to line their pockets and keep their people oppressed. One World Bank study revealed that in some cases, 85 percent of aid was diverted from its intended uses, leading one deputy director to note that "when the World Bank thinks it is financing an electric power station, it is really financing a brothel."[7] Despite trillions of dollars in foreign aid, millions of people still die every year in places like Africa for want of medicine and mosquito nets that cost a few cents apiece.[8]

There are smart, well-meaning people on all sides of the "aid debate," but one thing is clear: Foreign aid doesn't get countries out of the poverty trap.[9]

In fact, according to Zambian economist Dambiso Moyo, the aid system has made things *worse* by creating a corrupting dependency that prevents many poor countries from developing. In her book *Dead Aid*, Moyo calls on Africa "to rid the continent of aid-dependency, which has hindered good governance for so long."[10]

This is true even of aid in more recent years, which has been tied to practices of good governance and economic reforms. As Moyo says:

> The notion that aid can alleviate systemic poverty, and has done so, is a myth. Millions in Africa are poorer today because of aid; misery and poverty have not ended but have increased. Aid has been, and continues to be, an unmitigated political, economic, and humanitarian disaster for most parts of the developing world.[11]

Maybe some form of foreign aid can help some people, but there's no reason to believe it will ever cure poverty.

A Compassion Connection

Many private charities are doing wonderful work overseas. As a rule, the most successful endeavors have local connections. Rather than trying to "end poverty as we know it" from an office in New York, they focus on specific tasks in specific places. For instance, one nonprofit, Population Services International, has distributed bed nets treated with insecticide throughout Malawi by selling them to poor mothers through birth clinics and allowing the nurses involved to keep part of the proceeds of every net sold. This strategy not only has worked better than government-funded efforts that give the nets away, but has gotten nets into the hands of the people most likely to use them.[12]

A project of LIFE Outreach International is called Water for LIFE. Every day, children all over the world walk miles to fetch water filled with disease-causing pathogens that kill 1.8 million people every year. Because of unclean water, up to 50 percent of all people in poverty-stricken nations suffer severe health problems. Trillions of dollars in foreign aid spent in the last six decades haven't solved this tragedy. Water for LIFE drills wells that not only stop disease and promote healthy bodies but help families to grow their own gardens and care for their own animals.

More than 7,700 of these wells—each serving about a thousand people—are now in use in more than twenty countries around the world; the estimated number of changed lives reaches more than 7.7 million. In 2023, the twenty-third year of Water for LIFE, 415 new wells were established in needy areas.[13]

These efforts rely on an intricate web that links funding and ministries with people on the ground who have local knowledge. That makes them much better at helping people who suffer in poverty or crisis, or who are recovering from natural disasters.

What Should We Do?

Thousands of domestic charities also have a winning track record. One of the worst ideas of the left is that government-run welfare programs can replace private charity. But they're not the same thing. Charity comes from the Latin word meaning "love" (*charis*). Love can only be given freely. So, charity is different from "help" given impersonally by a government agency using tax money.

Of course, well-meaning people often provide private help based on emotions without thinking through the effects of their giving. This can be a tragic mistake. The more personal and concrete a gift is, the greater its chances of success. Imagine, for instance, a married man with two children in Detroit who loses his job. He and his family attend a large church that helps unemployed members, and it provides the man with temporary help, overseen by an experienced group of volunteers. It also connects him with a mentor who is a successful businessman.

Now imagine the same man does not attend church. He loses his job and signs up for unemployment insurance. He must show that he's applying for jobs, but that's not too hard. When the insurance payments end, he applies for several federal welfare programs. He lives in Detroit and the check comes from Washington, D.C.

In which scenario do you think the man is more likely to get back on his feet quickly? Clearly, the first one. All things being equal, smaller, local, and private sources of help are better than large, distant, government-run ones.

The Web of Responsibility

One reason that local, private efforts are better has to do with information and incentives.

Over time, government welfare tends to do more harm than good because it tears through an intricate web of overlapping jurisdictions of responsibility. When the state or any larger entity takes over a task that is better handled by someone closer to the problem, it violates its proper boundaries and creates more problems than it set out to solve. When helping those in need, voluntary, private, and informed is better than government-run and distant.

Good charity is compassionate. That doesn't mean you feel warm fuzzies in your heart; it means "to suffer alongside." You can't really suffer alongside people unless you know them and what they need.

Some of the best charity starts with one person, or one family. Our friends, Geoff and Tami Biehn, had felt glimmers of a call to help orphans for years, but weren't sure what to do. As they prayed, they each received strong impressions about selling their house to start an orphanage. That was hard. Geoff is a financial advisor, and the Biehns had been able to buy their house in an idyllic, mature neighborhood in a suburb of Columbus, Ohio, for cash. They loved everything about it. Besides, they had always dreamed of having extra money to buy a beach house for their children to enjoy.

Still, they kept listening and praying. They asked trusted family members and friends for prayer and advice. Their then seven-year-old daughter, Brianna, began sensing that God wanted them to sell their house and help orphans, even though moving would mean she and her older brother would have to leave their school and friends.

Geoff and Tami finally concluded that God was indeed asking them to sell their house, even though the depressed 2011 housing market seemed like a terrible time to do so. Within three weeks of listing it, they received a full cash offer from a buyer. Meanwhile, they found a smaller version of their beloved house in a nearby neighborhood. Brianna told them, "I think God has a house for us on the Big Hill, and it would be great if it was on a court." Without knowing it, she had described the house.

The price of the new house was about 60 percent of the selling price of their old one, so after the move, they had a hefty balance to help orphans.

The Biehns knew they wanted to work with (1) a Christ-centered organization with ties to a local church, that (2) was operating in a poor country, and (3) was close enough—and safe enough—for them to visit with their young children in tow. They found just such a ministry working in the Dominican Republic, so they flew there to learn more about it.[14]

The orphanage with thirty young girls was being run by Ketty Figueroa, a local pastor's wife. When the Biehns visited, the ministry was renting the property, but the landlord needed to sell it and offered Ketty a discount if she could come up with a few thousand dollars for a deposit. She had managed to scrape the money together on faith that God would bring the rest needed to buy the house. He did—and He used Geoff and Tami Biehn to deliver it.

Because of the Biehns' willingness to pray, listen, and sacrifice, God used them to help bless thirty orphaned little girls. But the Biehns will tell you that God blessed *them*. They can now visit the orphanage every year as a family, help out, and then spend a few days vacationing on a beach in the Dominican Republic—much better than their dream beach house.

God does not call every family to sell their house; but He does call each of us, in our own way, to help those in need. We just have to listen.

How Is Poverty Eliminated?

The Biehns' story is one example of how charity can work. Alas, charity doesn't always help, at least on large scales. Haiti has more aid workers per capita than any country in the world, yet it's still the poorest nation in the Western Hemisphere and one of the poorest in the world.[15] Even when charity helps, it has never lifted a whole culture out of poverty. We have no reason to think it can.

We should support good charities but should not expect them to work miracles. We can deliver vaccines and hydration packs and dig wells for the poor in Africa and elsewhere. We can volunteer at homeless shelters in our city. We can even buy an orphanage for little girls in a Caribbean country. But all these acts are funded by wealth produced elsewhere. There must be fertile fields and an abundant harvest before there can be any leftover stalks of grain for sojourners. The greater the bounty, the greater the gleanings. But where does the bounty come from?

If we want to alleviate widespread poverty, rather than just offering platitudes, we need to focus on how wealth is created. In the next few chapters, we'll tackle that question.

CHAPTER 13

A Place to Call Our Own

The right to private property is the foundation of limited government and economic growth. For a decade after the Soviet Union collapsed, almost every American agreed. But that didn't last long. The enemies of private property are back, and they're serious. They might not be calling for the collectivization of farms, as Russian leader Vladimir Lenin did a century ago—at least, not yet—but the Marxist hatred of private property is more mainstream now than at any time in American history.

Was the Early Church Socialist?

Even many Christians only half-heartedly defend private property since they feel selfish in insisting on a right to own things. They half-recall a story from the Book of Acts in which members of the early Church sold their personal belongings and shared everything in common. If this describes the Christian ideal, they wonder, why should we worry about the erosion of private property rights?

Let's examine that text:

> Now the company of those who believed were of one heart
> and soul, and no one said that any of the things which he
> possessed was his own, but they had everything in
> common. . . . There was not a needy person among them,
> for as many as were possessors of lands or houses sold
> them, and brought the proceeds of what was sold and laid
> it at the apostles' feet; and distribution was made to each
> as any had need. (Acts 4:32–35)

This was neither "socialism" nor "communism." Socialism, strictly speaking, means the abolition of private property. Communism views private property as a source of oppression. It's based on Karl Marx's theory of class warfare, in which the capitalists (bourgeoisie) slowly extract most of the wealth from the workers (proletarians). At that point, the workers revolt and seize the means of production. The state owns all property on behalf of the workers. This is "socialism" in Marxist theory. At some point, however, this socialist state is supposed to wither away and give rise to a communist utopia in which everyone is free and has everything he needs. (A good story, which never happens in real life.)

There's not one word about any of this in Acts. No one denounces private property as oppressing the poor. The state isn't confiscating anything. No one is coercing or being coerced. The Church in Jerusalem had no political power. Those early Christians were selling their belongings and sharing freely.

The story of Ananias and Sapphira doesn't help the communist reading of the text. This couple sold some land but kept part of the money for themselves and then lied about it when they took the rest to the Church. "Ananias," Peter asked, "why has Satan filled your heart to lie to the Holy Spirit and to keep back part of the proceeds of the lands?" A few seconds later, Ananias lay dead on the floor, apparently struck by God. Next, Peter questioned Sapphira. When she also lied about the price of the land, she died as well.

Was Ananias's sin that he didn't give up everything he owned? No. Just read the rest of Peter's statement:

> "While [your property] remained unsold, did it not remain your own? And after it was sold, were not the proceeds at your disposal? How is it that you have contrived this deed in your heart? You have not lied to men but to God!" (Acts 5:4)

Private property was not the problem, nor was selling it. Peter condemns Ananias and Sapphira not for keeping back part of the proceeds of the sale, but for lying about it.

The early chapters of Acts describe a unique situation—the birth of the Church—when the apostles' preaching at Pentecost added thousands of new believers overnight. Many of these new believers had traveled from other regions and spoke different languages. As a result, they needed to stay in Jerusalem much longer than they'd expected (before converting) to be discipled; thus, the local believers began selling their property so they could share with these new, displaced brothers and sisters.

This was a unique, short-term fix. At some point, many of these new Christians returned to their homes, taking their faith with them. Scripture nowhere records that they went home and founded communes; this never became the norm for all Christians everywhere. In fact, when some Thessalonian Christians later took advantage of fellow believers' generosity, Paul ordered them to "earn their own living." He even laid down a stern rule: "If anyone will not work, let him not eat" (2 Thessalonians 3:10, 12).[1]

The Roots of Private Property

Socialism has no basis in Scripture, but private property does. Two of the Ten Commandments assume this right and would make zero sense without it: You shall not steal, and you shall not covet your neighbor's possessions (Exodus 20:2–17 and Deuteronomy 5:6–21). Genesis 22 is devoted to describing—in detail—Abraham purchasing a plot of land for Sarah's burial. This suggests that Near Eastern standards for buying and selling property were already well developed in 2000 BC.

As Westerners, we benefit from four thousand years of laws, customs, and thinking about the concept of property. Drawing on ideas from Christian theology and Greek philosophy, the Western world slowly developed a sophisticated system of property law and titling. That system protects property rights, reinforces our other rights, and fosters the widespread creation of wealth.

Property Protects Our Other Rights

The Founders saw our right to property as an extension of ourselves and our liberty. John Adams said that property "implies liberty because property cannot be secure unless they have his personal liberty of life and limb, motion and rest for the purpose."[2]

The right to property not only protects our families and freedom, but also limits government. If millions of people own their own homes, cars, land, clothes, and labor, then much of our daily life remains outside the government's jurisdiction. If it wants to take your land to build a road, for instance, it must compensate you fairly. With no right to property, in contrast, we're at the mercy of either the strongest person or an all-powerful state.

If You Care about the Poor, Defend Private Property

Not everyone agrees, however. The first plank of *The Communist Manifesto*, written in 1848 by Karl Marx and Friedrich Engels, calls for the "abolition of private property." The 1917 Russian Revolution, led by Vladimir Lenin, tried to put Marx's ideas into action.

The revolution, as it turned out, provided a trainload of evidence that Marx didn't know what he was talking about. By 1920, industrial production in Russia had dropped to 18 percent of its 1913 level.[3] When Lenin tried to collectivize farms in Russia in the 1920s, more than five million peasants starved to death. It got so bad that he had to tweak the policy. Although hard industry and most of the land continued to be state-owned, he allowed families to cultivate small private plots.[4]

These plots made up only 2 percent of the cultivated land but contributed one-fourth of the output of Russian agriculture. That is, "the output per acre of the private plots was about sixteen times the per-acre output of the state-owned farms."[5]

The Communist Chinese discovered the same thing in the 1970s, but not before trying their hand at creating a so-called "new heaven and earth for man." Attempts to collectivize both farms and industry led to the deaths of some twenty million Chinese from famine and put another twenty million in labor camps.[6]

These are just two of dozens of horrific examples of communist catastrophes in the twentieth century. Abolishing private property is unjust: It helps neither the economy nor the poor. On the contrary, private property is the first and most basic way to reduce poverty and create wealth. Pope Leo XIII put this point well in his 1891 encyclical *Rerum Novarum*, "The first and most fundamental principle . . . if one would undertake to alleviate the condition of the masses, must be the inviolability of private property."[7] Both common sense and decades of research bear it out.

The Founders knew that if people enjoy the fruits of their labor, they're more likely to be good stewards, to work hard and produce wealth for themselves and others. Socialism detaches income—such as it is—from performance. It gives everyone the incentive to do as little as possible. Communists learned this lesson the hard way in the twentieth century. One of the best ways to destroy the hard work of peasants, factory workers, and everyone else is to collectivize their efforts.

In contrast, if hard work pays better than freeloading, people have a reason to work harder. The Greek philosopher Aristotle knew this 2,400 years ago. "That which is common to the greatest number has the least care bestowed upon it," he said. "Everyone thinks chiefly of his own, hardly at all of the common interest."[8] We can count on most people to act in their own self-interest. That doesn't mean everybody always does the *selfish* thing. It just means that if you can acquire property, then your self-interest will orient you to provide something for others—whether you're selfish or not—since you'll want to have something to trade in the marketplace (more on this later).

The Founders understood the power of legitimate self-interest so well that they even provided in the Constitution for writers and inventors to have "exclusive Right to their respective Writings and Discoveries." This right to intellectual property is the basis of our patent system, which is one reason there have been so many great American inventors. As Abraham Lincoln explained, by protecting intellectual property, our Founders "added *the fuel of interest to the fire of genius* in the discovery and production of new and useful things" (emphasis added).[9]

The Mystery of Property

One of the main reasons "developing" countries are poor is that they lack real property rights. A farmer might work the same plot of land for decades but never get beyond producing just enough to survive. The land serves only its basic purposes, and that very poorly. The farmer acts for the short term, not the long term. He prefers crops that come quickly to harvest to crops that are more profitable in the long run but take several years to mature. This "dead capital," according to Peruvian economist Hernando de Soto, is held informally or "extralegally."[10]

In the 1990s, de Soto sent research teams to several South American and Caribbean countries to study their property laws. They found that the same governments that fail to protect property rights also erect bureaucratic roadblocks that seem designed to keep citizens from opening businesses or owning legal property. To buy a home legally in Peru, for instance, a person had to wind his way through a five-stage maze, with 207 steps in the first stage alone.[11]

Haitians had it far worse. At the time of the study, they had to jump through sixty-five bureaucratic hoops just to lease land from the government. If they wanted to buy the land, another 111 hoops awaited them. It would take a Haitian nineteen years to buy property.[12]

Things haven't improved much in the last few decades. Imagine that poor Haitian manages to steer his way through this maze. He still lacks secure property since the country tends to go from one dictator to the other with alarming speed. Who's to say that a land contract secured under one regime will be recognized by the next? Can you imagine conducting business, investing in, or developing property in such a climate of uncertainty? No one else can, either.

De Soto argues that what the poor in the developing world need to improve their standard of living are strong private property laws. Robust property laws and titling, he argues, are the "mystery of capital" that has allowed the West to create vast wealth and raise the living standards of the poor. The problem is not that people in the developing world are stupid or predestined for poverty. The problem is that they don't enjoy the property and contract laws we do.[13]

Under a solid system of private property, a house or plot of land is transformed into more than just a house or patch of dirt. Rules, symbols, meanings, contracts, attitudes: These ethereal things turn dirt, wood, Sheetrock, and concrete into assets and wealth, which in turn can be used to create more wealth.

Of course, a formal property system is not the only thing a culture needs to prosper. It's one of the first rungs on the ladder to creating wealth. Without it, an economy will tend to stagnate, with much of the population living hand-to-mouth while a few lucky kings, princes, and scoundrels get fabulously wealthy. Places that have robust ways for ordinary people to acquire and keep property, in contrast, tend to get richer overall in the long run.

The right to property channels and orients our behaviors in wealth-enhancing ways. It alters not just our actions but the very way we view ourselves and the world around us.

We find this with squatters who gain property rights. Squatters are people who live on land that they don't own or rent. Cities in poorer countries are often surrounded by shantytowns where thousands of squatters live in dilapidated shacks. In 2007, a team of economists studied a settlement of squatters in Argentina. The people in one section of town were granted titles to their small properties. The people in the other part were not.

The economists found that the squatters who had become property owners were more optimistic than the others. They tended to trust others and to believe people could achieve something good if they worked hard.[14] As a result, they pursued their longer-term economic interests and tended to grow more prosperous as a result. Most squatters know that any day, the police could come and bulldoze them off their plot, so they don't bother making long-term plans.

What Should We Do?

The right to property is not legalized selfishness. It's the right that protects many of our other rights. When people can't acquire, hold, and sell property, they can't expect to enjoy the fruits of their labor and the benefits of a global economy. Nor can they create much new wealth.

A private property system needs a state strong and honest enough to enforce the law and punish those who violate it. At home, we need to remain vigilant against efforts to chip away at our property rights, especially in the form of burdensome regulations. These efforts never look like theft on the surface. Instead, they appeal to safety, equity, or sustainability. But slowly, surely, they chip away at property rights.

The communist government in Beijing and its state-controlled companies also threaten this right. They steal American's intellectual property as a matter of policy. Any serious trade and foreign policy should include a plan to deal with this.[15]

Finally, if we want to fight poverty overseas, we need to support policies that strengthen rather than weaken the property rights of citizens and families. This will probably take the combined efforts of missionaries, ministries, development groups, and enlightened foreign policy over many years, but it can happen.

Private property is the first step a country must take to traverse the steep path from poverty to prosperity. But, as we'll see in the next few chapters, it's just a start.

CHAPTER 14

Free to Prosper

C ritics claim that free markets follow the law of the jungle, where the strong are free to prey on the weak. The sloganeers of Marxist-led movements like Black Lives Matter and far-left politicians preach that "unfettered capitalism" allows the richest 1 percent to get richer by making the bottom 99 percent poorer. The oligarchs at the World Economic Forum want to dismantle that fallen system and "build back better." They promise a more humane economy—a "Great Reset"—that just happens to transfer massive power into their hands.

Many Christians also think this way. Jim Wallis paid lip service to the market, but he accuses his critics of believing in "free market fundamentalism."[1] In recent years, it's become a term of derision even from some social conservatives such as Sohrab Ahmari, who dismiss the market economy as a form of slavery to Mammon. They dream of a top-down Christian order that yokes each person's economic choices to doctrinal truths enforced by the state.

One thing that critics of the market economy on the left and far right alike share: They don't understand economics. They are like South Sea primitives plucking a radio from the "cargo" that fell off a U.S. Navy plane. They stare at the vast, complex network of cooperating people and firms called the "market economy." On some level they realize that it has produced the modern world and now feeds almost eight billion people (seven-eighths of whom would starve to death without it), but that doesn't drive them to respect a system that works such wonders. Instead, they opt for puzzlement, fear, and resentment.

Despite the turmoil of recent years, we think economic freedom is worth preserving. So let's consider how a free economy works—one worthy of human beings made in God's image. Socialists over the centuries have pointed to beehives and ant colonies as examples of their system in action. But human beings aren't termites or ants. And if the twentieth century taught us anything, it's that free economies are good for us, and socialist ones are not.

A "Free" Economy

We're using the common terms "free market" and "free enterprise" as shorthand for the freedom of people, families, and firms to decide what they will buy and sell without undo coercion by either the state or other people. We're not talking about some entity called a "market" that has power over such choices. That's an abstraction. Picture instead millions of human beings buying and selling goods and services freely, and you won't be far off. Unfortunately, bad mental images have led many people, including many believers, to think of a free market as a burden rather than a blessing. So, let's spend some time dissolving these mental images.

I (Jay) grew up in Amarillo, Texas. When I was in sixth grade, we had one of the ice storms common to the Texas Panhandle. The weatherman must have predicted it because our teacher, Mrs. Hubbard, came to school prepared to deal with rowdy students trapped inside during recess.

I assumed she had shopped the dollar section of a store because she brought a bunch of cheap toys and told us we were going to play a "trading game." Then she passed out the goodies, one to each student: a paddleboard with one of those red rubber balls tied down with a rubber band, an egg of Silly Putty, a set of Barbie trading cards. Nobody got the same toy, and we could all see what everybody else got.

She then asked us to write down, on a scale from 1 to 10, how much we liked our gift. We didn't have to consult anyone. Mrs. Hubbard then had us call out, one by one, the score we had given our toy. She added them all up and wrote down the total on the board.

Next, she told us that we could trade with the others in our row. This gave everyone four potential trading partners out of the twenty-five kids in class. No one had to trade, and no one could steal; but if one kid had the Silly Putty, another had the paddleboard, and each preferred the other's toy, then they were free to trade. Some students kept or got stuck with their original gift, but a lot of us ended up with a toy we liked more. Again, we wrote down how much we liked our new toys, on a scale of 1 to 10, called them out, and Mrs. Hubbard added up the scores. Guess what happened? The total went up after the trade.

For the second round, she told us we could trade with everyone in the room. Now we all had twenty-four possible trading partners rather than just four. Everyone, including the kid in the back row who hadn't said a word all year, suddenly snapped to attention.

The room was abuzz for several minutes with trades, trades, and more trades. Some toys changed hands several times. But the commotion died down when no new trades were possible. We again graded our toys and Mrs. Hubbard added up the scores; the total was much higher than the first two. Almost everyone ended up with a toy he liked more than the one he received at the beginning. No one had a score that had gone down.

This is a simple example of how genuinely free trade works.

Win-Win

A free economy isn't a utopia. It can't solve the problem of scarcity that began with the fall of man:

> "[C]ursed is the ground because of you;
> in toil you shall eat of it all the days of your life;
> thorns and thistles it shall bring forth to you;
> and you shall eat the plants of the field.
> In the sweat of your face
> you shall eat bread
> till you return to the ground,
> for out of it you were taken;
> you are dust,
> and to dust you shall return." (Genesis 3:17–19)

Not even the coming of Christ reversed this side effect of Adam's sin. It won't go away until the New Jerusalem. But freedom to work and trade can make our lot in life much better. These allow us to cooperate, specialize in what we're good at, and avoid wasteful effort.

Remember those win-win exchanges in my Texas classroom? If I traded my Barbie trading cards with Suzie for her paddleball, Suzie (who doesn't give a rip about paddleball) and I both win. In positive-sum or win-win games, nobody loses. Some players may end up better off than others, but everyone ends up better off than if they'd taken their toys and gone home. An exchange that's free on both sides, in which no one is forced or tricked into playing, is a positive-sum game. The partners wouldn't trade unless both saw themselves as better off as a result. Even though nothing new was added to the system, the total value goes up; the outcome is a win-win. If you understand this concept, you understand the free market better than most of its critics.

Of course, as adults we don't trade our toys, but our time and talents. We choose to specialize in what we're good at (such as speaking, teaching, and writing) and earn wealth from that to trade with other people who specialize in different things. So, we don't waste time and torture ourselves by trying to drill and repair our teeth or fix our cars.

There are two other kinds of games—win-lose and lose-lose—in which someone ends up worse off. No one plays lose-lose games intentionally, so let's ignore them.

That leaves win-lose games, which are often called zero-sum games. If your opponent takes one unit from you, he's at 1 and you're at –1. The sum of 1 and –1 is zero. If the game is, say, a form of gambling, you may have both started out with some money, but you haven't added any money to the total. The sum of what you have added is zero. No new wealth or value has been generated. To have a winner in a zero-sum game, you must have a loser. Monopoly, tennis, chess, and football are zero-sum games because a win for one side means a loss for the other.

Marxists view the economy as a zero-sum game of exploitation, group hatred, and finally, violent revolution. They assume that people don't really cooperate freely or fairly but will only cheat each other until the government controls their choices. This will then give rise to a "new socialist man." When that happens, the state will not be needed and will wither away, leaving a communist utopia.

This is all nonsense, including the first premise of argument. A free market is not a free-for-all in which the strong always prey on the weak. It requires a rule of law that allows only certain kinds of trades: We can't kidnap, enslave, threaten, or steal from each other. (And since every class has a bully, you need an authority like Mrs. Hubbard.) With these rules in place, free trade ends up being win-win. Free trades can happen only if both traders see themselves as better off because of the trade.

Economic Value Lies in the Eye of the Beholder

Each of the toys cost Mrs. Hubbard about the same amount, but we students valued them differently. For centuries, economists and philosophers tended to define economic value in terms of labor or cost of production—called the labor theory of value.[2] They thought something was worth what it cost to produce it. This sounds right when you first hear it, but the Trading Game shows that economic value is in the eye of the beholder. This may seem like a subtle point, but grasping it is vital if we are to avoid disastrous economic policies.

To see why the labor theory is wrong, imagine you decide to open a home baking business. You make delicious, fancy cakes with pricey ingredients. They cost you $100 each to make, so you charge $110. Is that what they're *worth*? Are people being unjust by refusing to buy your cakes at that price? Are they trying to exploit you (to use Marxist language)?

No, they're deciding what's worth spending their money on. The customer, competing with others, is the one who decides what any product is worth *economically* by choosing how much to pay (or refusing to pay) for it. That's it. The alternative is to let the government dictate what each thing is worth to every person and punish people if they try to violate its rules. This leads to disaster.

The heart of the market economy is the price system, which doesn't rely on a central authority full of brainy experts to decide what everything in life is worth. Instead, it allows each of us to decide, based on what we need and want, and to coordinate our choices accordingly. It's that profound and that simple. On that choice rests the difference between South Korea and North Korea. Guess which country needs razor wire and armed guards to keep its people from fleeing?

Prices and the Mystery of the Market

A free market sets up win-win exchanges. It also distributes goods and services far better than any system we could plan. This is what Adam Smith had in mind when he described the market as an "invisible hand." His idea is that a free market will "guide" the acts of business-people "to promote an end which is not part of [their] intention."[3]

The butcher, brewer, and baker don't need to know all the outcomes of their work. They don't need to visualize world peace or think nice thoughts to benefit others. They could just as well be thinking about their electric bill, their car insurance, or their desire to win the "best business owner of the year" award from the Chamber of Commerce. They might even be selfish. Nevertheless, in a healthy market economy, they will still try to provide something that others will freely buy. Smith saw this invisible hand as God's providence over human affairs, since it creates a more harmonious order than any human being could contrive. The great Austrian economist Friedrich Hayek also marveled at what he called the "spontaneous order" of the market.[4]

Common sense might lead you to suspect that a free market, where no one dictates prices, production quotas, and the like, would lead to chaos. To distribute goods and services well, won't someone have to oversee the whole system? This is what socialists thought in the twentieth century, and because they gained control over whole nations, they could test their beliefs on a broad scale. The result was misery and oppression, food shortages, overproduced goods that gathered dust on store shelves, widespread poverty, and at the extreme, mass death.

In the 1980s, the last premier of the Soviet Union, Mikhail Gorbachev, met with British Prime Minister Margaret Thatcher. According to a popular story, Gorbachev was surprised to see how well off the British seemed to be. He asked Thatcher who made sure the people got fed. "No one," she told him. "The price system does that." The British people got fed far better than the subjects of the Soviet Union, who languished under a planned economy.[5]

Think of the trading game again. What if, instead of the students trading freely, Mrs. Hubbard dictated or tried to guess which toy each of her twenty-five students preferred? Would all the kids have gotten what they liked most? Probably not. The fact that they traded when given a chance proved that most of the kids hadn't gotten what they preferred at the start.

Mrs. Hubbard's random distribution illustrates the dilemma that would beset any economic planner. Such planning can't work because humans are not all-knowing. To plan a whole economy, one would have to know the value of every product for every person in the economy at every time and place, since the value of things can change drastically from moment to moment.

Much to socialists' surprise, planned economies create all sorts of crazy distortions. For a time in the Soviet Union, glass factories were paid according to how many tons of sheet glass they produced.

Since they didn't need to bother making what people wanted, the factories started producing glass so thick that it was useless. The planners then changed the rules and paid factories by the square meter. Guess what happened? Factories started producing glass that was so thin that it broke at the slightest touch.[6]

By now, you might be wondering: If economic planners can't know the right price of anything before the moment of free exchange, how is free trade possible?

This is the central mystery and wonder of the market order: We can learn the value of any economic good—a one-hour aromatherapy session in Monaco on June 6, 2024, a cantaloupe at Trader Joe's in Santa Monica on May 5, 2025—but only through the market process in which free choices are channeled by a stable rule of law.

The purchased price of a good or service in a free economy is like a label packed with information. It tells us what that thing is worth (economically) at that moment. This price compresses a vast amount of information since it represents thousands of underlying facts. Based on current prices, savvy entrepreneurs can make educated guesses about how and where to invest. Savvy suppliers and producers can do the same.

When prices are "free" to move up and down in a market, they have an amazing power to summon goods, services, and resources to the place they're most valued. If there's a housing boom in Houston, Texas, the prices for lumber, bricks, concrete, and construction skills will go up there, and before long, supplies will appear there to meet the higher price. But other parts of the country don't normally end up with a shortage. If there's any demand for these things in Poughkeepsie or Pawnee, the prices will rise there, drawing some of the needed resources back there. Unless there's a literal shortage, the freedom of prices to go up and down will keep supply and demand for scarce goods in an exquisite equilibrium.

A free market is not the New Jerusalem, but it's a much better system than any human planners can devise. If we're interested in prosperity and helping the poor, we must recognize the power of the free market at home and abroad. Of course, "abroad" raises its own set of questions, which we'll discuss in the next chapter.

CHAPTER 15

Global Trade, Globalism, and the Threat of Communist China

The trading game reveals why real free trade is a win-win game; the larger the pool of trading partners, the greater the benefits overall.

A truly free market also allows people and firms to specialize in those tasks they're best at—instead of trying to, say, grow avocados in greenhouses in Iceland. The supply chain that gives rise to smartphones, Boeing 747s, and the internet is the outcome of international markets. These webs of cooperation have, in the last few centuries, allowed vast wealth to be created and enjoyed, much of it by relatively poor people.

Unfortunately, many global corporations and corrupt governments have given free trade a bad name. Woke companies blather on about "systemic racism" and force employees to endure training in diversity, equity, and inclusion (DEI) here at home while using slave labor in China. For its part, the regime in China has for decades exploited Western openness and goodwill to lie, cheat, and steal while pretending to give up its communist past. These facts have undermined public support for free trade. But we should not throw out the baby with the bathwater.

Basic Economics

The most toxic ingredients in that water are globalism and the communist regime in China. Before we flush that putrid sludge, though, let's get the baby (free trade) out and have a look at it.

In their book *Superabundance*, Marian Tupy and Gale Pooley show the miracles this system has wrought. The real cost of scores of key goods—determined by the amount of work needed to acquire them—has gone way down over the last couple of centuries, even as the number of people has exploded.[1] That's right: more people *and* more abundance. On this measure, the world is 423 percent more abundant now than it was in 1980.[2]

How did this happen? Expanding circles of trade, plus specialization, plus human innovation.

To grasp this, it helps to imagine the alternative: Let's say the citizens of Fargo, North Dakota, decide they are only going to buy locally produced goods. They resolve not to wear, eat, drive, or live in anything that came from anywhere outside the Fargo metropolitan area, which includes a few hundred thousand people.

To live as they do now, they would need to have mines and smelters of all sorts, steel mills, oil wells, oil refineries, car manufacturing and computer chip fabrication plants, light-bulb factories, leather tanners, farms, ranches, butchers, dairy farms, fruit orchards, paper and textile mills, chemical and drug factories, movie studios, and on and on and on—all in and around Fargo. Few folks in Fargo have either the time or the talent to handle all these tasks.

Without large markets that draw on specialized labor, most of what the folks in Fargo now take for granted would disappear. Their lives would soon resemble the lives of isolated villagers long before the Industrial Revolution. They would work much harder and produce far less. Everything would be much more expensive. Everyone would be vastly poorer. Their lives would be nasty, poor, brutish, and short.

If this doesn't seem clear, then keep shrinking the circle of trade in your mind from the city to a neighborhood in Fargo, or one street, or one household, or one person. At each smaller circle, people would be poorer than in the larger one. In fact, at such scales, most people would starve to death. Sometimes economic truth is only obvious at the extreme, but it applies everywhere. Keep this lesson in mind, along with the lessons of the trading game, when you're thinking about trade.

Global Trade, Not Globalism

Unfortunately, the demise of the Soviet Union didn't simply lead to freedom: It also cleared the way for some Western elites to push their alternative utopian vision of globalism. Indeed, many former communist leaders didn't repent—they pivoted. They chatted up the values of liberal democracy while rejecting the foundations that allowed the free world to defeat the Soviet Union. The result is that our culture is now awash in wokeness, which is a new, more subtle type of totalitarianism.[3]

"Globalization" refers to the growth of trade and specialization among the peoples of the world. On balance, this is a good thing—as long as cheaters don't get a free pass. There are still a billion people languishing in severe poverty, and billions more who could be doing far better. These people will stay poor unless they get plugged into global markets.

One-world globalism, on the other hand, is a toxic ideology. Globalists such Klaus Schwab of the World Economic Forum see nation-states as obsolete. They seek to dissolve national borders and grow transnational entities—such as the United Nations and the European Union—to manage eight billion world citizens.[4] Global trade is about the spread of economic freedom. Globalism is about the spread of political control—of one world government. Don't confuse these two things.

What about Outsourcing and Offshoring?

Global trade is a sore spot for many Americans, though—especially those in manufacturing, who worry about competing with cheap foreign labor. And the rise of a hostile China has made it even harder to think clearly about trade in general.

Most people assume that the U.S. lost millions of manufacturing jobs to China after trade deals in 2000 and 2001. Both of our political parties now use this "China Shock" as a talking point. But what really happened, what caused it, and what was its effect overall? As it turns out, the answers are hard to nail down.

We know that some 7.5 million lower-skill factory jobs have disappeared in the U.S. since 1980—especially in textiles, furniture, printing, and electronics. About five million of those have been lost since 2000. There are towns and areas across the Midwest—the "rustbelt"—that have suffered with opioid addiction and "deaths of despair" from overdoses and suicides.[5] These are tragedies no matter what caused them.

The loss of these jobs doesn't mean there are 7.5 million fewer *net* jobs. Over the same period, millions more service and tech jobs appeared—though many low-skill service jobs pay less well than the low-skill factory jobs. And these new jobs may be spread out, rather than concentrated where factories used to be in Michigan or Ohio. Such jobs may also be a mismatch for male heads of households without college degrees—especially for the men stuck in a town that has lost its factories and doesn't have a plan B.

There were, of course, benefits to the U.S. during this time. Chinese companies were investing here; cheaper goods from China often became inputs for other goods higher up the supply chain produced in the U.S. or elsewhere. And prices for many goods have gone way down for everyone over the same time, while the market for U.S. goods is now much larger as a result of trade. Computer chips are largely an American product, for instance—even if they're fabricated in Taiwan or Korea—and China is the world's top consumer of such chips.

Now the story gets even more complex. The loss of all these manufacturing jobs doesn't mean U.S. manufacturing is less productive. On the contrary, output has gone up over the same period because of automation and greater efficiency. We produce more, both in total and per worker, with fewer workers. So how much of the job loss in manufacturing is due to automation and how much to trade? Economists have spent years trying to figure this out. (See the notes for a few key sources.)[6] Long story short: At least half of the jobs, and maybe far more, were lost to technology, not to trade with China.

Globally, far more is produced now than in 2000. At the same time, the *share* of the value-add in global manufacturing has changed. China has risen from less than 10 percent to almost 30 percent while the U.S. has fallen from about 22 percent to about 16 percent of global manufacturing. That makes China number one in the world. But the U.S. is still number two—as much as the following three countries combined.[7] That may be worrisome, but it's absurd to say that "America no longer builds anything."[8]

In any case, the crucial question now is not what happened to these jobs, but what's the best way to create new ones, especially for

men without college degrees? And what do we do with a more powerful, and hostile, communist China?

How to Think about Trade and Competition

We'll answer these questions. But first, let's get clear about how
trade works when crime and slavery aren't involved, so we don't fall
for the cartoon caricatures beloved by politicians on the left and the
right.

If you have a manufacturing job in Detroit and your plant closes
and relocates to Montgomery or Mumbai, that's painful and disrup-
tive for you. Ditto if you have a coding job in Austin. No one likes
competition. Every worker and every company might prefer monopoly
control. If you're getting paid $50 an hour to build motherboards for
computers, you're not going to like it if someone across town or across
the ocean will do the job better or for less. You might favor policies
that "protect" your job by making it harder for those other workers
to compete. If the government makes it hard for your employer to hire
and fire workers, or slaps steep tariffs on imported motherboards, for
instance, you'll have less competition. But you also likely won't per-
form as well.

The same thing is true for companies. Walmart would love for
regulators to hobble Target and Amazon. That's why defending a free
market is not the same as defending business or big business. Most
businesses prefer markets jerry-rigged to favor them.

With any economic policy, though, we should ask first, is it just?
And second, will it really help? That is, are laws that limit trade to
protect a specific job or company—that restrict competition—just?
And do they really help you, or our country as a whole, in the long
run? Does the computer company have a duty to keep paying you $50
an hour, even if that makes the company less competitive, when your

neighbor or an Indian will do the same work for less money? Are you entitled to your exact job, and entitled to prevent your neighbor or the poor Indian from competing? And should your neighbor be forced to buy a higher-priced motherboard made by you instead of a much less expensive one made by someone else?

Note that such laws involve subtly forcing your neighbor to give up some of his property—the extra cost of the motherboard. What's more, with such regulations, all the goods you need to buy will be more expensive as well, especially when everyone catches on to the protectionist trick of limiting competition. Your wages might stay higher for a while, but prices will shoot up for you and everyone else. And both your company and the economy will get more decrepit and less competitive over time.

That's why most economists argue that all this sludge in the system is lose-lose for almost everyone in the long run. It trades targeted, short-term gains for some people for sweeping, long-term pain for almost everyone. Much better to accept the tradeoffs of free and competitive markets.

But what if the government slapped a tariff on all imported motherboards to raise their costs, and then used the money to subsidize the American company? Lots of Americans support policies like this. But again, this amounts to a government official making your neighbor give up some of his wealth to protect a company. It will also lead to the American company being less competitive in the long run—just as protecting a teenager from the consequences of his bad behavior will make him less likely to clean up his act.

Then there's the fact that such anticompetitive efforts are cowardly. Do we really think Americans can't compete with other countries unless the government "protects" us in this way?

Beneath all this is a more subtle confusion. Economists call it "the lump of labor fallacy," which leads people to imagine that there's a fixed supply of jobs. In truth, there's no "lump of labor" that gets depleted when someone gets a job, or someone creates a tool to make work more efficient. If there were, human history would be a long, dreary tale of rising poverty and unemployment. Instead, people—even the poorest 10 percent—are much better off now, with a global population near eight billion, than were their counterparts in any previous century.

So, where do more and better (real) jobs come from? Answer: enterprise. Entrepreneurs seek new ventures and risk their money to pursue them. Many of these fail, but the best ones produce new jobs and new prospects. There are no jobs stored ahead of time in a warehouse somewhere. Enterprise creates new wealth and new jobs.

But those come at a cost: Enterprise destroys older ways of doing things. This disrupts the lives of real people. The more enterprising an economy, the more of this "job churn" it will have, since a new way of doing something can make the old way of doing it obsolete. Economist Joseph Schumpeter called this *creative destruction*. If a company doesn't provide something people will freely buy, then it will have to change, or it will cease to exist—unless the government props it up.

The buggy whip industry was displaced by the auto industry, the whale oil industry by petroleum refining, and the electric typewriter by the personal computer. Better machines make our factories far more productive than they used to be. But that means the common assembly-line jobs of the last century are dwindling away.[9]

The question, then, is not how can we avoid all painful change and job displacement, but rather, what's the best system for everyone overall and in the long run? We know the answer in the abstract. Adam Smith, the father of modern economics, explained this more than two hundred years ago:

What is prudence in the conduct of every family can scarce be folly in that of a great kingdom. If a foreign country can supply us with a commodity cheaper than we ourselves can make it, better buy it of them with some part of the produce of our own industry, employed in a way in which we have some advantage.[10]

It's not a "wealth transfer" for us to buy coffee from another country better suited to growing coffee than we are. They get money and we get coffee. Assuming no one lies or cheats, both sides are better off because of the trade. The time and effort we save by not growing coffee badly can be employed more fruitfully. (We may have reasons for not trading with some foreign countries despite the extra cost. We'll discuss that below.) If, instead, we think we're entitled to our jobs at our current salary, and we support politicians who promise to "protect" them, we and our children will be worse off in the long run—with less freedom, less prosperity, and worse and fewer jobs.

It's hard to think clearly about this issue when we have a stake in it. So, consider Israel. The government there imposed heavy tariffs and protections on its citizens for decades after its founding in 1948. The Israeli economy lumbered along. Once those policies were reformed in the late 1980s and '90s, however, Israel's economy exploded. No doubt everyone who liked the earlier policies thought they were better off before, but they weren't looking at the long-term costs and benefits.

The value of widespread trade is not just theory; it's fact. Over the last several decades, per capita income has gone up in most countries around the world—though the COVID lockdowns and Biden inflation have caused a drop in the last few years. Total income has increased, including in many developing countries. The exceptions are communist and other oppressive countries such as North Korea that have remained mostly outside global markets.[11]

In general, the more economic freedom a country enjoys, the better it does. Every year, places such as Singapore, Switzerland, and New Zealand rank near the top in economic freedom. Zimbabwe, Cuba, and North Korea land at the bottom. The U.S. has been going down for years. In 2023, we ranked twenty-fifth, behind every Scandinavian country![12]

Free trade among nations, on balance, makes all of them more prosperous than they would be otherwise. That fact hasn't changed just because it's less popular to say so than it used to be.

What about China?

But what about trade with adversaries? Even during the free trade glory days of the 1980s, we had a trade embargo against the Soviet Union. Only a few rock-ribbed libertarians objected.

Why didn't we do the same with China? The short answer is that in the '80s and '90s, the regime in Beijing seemed to be moving away from Maoism. It opened enterprise zones, allowed private businesses to form, created a stock market, and signaled that it was reforming. As a result, its economy started to grow—fast. Many in the West hoped that with open trade, the Chinese middle class would grow and then press for reforms from within. Rather than a hostile communist nemesis, we would have a vibrant trading partner like Japan—to say nothing of the benefits for the Chinese people, most of whom were desperately poor.

That didn't happen. Instead, Beijing learned from the Soviets' mistakes to pursue a much shrewder strategy. Rather than building giant, state-owned farms and industries, Beijing built state-controlled firms that looked, from the outside, like the private firms in the U.S.

These firms invested in U.S. properties and did many of the other things we associate with market economies. As a result, they performed much better than the purely socialist alternative.

The truth, though, is that China built a fascist economy with no clear lines between the private and public sectors. The social media platform TikTok, for instance, is tied to the Chinese government.[13] It collects truckloads of data from American users while feeding us addictive trash that it blocks in China. Beijing also launched a huge effort to spy on American citizens and companies, cheat shamelessly on trade deals, steal intellectual property, buy up American farmland, harass and arrest Chinese citizens inside our borders, and infiltrate our universities.[14] Within its borders, the regime has imprisoned at least a million Uyghur Muslims—often just for practicing their religion.[15]

Meanwhile, we granted China most favored nation status—as if it were the Philippines or South Korea! Though the details are complex, this surely distorted our labor markets since we weren't dealing with an honest trading partner.

The world now finds itself entangled with a global adversary much richer and more powerful than the former Soviet Union. It owns about a trillion dollars of U.S debt, and, like the Soviet Union, wants to be the world's sole superpower. Many of our largest companies—including the NBA—are compromised. They enjoy access to the massive Chinese market and don't want the money train to roll to a stop.

What Do We Do?

This is the greatest foreign policy challenge we face, and it presents us with nothing but hard choices. A few things are clear, though. First, we can't keep pretending this problem will go away. China is a totalitarian foe, not a budding liberal democracy. As Heritage Foundation

President Kevin Roberts puts it, "It is past time for a whole-of-government and whole-of-society effort that serves American interests and protects the American people and economy from malicious actions by the CCP."[16]

Second, we should not pretend that "decoupling" from China will be painless. For instance, about half of the world's semiconductors, the brains of our information technology, are fabricated in Taiwan—an island nation that China considers one of its provinces. (Only 12 percent of this chip fabrication is in the United States. Mainland China comes in fifth.[17]) This work is vital to the U.S. and global economy, but it's exquisitely complex. It requires costly, high-tech plants, the expertise of thousands of engineers, and hundreds of related nearby companies, as Taiwan has. This capacity can't just be beamed from one place to another, though politicians looking for votes like to pretend it can be.[18]

Vast numbers of computers, smartphones, and other electronics—which use U.S.-designed chips fabricated in Taiwan—are assembled in mainland China for use around the globe.

Add to this the fact that we depend on China for the manufacture of many drugs, batteries for electric cars, and all sorts of "rare earth minerals" that are vital to key technologies. China also (falsely) claims jurisdiction over sea lanes that are among the busiest in the world. This is the mother of all trade bottlenecks.

Extracting ourselves from China will likely cost us both jobs and national wealth. Prices on all sorts of goods will go up. But the alternative—a world dominated by communist China—would surely be worse.

We can, however, make this less painful than it would be otherwise. China has far fewer options than we do, and its economy is almost certainly more fragile than it appears from the outside. To win this Cold War, we must persuade the Chinese leadership that it has more to lose than to gain from its current policies. This will require us to slash bad regulations at home to make it easier for U.S. firms to compete and for entrepreneurs to start new ventures. Many of these regulations supposedly protect the environment. What they really do is throttle our industry and give China—the world's largest polluter—the advantage.

We must also quit pining for the low-skill factory jobs of the last century. If we want our factories to compete, they must be automated. As a result, they will provide fewer low-skill jobs even as they produce more goods. It would be wasteful and foolish to try to recreate the factories common in the 1950s. Instead, in the blue-collar sector, we need to focus far more on the skilled trades that are in high demand—plumbing, painting, electrical work, welding, higher-end construction, and the like. These jobs pay well, can't be outsourced, and won't get replaced by robots anytime soon.

Finally, we need to create an international trade alliance. Beijing is building trade relations around the world, and we need to do the same. We won't magically grow our economy by shutting down our trade while China expands its own. Instead, we need to build the largest free trade zone we can—with friends, potential friends, and fellow belligerents in Asia, Africa, the Middle East, Europe, and Latin America. We must do this too if we want to stop Beijing's efforts to become the next global hegemon.

We should reward politicians who tell us the truth about all these challenges and display the competence and bravery to face them head on. We should reject the ones who just tell us what they think we want to hear.

CHAPTER 16

Peace in Our Borders

In 2016, Donald Trump rode the issue of illegal immigration all the way to the White House. For decades, most Democrats had turned a blind eye to the topic, as had most Republicans. Efforts at "immigration reform" failed, in part, because they always amounted to amnesty, with nothing gained in return, such as secure borders. Trump sensed widespread anger among voters over the issue and made building a wall on our southern border the literal and figurative symbol of his campaign.

The left did its best to tar the brash businessman from Queens as a racist, but there was never any evidence of that. He just voiced the thoughts of millions of Americans: Every country gets to say who can enter its territory. It's foolish and unfair to reward people who come here illegally while throwing up barriers to legal immigrants and to both low- and high-skilled workers who were born here.

Views on immigration don't divide up neatly into "liberal" and "conservative." Some, such as the editorial page of the *Wall Street Journal*, focus on the economic perks to the free flow of labor. Just as capital in a free market will flow to the places it is most valued, labor will do the same.

This has always happened within our borders. In the nineteenth century, farmers moved west in search of soil more fertile than the rocky ground available in New England. Right now, there is an exodus of workers from California to Texas and Florida because the Lone Star and Sunshine states have much better business environments. In the long run, this freedom of movement is not just good for Texas, Florida, and workers, but for California as well.

The main problem with foreign immigration is not so much economic as social and cultural. "Labor" is an abstraction. It can't rent a U-Haul, be transferred by wire, or be shipped by FedEx. Labor is people—men and women, families, religious beliefs, political histories, and cultures. People shape the culture of the country and get to *vote on its laws*. If they hold hostile ideas (such as socialism or sharia), they could change the country to match their own ideas instead of the other way around.

That's why many worry about the long-term cultural impact of unlimited immigration. To maintain our laws and culture, they want the inflow of people to be gradual enough to allow immigrants to gain allegiance to our culture and Constitution. That's common sense, not racism.

Of course, others focus on the people, not the consequences of the policy, and want to grant blanket amnesty to illegal immigrants. But these folks often confuse refugees fleeing true danger with people who just want to come here while bypassing the legal path for doing so. And then there are those on the left who want to grant blanket amnesty so that the new citizens will vote for their candidates.

Labor unions also weigh in on this; their leaders are staunchly on the left, even if their members dislike immigration (legal or otherwise) because they fear it will undercut their union wages.

Love the Sojourner

There's no simple "Christian" policy on immigration, since it involves lots of competing goods. God commanded His chosen people to treat *sojourners* kindly:

> [God] executes justice for the fatherless and the widow, and loves the sojourner, giving him food and clothing. Love the sojourner therefore; for you were sojourners in the land of Egypt. (Deuteronomy 10:18–19)

God has special compassion for sojourners, and we should, too.

Over the last decade, both the U.S. Conference of Catholic Bishops and the National Association of Evangelicals[1] have called for "immigration reform" that amounts to mass amnesty, claiming it is based on Scripture. But nothing in Scripture suggests that nations must have open borders. Critics have suggested that the Catholic bishops and the NAE are self-interested, since Catholic Charities and others receive millions of dollars from the federal government for processing immigrants.[2] In any case, neither has offered a wise or just plan to fix the problem. Justice and kindness entail neither mass amnesty nor the crazy mess we have now.

Immigration no longer means what it did when the Pilgrims sailed from England by way of the Netherlands, the Irish came here during the potato famine, and Chinese people sailed to California. These people often left everything in hope of a better life for their children. They came legally and worked hard when they got here. They sought to become Americans.

But the U.S. is now lax in securing its borders and has become a vast entitlement state, so that even immigrants who want to make a life for themselves can end up on the public dole. Many of our schools now discourage assimilation and encourage cultural relativism. These policies often have turned immigration into a liability rather than an asset. No plan for reform that ignores these facts has a prayer of passing muster with voters. Nor should it.

The problem is often boiled down to a short proverb: "Democracy, immigration, multi-culturalism . . . pick any two."[3] These three are like territorial cats. You might get two to live under the same roof, but not three. Democracy—that is, voting for all adult citizens—and immigration can coexist if immigrants adopt the same constitutional values as their adopted country. Immigration and multiculturalism can coexist in a dictatorship because, even if a million *Mayflowers* arrive with pilgrims who don't assimilate, they lack the political power to transform the country. And democracy and multiculturalism can coexist if the cultural variety was present at the beginning and no new immigrants with contrary values are admitted afterward.

Here's the key point: Immigration plus cultural relativism plus democracy creates dangerous ethnic and religious factions, which over time will tear apart the country. This is obvious in the extreme: Imagine granting American citizenship all at once to three hundred million people chosen at random from cultures that oppose human rights and religious freedom. How do you think the next election will turn out? And the one after that?

Illegal Immigration

Now add the extra wrinkle of illegal immigration. How bad is this? Our immigration authorities encountered two million illegal immigrants, mostly on our southern border, in 2022 alone![4] The influx started within weeks of Joe Biden's inauguration.

Confusing legal with illegal immigration is "like saying that because you don't like people breaking into your house, you are anti-guest."[5] It's easy for those of us who live hundreds of miles from our southern border with Mexico to accuse ranchers there of being anti-immigrant. But what happened when a planeload of immigrants from Florida was sent to Martha's Vineyard—home to cultural elites including former President Barack Obama? Residents responded by calling the National Guard to round them up within twenty-four hours.[6]

It's no surprise that millions of people want to come to the U.S. For all our problems, life here, especially for the poor, is much better than in the countries south of our border. American employers often benefit from the work of illegal immigrants, which creates a strong demand for it. And, because of absurd policies, it's easier and cheaper to come here illegally than to work your way through the bureaucratic maze toward citizenship.

Real reform is tough because we don't have the luxury of crafting a policy from scratch. At least twelve million people live in the United States illegally.[7] Millions of them have been here for years, are working, and have kids in schools (also illegally).[8] That makes the problem different from crimes like shoplifting.

Let's say your state informed you that it had been secretly monitoring your driving for the last two decades and was going to fine you for every time you had exceeded the speed limit. Then they send you a fine for $20,000. If they had stopped you the first few times you sped, you would have adjusted your behavior. Most Americans would reject such a policy as unfair.

Our immigration problem is like that. It's due partly due to illegal acts and partly to decades of lax enforcement of our laws. Government mismanagement has allowed illegal immigrants to evade the law and unfairly compete against other lower-income workers—yet their illegal status has kept them from becoming Americans. This rends the social fabric in ways that aren't easy to mend.

That, combined with dysfunction in Mexico and other countries to our south, means no solution will be perfect. What we do with illegal immigrants who have been here for years is one thing; how we handle recent and future illegal immigration is another.

On the one hand, we can't just deport twelve million people. The cost, logistics, and tragedy would be immense. Likewise, granting blanket amnesty would reward the lawbreakers, discourage the law-abiding, and encourage even more illegal immigration.

But we can do a lot to fix the system between these two extremes. Any viable proposal should include the following elements, and in the right order.

Fix and Enforce the Law

First, the government needs to secure the borders, both to gain the public's trust and to prevent more people from crossing illegally. Many countries, including Mexico, treat illegal immigrants in their own countries as foreign enemies of the state. Meanwhile, criminal cartels largely control the illegal flow of people along our southern border. This also allows them to smuggle in drugs and engage in horrific child and sex trafficking.[9]

In response, the least we can do is secure our borders. That includes ending the crazy "catch-and-release" policy of the Biden administration, which draws illegal immigration like an electromagnet draws iron filings. Fences, walls, border guards, National Guard, drones, cameras, fast deportation, and stated resolve would reduce the flood to a trickle.

We must also keep track of immigrants who come here legally but overstay their visas (such as most of the 9/11 terrorists). If the federal government can keep track of Social Security checks and income tax returns, it can keep better track of these visa holders; it just hasn't been a priority.

In the last few years, countless people have come here by falsely pleading asylum. This is yet another crime, and traffickers and church-linked nonprofits often coach immigrants on how to do this.[10] Asylum laws are for people fleeing for their lives from a war-torn country; anyone truly seeking asylum should do so in the first safe country he enters. Instead, millions pass through several safe countries on their way to the U.S. and then apply for asylum. They're not fleeing near-certain death; they're shopping. As Heritage Foundation border expert Lora Ries puts it, Biden has tried to use "an erroneously named gimmick on top of a shell game to cover up bad optics on surging illegal immigration."[11] This needs to stop.

Assimilate

Second, we must pursue an energetic legal policy of assimilating immigrants, which includes solid civics education and training in English. There's nothing magical about English, but it's the primary language of the United States and of international trade. A common language unites people. Those who come here are much more likely to succeed if they learn it.[12]

The alternative isn't live-and-let-live, but "reverse assimilation," whereby the immigrant culture displaces the native one. This is already happening with Muslims to Europe. We're *not* talking about well-assimilated Muslims who are happy to be free of tyranny in Iraq or Iran. We mean large, unassimilated, hostile Muslim populations living in enclaves. Strict Islam is both religious and political, and secular Europe is ill-prepared to handle it.

Teach American Culture

Third, we must pass American culture on to immigrants. We're all for cultural and ethnic variety, but many of our schools now teach woke relativism. A woman who moves here from Vietnam or Venezuela and enrolls in an American history class at a community college is likely to learn that America enslaved Africans and massacred

Indians. She'll learn little to nothing about the U.S. Constitution or our role in defeating the Nazis and Soviets. This is not the way to cultivate new citizens.

We must roll back the influence of relativism and anti-Americanism in our public institutions. These trends harm immigrants by keeping them from embracing American culture. There are already many ministries that work with immigrants and refugees. The government should focus its efforts here.

Work, Not Entitlements

Fourth, we must reform entitlements and welfare programs that tend to suck immigrants into a cycle that discourages work. We have seen immigrants come to the United States as refugees with help from Christian ministries. Rather than seeking gainful employment, however, some of these ministries help the refugees get Social Security income and other unearned perks from the federal government. This is false compassion that prevents immigrants from contributing to society. It also creates resentment. People of faith should take the lead in helping immigrants find jobs and fight the temptation to become wards of the state. They should not show immigrants how to game the system.

Verify Employment

Finally, Congress should mandate that employers use the E-Verify system. This is an electronic version of a paper process we already have that lets employers verify that ID forms from job applicants, such as a Social Security card or state driver's license, are valid. This would help employers comply with the law and encourage them to hire only legal employees.[13]

Make Immigration Great Again

Americans have long valued immigrants as a key part of our history and our future. For that to continue, the government must stop the flood of illegal immigration, maintain border security, enforce our laws, and help ensure that those who come here become good citizens. Otherwise, our country as we know it will cease to exist—for both Americans and those future immigrants we invite to join our great nation.

CHAPTER 17

Be Fruitful

In Genesis 1, God's blessing to the first man and woman bundled together two things we tend to separate: the family and the economy. That's not an accident.

"Be fruitful and multiply, and fill the earth and subdue it; and have dominion over the fish of the sea and over the birds of the air and over every living thing that moves upon the earth" (Genesis 1:28). This idea of man as the *imago Dei* ("image of God") has given theologians gainful employment for two thousand years. They have often equated the image with our reason or our soul; but the text simply says that human beings—both male and female—are true icons of God. He is the sovereign King over the heavens and the earth who, in turn, appoints us to have dominion as kings and queens over the tiny part of creation we can touch. God creates by calling things into existence. He then commands us to create according to our power, by "[filling] the earth and [subduing] it." All our creativity comes from God, who calls us to be cocreators alongside Him.

Where Genesis 1 gives the cosmic overview, Genesis 2 zooms in tight. Here God fashions man from the ground, breathes into him the breath of life, puts him in a garden and tells him to "till it and keep it."[1] We're made of dirt and are made to work with dirt—and yet we have within us the very breath of God. Work itself is part of God's original blessing, not His curse after the Fall. We are a unique mixture of Heaven and Earth, so the way we work should reflect the fact that we are a unity of matter and spirit, neither pack animals nor angels.

Though the Bible is not an economics textbook, it casts light on an important truth of economics: With our hands and our minds, we can create wealth—and in the right setting, that wealth becomes the source of more wealth.

How Wealth Creation Started

Early humans first roamed the earth as hunters and gatherers; then they began to domesticate animals and to cultivate plants such as wheat and barley. These farmers started with what God had provided—seeds, land, rain, animals—and enriched it. Today, economists list the three factors of production as land, labor, and capital.

After man developed ways to store food and irrigate land, cities appeared with growing populations not tied directly to farming, which gave rise to much larger civilizations. Metal plows and wheeled carts slowly replaced stone and wooden tools; horses replaced oxen for plowing; and tractors replaced horses. Thousands of innovations—from seed drills, reapers, combines, and hybridized grains, along with countless new farming techniques—made agriculture much more productive.

With world exploration came new crops such as the potato, ending the cycle of regular famines in Europe. After World War II, the Green Revolution saw Western technology transform agriculture in places like India. This allowed the vast subcontinent to start exporting food. Even though there are many times more people now than there were even a few centuries ago, we don't suffer global famines. So much for the "overpopulation" panic-mongers! Now, when food shortages do occur, it's because of corrupt governments.

As recently as 1900, 80 percent of the world population still lived on farms. By the 1970s, that number had dropped to 50 percent.[2] Millions of people still engage in primitive subsistence farming, as they have for centuries—growing just enough to feed themselves, if they're lucky. With solid private property laws and high technology, however, less than 2 percent of the American population now lives on farms, and yet they produce enough not only to feed the U.S., but to export abroad.[3] Most of history was marked by scarcity, but we now live amid both great abundance and scarcity.

Better farming opened the way to developments in art, music, philosophy, literature, and all sorts of new technologies. From mastering fire and inventing the wheel, building levers and pulleys, learning to draw metal ores from the earth with mining and smelting, to harnessing the energy of rivers and wind with water and windmills, our ancestors slowly transformed the material world around them to create new wealth. But technology is only the tip of the iceberg.

More and More Mind

Though the word "capital" first referred to cattle, it also looks like the Latin word for "head," *caput*.[4] In modern economies, the mind matters more than matter. Hernando de Soto points out that property laws make capital "mind friendly," since they allow physical assets such as land to take on a parallel existence in the realm of representation. For instance, if a farmer owns 100 acres in the Mississippi Delta, his relationship to that chunk of land opens other avenues for creating wealth. He can translate his ownership of that land into a line of credit with a banker or a loan for farm equipment and then start farming.

Most of the vast new wealth created in our economy comes not from land, but from intellectual capital, such as information encoded on computer servers. Knowledge is being applied to knowledge itself. Knowledge "is now fast becoming the one factor in production," said the great management guru Peter Drucker, "sidelining both capital and labor."[5]

This hints at a startling trend. Over time, we can create more and more wealth with less and less stuff. It took six thousand years to go from the first farms to the invention of the wheel. Everything from cars, toilets, telephones, electric lights, planes, rockets, computers, the internet, and antibiotics was invented in the last four generations.[6]

Often, we're able to use less costly stuff to do more. We now use virtually free material, silica—like beach sand—to make computer chips and fiber-optic cables. A fiber-optic cable made from sixty pounds of cheap sand can carry a thousand times more information than one made from two thousand pounds of expensive copper.[7] God gave us sand—and the ability to transform it into chips and cables. New wealth comes from how we represent, inform, and transform matter—from our minds working together.

A Wealth-Creating, Not a Wealth-Hoarding, Culture

Such wealth creation isn't universal, though. Like learning to walk or speak a language, people differ both in what they can do and to what degree their environment amplifies or diminishes their innate creative gifts. If Apple cofounder Steve Jobs had been born and raised in, say, Haiti or Burma, he would not have created the wealth that he did growing up in the United States.

Jobs and Apple cofounder Steve Wozniak gave the world Apple I and Apple II, which, early on, were commercial flops. But Jobs lived in a society where he could learn from his failures and make them a foundation for future success. As a result, his company went on to create iTunes, and the iPod, iPad, and iPhone.

There are still large swaths of the planet where this just doesn't happen. And years of stifling regulations have made it harder to do in the U.S. as well. Wealth creation is one sign of human flourishing, especially when a culture once in extreme poverty creates enough wealth to move beyond destitution. We should celebrate it when cultures reach a point where they can feed, clothe, and shelter themselves and begin teaching their children to use their God-given abilities more fully. Still, there are two extremes we must avoid: the prosperity gospel and the poverty gospel.

Scripture is chock-full of warnings about greed and the love of wealth:

"Do not lay up for yourselves treasures on earth," Jesus says to his disciples, "where moth and rust consume and where thieves break in and steal, but lay up for yourselves treasures in heaven. . . . Where your treasure is, there your heart will be also." Elsewhere, He insisted, "You cannot serve God and mammon" (Matthew 6:19–24). And when the rich young ruler asks Jesus what else he can do to inherit eternal life, Jesus tells him to sell everything he has, give it to the poor, and follow Him. When the man turns away, Jesus tells His disciples, "It is easier for a camel to go through the eye of a needle than for a rich man to enter the kingdom of God" (Luke 18:25).

The Apostle Paul describes greed as a form of idolatry (Ephesians 5:5) and wrote that "the love of money is the root of all evil" (1 Timothy 6:10). James even tells certain greedy people in one church that the rust from their ill-gotten bullion will eat their flesh (James 5:3–6)!

Contrary to extreme versions of the prosperity gospel, the Bible never says that all believers will be materially rich if they just have faith. This idea that faith must produce material riches is false. Nevertheless, the Bible often treats material wealth as a blessing from God. This is a recurring theme in much of the Old Testament. If wealth can be a blessing, then it can't be bad in itself.

In the New Testament, Jesus didn't avoid the wealthy. He often stayed in their homes and associated with people like Mary and Martha, who were apparently far from poor. And Luke, who writes about the rich young ruler, also informs us that wealthy women provided for Jesus and the disciples (Luke 8:3).

The opposite extreme from the prosperity gospel is to treat involuntary poverty as a blessing. The poor are blessed, as Jesus says in Luke, not because poverty is good, but because they know they depend on God. In Matthew, Jesus says, "Blessed are the poor in spirit." To be poor in spirit is to be so free of false attachments that God can fill you with His Spirit. That's why missionaries and monks can be so blessed spiritually when they freely embrace material poverty. But that doesn't mean we should welcome mass poverty. Fasting is a path to spiritual growth, but we don't pray for famines.

Jesus commanded the rich young ruler to sell everything he had, but He didn't issue that command to everyone in the way He commanded us all to love our neighbors. Jesus knew that this man's wealth was a profound hindrance to his salvation.

When James warned the rich that their money would eat their flesh, he was speaking to wealthy people who were defrauding the poor of their promised wages. Talk about idolizing money!

If a person is hoarding his wealth, then that wealth is a stumbling block. The classic hoarder, of course, is the miser, like Ebenezer Scrooge. The Bible has nothing good to say about misers.

Free economies, however, discourage miserliness and encourage its near opposite: enterprise.

The miser prefers the security of his possessions to the risk of investment. Entrepreneurs embrace uncertainty in the hope of greater gains in the future. For the miser, money is the end; for the entrepreneur, money is the means to another end.

Great entrepreneurs succeed not by amassing fortunes, but by anticipating the needs of others and then risking whatever fortune they've acquired to meet those needs. Unlike the greedy miser who clutches his money, entrepreneurs use money to create or deliver something they imagine will fulfill some need or desire: a new institution that allows many investors to take on a small amount of risk in a huge business venture; a leaf that tastes delightful and delivers caffeine when dried and boiled in water; melted and dried sand that allows walls to become transparent windows; and so on. Long before these things exist, they appear as vague flashes of inspiration and imagination in the mind of an entrepreneur.

From Waste to Wealth

The documentary *The Call of the Entrepreneur* tells the story of dairy farmer Brad Morgan.[8] For five years, Morgan rented a farm near Evart, Michigan. He was eventually able to get a loan to buy it. In the early years, his efforts paid off, and he led the region in milk production per cow. In 1999, however, milk prices plummeted, and he was in danger of losing his farm. Morgan could have given up and tried to sell it.

Instead, he defied the odds and developed a way to make a profit by composting cow manure into organic fertilizer. All the experts thought this would never work, but Morgan was sure he could find a way to make a profit. Before long, he had developed a way to speed up the composting process from two years to sixty days.

With paid help from a soil expert, Morgan kept tweaking the formula until he had developed very high-quality compost. Then he set about marketing his "Dairy Doo" to gardeners, farmers, and golf courses. Today, his organic fertilizer sells out before it even hits the market. Morgan is literally turning waste into wealth.

No one, not even Brad Morgan, knew how popular his fertilizer would become, but he anticipated it. That's the nature of enterprise: risk, initiative, and invention precede supply. And supply of a new good or service precedes—even creates—demand. At the base of the free enterprise system is not greed or consumption, which is everywhere, but intuition, imagination, and creation.

Free enterprise requires a host of virtues. Before entrepreneurs can invest capital, for instance, they must first accumulate it. So unlike gluttons, entrepreneurs must save rather than consume. Unlike misers, they risk rather than hoard. Unlike the self-centered, they anticipate the needs of others. Unlike the impulsive, they make prudent choices. Unlike the robot, they freely discover new ways of creating and combining resources. Unlike cynics, they trust their neighbors, their partners, their culture, their employees, and "the compensatory logic of the cosmos."[9] Not everyone is cut out to be an entrepreneur, but everyone can gain when entrepreneurs can freely pursue their calling.

No one can predict what an entrepreneur will create ahead of time—not even the entrepreneur! We see their work after the fact. Supply and demand kick in after there's a supply. And in a modern economy, supply depends on enterprise, and enterprise depends on the freedom to save, gather, and risk capital in pursuit of entrepreneurial visions. This is how new wealth is created.

Land, labor, and capital are still important, but in the modern age, entrepreneurs are largely responsible for orchestrating those resources, with the human laborer joining the entrepreneur's orchestra as part of a win-win exchange. When this happens, even somewhat unskilled labor can generate more wealth than in other settings. A maid, for instance, can make far more money in the vicinity of a Michael Dell than in a rural setting or a developing country. The result of enterprise is a wealth-creating zone that extends far beyond the entrepreneur.

Therefore, we should purge our unhealthy biases against wealth creators. We can't expect unbelievers to retire the rhetoric of envy when even Christian leaders encourage it. We need an economic system that allows the poor to work their way out of poverty and allows entrepreneurs the freedom to create wealth for themselves and others.

Only free and virtuous economies can do both.

CHAPTER 18

Have Dominion

In a famous 1967 paper published in *Science*, Lynn White blamed the "ecological crisis" on—of all things—the Bible.

> By destroying pagan animism Christianity made it possible to exploit nature. . . . We shall continue to have a worsening ecologic crisis until we reject the Christian axiom that nature has no reason for existence save to serve man.[1]

This claim is pure hogwash. It's not a Christian axiom that creation exists only for our sake. When God confronts Job and his accusers, for instance, He spends three chapters explaining that He has all sorts of purposes in the world involving creatures and objects great and small, of which Job and his accusers know nothing!

Or take Genesis 1. At the end of each of God's days of creation, God looks at what He has made and pronounces it good. He does this five times before man ever arrives on the scene. Since all the earth is God's creation, it has inherent value apart from what we do with it.

No conservative, and no serious Christian or Jew, should resist a call to care for the environment. Unfortunately, the environmental movement goes far beyond that and often treats human beings as the problem. Decades after White's paper was published, many environmentalists still claim we must replace the biblical view of man with a more nature-centered faith by ceding control to the UN and activists who attach "environmental, social, and governance" (ESG) scores to every business. What's more, many so-called green policies merely cede power to bureaucrats in Washington or the UN while doing little or nothing to protect the planet.

Climate Change

The term "climate change" is shorthand for the claim that man is causing abnormal changes in the climate, mainly by adding carbon dioxide to the atmosphere, and that we need a political fix—fast!—to prevent droughts, mega hurricanes, big mosquitoes, and rising seas that will drown polar bears while submerging our coasts and low-lying islands. This means we need to somehow stop releasing carbon dioxide into the atmosphere. Since we won't do that on our own, the government or the UN must find a way to make us do it.

There are several different claims here masquerading as one. Let's tease them apart.

1. Is the earth warming?

Behind this question, another is hiding: Since when? If we start measuring in 1998, for instance, and end in 2023, the best evidence suggests we've had little or no net warming. But if we measure from 1940 to 1979, and take the average, we'd say the planet's average global surface temperature was cooling. As a result, the big scare in the mid-1970s was the looming threat of runaway global cooling. The press at the time treated this as a scientific near certainty.[2]

If we measure from AD 1000 to the present, we see a bit of cooling. Or, if we pick a baseline of 1850 and look at the best data we have, we'll conclude that it's warmed slightly since then—about two degrees Fahrenheit.

In short, the global temperature has gone up and down a bit at different times over the last thousand years, and the current average temperature, best we can tell, is in that range.

2. If the earth is warming, are we causing it?

The average global temperature seems to have risen about two degrees Fahrenheit in the past 160 years. Humans have been adding carbon dioxide to the atmosphere during that time. In 1960, there were about 320 parts of carbon dioxide per million (ppm) in the atmosphere. Now there are about 420 ppm. That's about 50 percent higher than it was just before the Industrial Revolution.[3] Is this causing the warming?

Note that warming effect and its cause are two different things. This is a point of logic, not science. Retreating glaciers in Alaska, polar bears mournfully looking at the ocean from the edge of a chunk of sea ice, and ever-shorter winters could be evidence of warming—if they were happening. But these events could not tell us *why* the earth has warmed.

Still, we know that carbon dioxide is a greenhouse gas, as are methane and water vapor. That means it's good at absorbing infrared radiation. But how much heat can it hold? Almost all climate scientists agree that carbon dioxide alone won't contribute much to global warming. We would have to double the amount in the atmosphere just to get one degree (centigrade) of warming. We've only added about 30 percent in the last sixty years, well short of the 100 percent increase needed to raise the temperature one degree. We'd then have to double that amount just to get another degree of warming. In other words, it gets harder and harder to raise the temperature another degree.

So why do many scientists think climate catastrophe is right around the corner? They assume that feedback processes are enhancing the warming of the extra carbon dioxide. Those assumptions get plugged into the computer models that are supposed to represent the climate system. Those models "predict" more warming soon, which will "change" the climate in harmful ways.

But extreme warming is not what we observe from ground measures, weather balloons, or satellites. This has led some researchers to suspect that the models—or the assumptions plugged into them—are wrong. How? Some of the feedback may counteract the modest warming effect of the extra carbon dioxide rather than magnify it.[4] Several scientific papers suggest that certain clouds are doing some of the counteracting.[5]

We have little reason to assume the climate system is fragile. After all, the earth has warmed and cooled throughout history. The concentration of carbon dioxide in the atmosphere has varied widely—often being much higher than it is now. If tiny changes in this trace gas in the atmosphere led to huge changes in temperature, we would see that in the earth's records (such as the ice cores from Antarctica and Greenland).

Those records show major changes in temperature, but these don't follow slight increases in atmospheric carbon dioxide. On the contrary, when the global temperature has varied in the past, changes in carbon dioxide in the atmosphere have changed several hundred years *afterward*.[6] Here's why: The warmer the oceans, the less carbon dioxide they can hold. So, when the earth warmed in the past, the oceans would release carbon dioxide into the atmosphere. Yet this process did not lead to a runaway disaster with warmer temperatures releasing more carbon dioxide from the oceans, which then warmed the planet further, which then released more carbon dioxide from the oceans, and so on. Rather, it suggests that the changes in carbon dioxide we see today won't lead to major changes in climate.

Despite the media hype, the current changes in global climate aren't unprecedented.[7] For all we know, our slight warming trend is normal, and there may even be other causes for it. Some scientists argue that changes in the sun's energy output or magnetic activity are the main actors in Earth's changing climate.[8] Others point out that Mars has also gotten warmer in recent years.[9] Earth and Mars don't have Exxon, BP, and Chevron in common; they have the sun.

It's plausible that human beings affect the climate. But to say we're the main driver of climate change, you must assume that the climate is supersensitive to changes in the concentration of carbon dioxide in the atmosphere. There are lots of reasons to doubt that.[10]

3. If we are causing the earth to warm, is that bad?

Even if we're warming the earth, it doesn't follow that this is bad. First, *none* of the predicted extreme weather events are happening in the real world—as Steven Koonin shows in his 2021 book *Unsettled*, in which he surveys the scientific literature.[11] Koonin is no oil company shill. He's an accomplished physicist who served as Undersecretary for Science in the U.S. Department of Energy under President Obama. No doubt you've heard that hurricanes, tornadoes, droughts, and heat waves are getting worse and more frequent, and that the Greenland ice sheet is shrinking. None of this is true. There's a yawning chasm between the evidence in the scientific literature and the propaganda churned out on the evening news.

Besides, even if warming led to droughts or floods in some places, it might lead to milder, wetter, and more productive weather in many others. People prefer warm to cold weather. Much of the landmass in the far north of the globe could become fertile, pleasant territory in a warmer world. Also, we use less energy when it's warm than when it's cold, so some warming is likely a net positive.[12] Koonin notes that even the UN's climate alarm arm, the Intergovernmental Panel on Climate Change, doesn't predict warming will have a net economic cost until the end of this century.

As a logical point, to know whether warming is good or bad, we'd need to know what the optimum global temperature is. Then we could see whether we're moving toward or away from it. But we don't have that information.

What we do know is that carbon dioxide is plant food—*not* a toxic pollutant. Plants, to various degrees, thrive in rising levels of carbon dioxide growing faster and fuller. These plants, in turn, slowly sequester carbon dioxide that would otherwise be in the atmosphere.[13] This and other evidence lead us to suspect that moderate warming, even if we're causing it, is a net benefit.

4. If we're causing the earth to warm and that's bad, would the proposed "solutions" make any difference?

Most informed experts agree that any feasible policy to reduce greenhouse gas emissions would do little if anything. For years, the UN pushed the Kyoto Protocol, calling for nations to reduce their carbon dioxide emissions to 5.2 percent below 1990 levels. According to the official estimates, it would have reduced the rate of warming an undetectable 0.05 degrees centigrade after about fifty years. And yet complying with it would have cost the worldwide economy a huge amount of money—in the many trillions of dollars.[14]

Now the UN is pushing the Paris Climate Accords, which also calls on nations to reduce greenhouse gas emissions. Danish expert Bjørn Lomborg calculates that if every country that signed the agreement really did what they promised—didn't shift emissions to another country, and kept their emissions down for the rest of the century—this would at best reduce warming by 0.17 degrees Fahrenheit by 2100.[15] The price for this trivial effect? One to two trillion dollars every year!

In the real world, most countries aren't complying because they don't have good substitutes for hydrocarbons—that is, coal, oil, and natural gas. The one viable alternative for the electrical grid is nuclear power, but the environmental lobby has managed to scare most countries out of developing it. That means that, unless you live in France—with a grid that's almost 70 percent nuclear—even electric cars get most of their power from fossil fuels.[16]

That leaves so-called "sustainable" energy sources such as wind and solar. These have their uses but can't come close to meeting the current or future energy needs worldwide. First, wind and solar sources go dead when the wind stops or the sun sets. Second, the basic physics are unforgiving. They're not nearly as energy dense as coal, oil, and gas. That's why fossil fuels still provide about 80 percent of the world's energy. For many uses, there are no better, affordable substitutes.[17]

Given these constraints, it's absurd to expect anyone to stop using fossil fuels without abundant and affordable alternatives. Even if we assumed the worst about human-induced climate change, the extreme costs and meager benefits would lead us to oppose efforts to restrict CO_2 emissions by force. Such attempts to spike the cost of energy would hit the poor the hardest.[18]

If the U.S. and other countries committed to such a pact, the only big winner would be Communist China. Wind and solar technology require "rare earth" metals, much of which is mined there. So, until someone invents a new source of energy, any push to substitute "renewable" energy for fossil fuel will help China, which is rolling out about two new coal plants per week. That's six times more than the rest of the world combined.[19] China also is lending money to poor countries to do the same—something that the World Bank and International Monetary Fund refuse to do.[20]

Help the Poor Adapt

Almost any way you measure it, our environment is cleaner than it has been even in the recent past.[21] Nothing is risk- or cost-free. But over time, we have learned to use more efficient and earth- and life-friendly forms of energy—uranium or oil extracted from deep in the ground rather than wood from forests or dung from the pasture.

In the developed world, air and water quality, soil erosion, and toxic releases have improved, not declined, in the last several decades.[22] In general, the wealthier a country is, the better its environment.[23] Economists call this the Environmental Kuznets Curve. Here's the basic idea: In the early stages of industrial growth, a country can be hard on the environment (think China and India). But after a country reaches a certain per capita income, the environment starts improving.[24] Societies start to worry about the air and planet *per se* once they secure basic survival and comfort. Americans with two or three cars per household, HVACs, nontoxic air and water, safe streets, and too much to eat are more likely to fret about separating paper and plastics and protecting salmon runs than are poor villagers in the bush without plumbing or clean water.

The wealthier you are, the easier it is to adapt to change. You can buy different clothes, move, add insulation to your attic, go on vacation, install an air conditioner or heater, work inside, or whatever. The poor are far less flexible. Any change in the economy or the climate is going to hit the poor hardest because they have fewer means to *adapt*. So even if the climate gets harsher, it's much wiser for us to help nations become wealthier rather than to stage misguided campaigns to restrict energy use. Those restrictions will do little or nothing for the environment and trap billions of people in poverty, thereby making them much less likely to fret about the planet.

What Should We Do?

There's now a relentless campaign from the global left—including the UN, EU, and WEF—to push for a "Net Zero" carbon future with a very short timeline. Crazy talk about converting all cars, airlines, and military equipment to zero-carbon tech by 2030 or 2050 is just that—crazy. It can't and won't happen. If this were just left-wing virtue-signaling, we could ignore it. But globalists and their leftist acolytes seem determined to try it. This will not put a dent in greenhouse gas emissions. Over the last several years, the U.S. has moved to cleaner, less CO_2–intensive natural gas—thanks to fracking, not UN accords. But gas is still a fossil fuel.

The Net Zero campaign is so clearly absurd that we suspect most leaders behind it really want control and merely use the planet as a pretense. Sometimes, they even say the quiet part out loud. Ottmar Edenhofer, the cochair of the UN's IPCC Working Group III, once explained that the goal of climate policy "is redistributing the world's wealth and natural resources."[25]

When it comes to environmental policy, be as wise as a serpent. Study carefully before you adopt fashionable ecotrends. Find the best arguments for and against a policy.[26] Reject false dilemmas and fake appeals to "the science."

At the same time, tackle real environmental problems with gusto, especially at the local level, where we see the effects and can correct course more easily. In Texas, fresh water is a big deal. In Washington state, it's salmon. These are real problems that need hard thinking and tangible solutions.

Look for market solutions to environmental problems first.[27] Strong private property laws are often the best ways to encourage people to act in environmentally friendly ways. We tend to act less responsibly when we enjoy a benefit but don't suffer the cost, or when our bad behavior doesn't directly affect us. That's why we tend to treat our backyards better than the grass at city parks.

Sometimes, though, our work can produce what economists call a negative externality. That refers to a cost not fully accounted for in an exchange. If you buy some lumber from a sawmill, for instance, that's a win for the mill and a win for you. But what if the mill dumps toxic sludge in a nearby stream that flows onto a neighboring ranch? That's a cost someone else must pay. The simplest solution might be a law or regulation that would require the mill to bear the cost of cleanup—along with a penalty to discourage other sawmills tempted to pollute. Sawmills would then raise the cost of their lumber to compensate for the added expense. In this way, a market transaction would internalize an externality. That's simple justice.

In short, look at long-term historical trends and think clearly about real problems before acting. We can preserve the environment for our children and give poor countries a chance to develop as we have, but we must resist crazy calls from the left to ditch the best forms of energy we have right now.

Even if using fossil fuel won't destroy the climate, will we run out of it if we don't find alternatives soon? We'll take that up in the next chapter.

CHAPTER 19

Till It and Keep It

In 2011, British soccer star David Beckham and his wife, former Spice Girl Victoria Beckham, had their fourth child—a baby girl. While many fans celebrated the event, some media pundits denounced them as "environmentally irresponsible" parents.[1]

Experts propose sundry solutions to the supposed problem of children as "carbon footprints." Some recommend changing the tax code to punish overbreeders. Others hope for a quicker fix. "Until such time as Homo sapiens should decide to rejoin nature," wrote David Graber, a biologist working for National Park Service, "some of us can only hope for the right virus to come along."[2] Graber didn't post this on a fringe bulletin board; he published it in 1989 in the *Los Angeles Times*.

Graber was offering a new and darker take on an old idea first spawned by the Rev. Thomas Malthus, a nineteenth-century Anglican priest and amateur scientist. Malthus noticed that the human population was growing exponentially while the food supply was not. He concluded that worldwide famine would soon bring the population back to a manageable size. (Charles Darwin got some of his ideas from Malthus.) Doomsday never came, so Malthus later changed his tune; but his original song is still sung.

In the 1960s and '70s, the nonprofit Club of Rome warned that we were using up our natural resources. In 1968, Paul Ehrlich wrote in *The Population Bomb*, "The battle to feed all of humanity is over. In the 1970s the world will undergo famines—hundreds of millions of people are going to starve to death."[3] It didn't happen, of course, and this gave Ehrlich time to release new editions of his book. He kept moving the date of doomsday while raking in more royalties.

Here's the argument: Earth's surface is finite, as is the number of trees, the amount of water, oil, copper, fertile land, and so on. The earth now holds almost eight billion people—to say nothing of all the beetles and spiders. There must be some limit, some point beyond which we exceed the planet's "carrying capacity." When scientists calculate that point, columnists announce that "the earth is full," as Thomas Friedman did on June 8, 2011.[4]

The doomsday predictors are always wrong. Why? Because they make two basic mistakes, both of which were already present in Malthus's argument. First, he extrapolated a short-term trend of exponential population growth far into the future. Second, he assumed that organisms always reproduce until they meet the limit of available food, and then start dying off in mass numbers.

Bacteria will do this in a Petri dish. But, as it happens, not even rabbits "breed like rabbits"! And humans are neither bacteria nor rabbits.

If you graph the growth in human population over time, it doesn't just keep curving upward to infinity. It forms a flattened S curve. It starts with a mostly horizontal line, since, for thousands of years, human population was low by modern standards. Then, over a few centuries, industry and invention allowed us to produce far more wealth and food. That spurred rapid population growth, just when

Malthus happened to notice it. This is where the line curves sharply upward on the graph.

As societies develop more, however, their fertility rates drop. The line starts to flatten out again. Then the curve starts to slope downward. At that point, we have the opposite problem from the one Malthus feared: Most "advanced" countries are not replacing their current populations. Even the UN expects world population to level off at about nine billion in the year 2050, and to start declining after that.[5]

What Is Man?

But what about the other premise? Have we surpassed the known capacity of the planet? No. This is as baseless as the belief that we will keep breeding to infinity and beyond. It treats human beings as mainly consumers rather than producers.

When God blessed Adam and Eve, and told them to "be fruitful and multiply," He put them in a garden and commanded them to "till it and keep it." From the start, our dominion involved us transforming the world around us for fruitful purposes. Remember, this happened before the Fall into sin. The Fall didn't create work; it turned work into often-frustrating toil. In exercising our stewardship, we can mess up, pollute, and destroy. Still, God always intended us to work, to create, to tend the garden, to transform the earth.

We're not saying that we can blithely squander resources or that technology will always save us. But to think clearly about resources, we must first clean out the cobwebs that so often cloud our thinking.

What Is a Resource?

The cobwebs are thick when it comes to thinking about natural resources. When you see the word "resource," what picture appears in your mind? Most people think of stuff we can weigh or count: oil in the reservoir, land with barbed-wire fence around it, water in a lake or aquifer, gold coins buried in a mattress. Some resources, such as water, wood, and fish, are renewable if we don't overdo it. Other resources, like oil and coal, aren't. That's why we all tend to believe reports that say we're past the peak of oil reserves and they're now dwindling, even though those old arguments have proved wrong every time.

What's the problem? These warnings are only based on proven or known oil reserves. Discovering an oil reserve costs money. ExxonMobil or Arco must spend millions digging dry holes before they find one. "How much of any given natural resource is known to exist," notes Thomas Sowell, "depends on how much it costs to know."[6] It also depends on how much it's worth to know it.

As the current supply of oil dwindles or as demand spikes, the price per barrel goes up. This coaxes oil companies to look for new reserves in more costly places on the bet that they can make a profit at the new, higher price. But they won't spend the money to find more reserves if they don't think they can recoup those expenses later at the gas pump.

So, known reserves reflect *how much it's worth* to know about right now, not how much total oil there is to discover. If a barrel of oil were worth, say, a thousand dollars, but still in high demand, explorers would spend far more than they do now to find new deposits. The fact that oil is under a hundred dollars a barrel means we're not about to run out of it.

Other forms of oil deposits, such as oil shale and oil sands, differ from the crude oil coming out of wells. If crude oil is abundant and cheap, it doesn't make sense to search for ways to extract these deposits. If the price of oil gets above a certain point, however, lots of mining and petroleum engineers will turn their attention in that direction. In fact, that's already happening.

The amount of matter underground in Canada or Saudi Arabia, then, matters less than the newly discovered ways to access and use it. Because we develop new ways of exploring, mining, and refining, future resources are often cheaper to acquire than current resources, even under pressures of greater demand.[7]

If we only think of these resources as a fixed amount of physical matter, we will always fear that we're running out of them. But resources aren't just there in a lake or in a tank or in the ground: In a sense, we *create* resources.

We did not switch from whale blubber to oil because we killed off the last whale or because salty harpooners suddenly developed a soft spot for underwater mammals. We stopped because whale oil was pricey, and clever inventors and entrepreneurs looked for other forms of energy to produce heat and light.

They landed on petroleum, which had been considered a waste product for centuries. In the mid-nineteenth century, though, someone figured out how to refine oil into kerosene. Someone else figured out that kerosene could heat cold houses and light dark rooms. Sperm whales throughout the seven seas bellowed a sigh of relief.

Black gold really took off with the invention of cars and the internal combustion engine. Since then, we have devised all sorts of ways to explore, refine, and use it more efficiently. For most of history, oil wasn't a resource; it *became* one through man's vision and ingenuity.

The same is true with most resources, even something as simple as water. Most of the water we drink is mediated by human minds and hands. If it's fresh water from a deep aquifer, someone had to dig and maintain a well. Other water is recycled and purified. Most of it is transported by pipes and plumbing. It's easy to imagine that the water is just there, but little of it would be where we need it if someone had not brought it from somewhere else.

Of course, we don't create from nothing, as God does. We use what He has given us. Nevertheless, over time, the matter in many material resources matters less than how people transform them for some use. We transform wood into fuel, lumber, and houses; stones into walls and arrowheads; clay into pots, bricks, and ovens; fur into coats; fields into farms; manure into fertilizer; oil into gasoline, kerosene, and plastic; cotton into clothing; copper into phone lines and electric generators; sand into computer chips and fiber-optic cables; light into lasers; and plastic into DVDs bearing software read by lasers—until the songs themselves are just software (mp3 files) stored in the cloud.

Waste Not, Want Not

The lesson of history is clear: The fact that there's a fixed supply of dung, wood, coal, oil, or uranium doesn't mean we're doomed to run out of energy. This contradicts the mental image most of us have of a bright electrified pot of "energy." The rich kids, critics imagine, are getting more than their fair share. The obvious moral is that we need to use less so that others can have more. "Our world is characterized by an alarming discrepancy," says the National Religious Partnership for the Environment, "between those who consume too much and those who do not have enough."[8]

This is like the story we tell children who won't eat their peas: "Listen, buster, you need to eat what you're served, because there are children starving in Africa." But these facts aren't related. Gluttony and waste in our part of the world are serious moral problems. We can't keep consuming more than we save and invest. But our consumption is not causing want and hunger elsewhere. That's just not how it works.

The Ultimate Resource

For centuries people have feared they were running out of whatever resource they happened to be using. First it was wood; then it was coal. We've still got plenty of both. What happened in both cases was that scarcity led to rising prices, which spurred hard work and ingenuity. Necessity is indeed the mother of invention; but man is the father. Together they make a very fruitful pair. "The Stone Age came to an end not for a lack of stones," someone once said, "and the oil age will end, but not for a lack of oil."[9]

Technology disrupts old ways of doing things and often destroys jobs in the short run. Over the long haul, however, it gives rise to new and better jobs, since it allows our labor to be more productive and more valuable. We know this from history. So why do we often fall for claims that contradict it? Why do the UN, the WEF, the EU, and one of our two major political parties treat natural resources as mere matter? Because they forget what economist Julian Simon called "the ultimate resource"—the creative vision and imagination of human beings. The more people in healthy societies there are, the more laborers, inventors, producers, builders, farmers, problem solvers, and creators who can transform material resources and create new ones. Simon and Pope John Paul II both saw this. They taught that man, not matter, is the ultimate resource.

Of course, we don't spring from our mother's womb at our full potential. We must be taught, corrected, nurtured, and planted in the right cultural setting to become even a fraction of what we can be. We're now at great risk of losing a culture that allows us to develop our God-given creativity as stewards. If we can preserve it, however, we need not fear that we will exhaust the earth's resources.

Welcome to the Fight

O ur country—indeed, our civilization—is in peril from a foe that
threatens to dissolve us from within, thus making us a soft target
for enemies without. We might like to return to a lost Golden Age
without death, toil, or trouble. But we can't. Time only goes in one
direction. We can, however, build an alliance of faith and reason that
draws from the best of our past to fight a common enemy and forge
a better future. In these pages, we've tried to sketch the outlines of a
common platform for such an alliance.

The greatest challenge to this alliance is internal division—and
our adversaries know it. As it happens, a shining example of this
threat broke out just as we were putting the final touches on this book.
In the lead-up to the 2023 liturgical season called "Pride Month,"
two friends we admire—Yoram Hazony and James Lindsay—were
slugging it out on Twitter.

Hazony is an Orthodox Jew and a leader of National Conservatism.
He thinks a return to the God of the Bible is our only hope. Lindsay

is a mathematician, public intellectual, and insightful critic of woke ideology. Though he's a nonreligious "classical liberal," he often makes common cause with conservative believers.

Lindsay had been warning that the woke left was trying to provoke Christians with drag queen story hours and gender-bending swimwear for small kids. Why? So that some Christian hotheads would say or do something stupid. The media would then use these outbursts as "proof" that the real threat is right-wing "Christian Nationalists" (which, for the media, is code for "white supremacists"). The fear of this threat, in turn, would push moderates and liberals to ally with the woke left they were starting to disown.

Lindsay seemed especially worried that, in fighting gender ideology, Christians would attack same-sex marriage and people who identify as gay or lesbian—just when the "LGB" part of the Pride Coalition was breaking with the "T+" part. In other words, Christians would step right into the trap. After all, groups such as "Gays Against Groomers" oppose "drag queen story hour" and teaching kids they might be born in the wrong body. And far more people support same-sex marriage than things like sterilizing drugs and surgeries for kids. It can only help the gender fanatics for the public to think that it's "anti-gay" to oppose "gender-affirming" double mastectomies for fifteen-year-old girls. The trap would do double duty for the woke left, since it would both divide its opposition and expand its own base.

That part of Lindsay's argument seemed exactly right—the left set the trap, and Christians were in danger of walking right into it. But Hazony objected to another part of Lindsay's argument. Lindsay seemed not only to issue a warning, but also to suggest that the recent redefinition of marriage was right and just, and that Christians were wrong to oppose it. As a result, Hazony thought Lindsay was telling Christians to abandon the truth.

This is just the sort of episode that any stable alliance of faith and reason will have to weather. These days, few, if any, secular liberals— including classical liberals—see the problem with redefining marriage in law and culture. They can't imagine why anyone except bigots would disagree with them on this point. So, arguing with them about marriage is not a great way to win their support in a fight over gender ideology.

It should be clear that we think their view of marriage is mistaken. The sexual revolution started by downplaying the real differences between men and women, reducing sex to the physical urge, and defining freedom as the fulfillment of that urge, limited only by consent. It coaxed our culture to accept a series of lies: that sex need not be limited to marriage, for instance, and that it need not produce children. And when "unwanted" pregnancy resulted, intellectuals and judges found that to defend their solution—abortion—they had to deny a biological fact about when human life begins.

If sex and children have nothing to do with marriage, someone was bound to ask, "What is marriage exactly? How should the law define it? Why must it involve a man and a woman? And why just a pair?" The campaign to redefine marriage was baked into the logic of this revolution from the start.

In truth, marriage unites a husband and wife comprehensively, both enshrining and protecting what society needs to function: the bearing and raising of children. That's why every culture has marriage and sets it apart it in law and custom from other arrangements. This has nothing to do with bigotry. Until recently, everyone *knew* this, even without recourse to Scripture.

Gender ideology didn't just drop from the sky. It was the next stage of the sexual revolution after marriage was legally upended. In 2015, the U.S. Supreme Court claimed, in effect, that reproduction—the complementarity of male and female—has nothing to do with marriage. The "trans" campaign—which denies the sexual binary itself—kicked into high gear about five seconds later. The same groups that led the campaign to redefine marriage, from the ACLU to the Human Rights Campaign, pivoted from the LBG to the T without taking a breath. We can't pretend otherwise just because in 2023 most people don't want to hear it.

If we want a stable future, it won't be enough to close gender clinics for kids. Our culture will need to rethink the long legal and historical path that brought us to this gender madness. (That's why we've laid out these arguments in this book: People of faith need to be able to explain them to potential allies who don't share our faith.)

At the same time, justice requires that we treat different things differently. Gender ideology departs from what came before. It's infused with critical theory and postmodernism, which has carved a chasm between the LGB and the T+. LGBs believe males and females exist, for instance. They know a male doesn't magically become a female by identifying as one. Many of them abhor the campaign to expose young kids to porn. They fight the injustice of males competing in female sports, and male rapists enjoying the comforts of female prisons.

Moreover, as a strategic matter, far more people are willing to fight gender ideology than to relitigate issues like same-sex marriage or no-fault divorce. We should focus on the fights we can win, while reserving the right to have a longer conversation later. Arguing with allies about the birth control pill right now is a great way not to beat gender ideology. Ditto for many of the other issues treated in this book—from trade to climate change—on which any broad and diverse alliance may disagree.

This is the wisdom in Lindsay's warning to Christians. Indeed, it echoes two much earlier pieces of advice from Jesus. First, focus on the needs of the moment—"Sufficient unto the day is the evil thereof"

(Matthew 6:34 KJV). Second, "be wise as serpents and innocent as doves" (Matthew 10:16 RSV).

In short, exercise strategic wisdom, recognize what time it is, and anticipate the traps set by our foes. Whenever they provoke us, we should ask ourselves: "What do our opponents want us to do right now?" And then we should *not do that*.

To be innocent as doves is to model justice and compassion, both with allies and opponents. If we act meaner than a rabid junkyard dog, that's our problem. There are millions of potential allies who disagree with us on important matters. They may see only part of the truth, but they're willing to fight for the truth they can see. We need not abandon what we know just because they disagree with us. To beat back the darkness, though, we need them—and they need us. As Heritage Foundation founder Edwin Feulner advised, we should not make our 80 percent friends our 20 percent enemies.

But what of our enemies? Christians are under strict orders to love them—even when we fight them.[1] Indeed, we should fight *because* we love them. We can't do this in our own strength. To succeed, we can't just defend the truth, but must live within it. As Archbishop Charles Chaput explains:

> Living within the truth means living every day and every moment from the unshakeable conviction that God lives, and that his love is the motive force of human history and the engine of every authentic human life. . . . Living within the truth also means telling the truth and calling things by their right names. And that means exposing the lies by which some men try to force others to live. . . . Let us support each other—whatever the cost—so that when we make our accounting to the Lord, we will be numbered among the faithful and courageous, and not the cowardly or the evasive,

or those who compromised until there was nothing left of their convictions; or those who were silent when they should have spoken the right word at the right time.[2]

The history of our country is but a short, small chapter in God's grand, unfolding cosmic drama. Yet, it is the chapter in which we must live and choose and act. We may know how the story ends, but not how our chapter ends—perhaps because it is given to us to help write it. If we want our country's chapter to continue, we must build an alliance with all those who see the evil that is upon us and will fight to defeat it. Not just any fight—the good fight.

The gloves are already off. Welcome to the fight.

Acknowledgments

This book pulls together ideas and arguments that we've wrestled with for decades, so any complete list of acknowledgements would fill volumes. But we are grateful to many who helped us directly with the manuscript—providing us with editorial advice, vetting, and sometimes correcting our treatment of specific topics.

These include the following friends and colleagues: John Zmirak, Ryan T. Anderson, Guillermo Gonzalez, Delano Squires, Macy Petty, Sam Silvestro, Ellie Richards, Carol Stertzer, Victoria Beckham, Alexandra DeSanctis, Melanie Israel, Jason Bedrick, Jonathan Butcher, David Ditch, Richard Stern, Lora Ries, Trey Boyd, Russell Greene, and Scott Lincicome. This book is much tighter and less mistake-prone than it would have been otherwise. Any mistakes that remain are, alas, our own.

Going Deeper: What to Read

Anderson, Ryan T. *Truth Overruled: The Future of Marriage and Religious Freedom*. Washington, D.C.: Regnery Publishing, 2015.
———. *When Harry Became Sally: Responding to the Transgender Moment*. New York: Encounter Books, 2018.
Anderson, Ryan T. and Alexandra DeSanctis. *Tearing Us Apart: How Abortion Harms Everything and Solves Nothing*. Washington, D.C.: Regnery Publishing, 2022.
Arkes, Hadley. *Mere Natural Law: Originalism and the Anchoring Truths of the Constitution*. Washington, D.C.: Regnery Gateway, 2023.
Girgis, Sherif, Robert P. George, and Ryan T. Anderson. *What Is Marriage? Man and Woman: A Defense*. New York: Encounter Books, 2020.
Gregg, Samuel. *The Next American Economy: Nation, State, and Markets in an Uncertain World*. New York: Encounter Books, 2022.

Hall, Mark David. *Did America Have a Religious Founding? Separating Modern Myth from Historical Truth.* Nashville, Tennessee: Thomas Nelson, 2019.

Kirk, Russell. *Concise Guide to Conservatism.* Washington, D.C.: Regnery Gateway, 2019.

Pillsbury, Michael. *The Hundred-Year Marathon: China's Secret Strategy to Replace America as the Global Superpower.* New York: Henry Holt & Co., 2015.

Pluckrose, Helen and James Lindsay. *Cynical Theories: How Activist Scholarship Made Everything about Race, Gender, and Identity—and Why This Harms Everybody.* Durham, North Carolina: Pitchstone Publishing, 2020.

Richards, Jay W. *Money, Greed, and God: The Christian Case for Free Enterprise.* San Francisco: HarperOne, 2019.

———. *The Human Advantage: The Future of American Work in an Age of Smart Machines.* New York: Forum Books, 2018.

Trueman, Carl R. *Strange New World: How Thinkers and Activists Redefined Identity and Sparked the Sexual Revolution.* Wheaton, Illinois: Crossway, 2022.

Tupy, Marian L. and Gale L. Pooley. *Superabundance: The Story of Population Growth, Innovation, and Human Flourishing on an Infinitely Bountiful Planet.* Washington, D.C.: Cato Institute, 2022.

West, Thomas G. *The Political Theory of the American Founding: Natural Rights, Public Policy, and the Moral Conditions of Freedom.* Cambridge, UK: Cambridge University Press, 2017.

Notes

Introduction

1. Joe Bukuras, "Acquitted Pro-Life Activist Mark Houck Reveals Details of 'Reckless' FBI Raid; Will Press Charges," Catholic News Agency, February 1, 2023, https://www.catholicnewsagency.com/news/253523/acquitted-pro-life-activist-mark-houck-reveals-details-of-fbi-raid-will-press-charges.

2. Divorce rates have leveled off in recent years. But this is because far more people are now living together and having children without getting married. So fewer children are being raised by married parents, even though divorce rates per se aren't going up. See detailed statistics at "2016 Index of Culture and Opportunity: The Social and Economic Trends That Shape America," Heritage Foundation, July 11, 2016, http://www.familyfacts.org.

3. Isabel Keane, "Vermont School Removes 'Male,' 'Female' Terms from Reproductive System Lessons," *New York Post*, April 26, 2023, https://nypost.com/2023/04/26/vermont-school-removes-male-female-terms-from-reproductive-system-lessons.

4. David Ditch, "These 7 Charts Show Why Congress Must Get Spending under Control Immediately," The Daily Signal, July 5, 2022, https://www.dailysignal.com/2022/07/05/7-charts-show-why-congress-must-get-spending-under-control-immediately-if-not-sooner.

5. Max D, "How Federal Reserve Printed More Money in 2020 & 2021 than in the History of the World," aMarketology, July 11, 2022, https://www.amarketology.com/how-the-us-government-caused -inflation-by-printing-record-amounts-of-money-in-2020-and-2021.

6. Jonathan V. Last, *What to Expect When No One's Expecting: America's Coming Demographic Disaster* (San Francisco: Encounter Books, 2013).

7. Genevieve Gluck, "Transgender State Representative Moves to Allow 'Sexual Attachment to Children' to Be Classified as Protected 'Sexual Orientation,'" Reduxx, April 26, 2023, https://reduxx.info/transgender -state-representative-moves-to-allow-sexual-attachment-to-children-to -be-classified-as-protected-sexual-orientation.

8. Tom Cotton, "The BLM Effect," Tom Cotton Senator for Arkansas, July 29, 2021, https://www.cotton.senate.gov/news/op-eds/the-blm -effect.

9. Edward Feser, "How to Define 'Wokeness,'" *Edward Feser* (blog), March 18, 2023, http://edwardfeser.blogspot.com/2023/03/how-to -define-wokeness.html.

10. The best book on the topic is Helen Pluckrose and James Lindsay, *Cynical Theories: How Activist Scholarship Made Everything about Race, Gender, and Identity and Why This Harms Everybody* (Durham, North Carolina: Pitchstone Publishing, 2020). For a shorter treatment, see Wilfred Reilly, "How to Define 'Woke,'" *National Review*, March 19, 2023, https://www.nationalreview.com/2023/03/ how-to-define-woke.

11. When Pope Paul VI issued his encyclical *Humanae Vitae*, high-profile critics in media, culture, politics, and even in the Catholic hierarchy denounced him for failing to join the right side of history. But his predictions of where the "contraceptive mentality" would lead now look like confirmed prophecies. Chloe Langr, "50 Years Later: How 'Humanae Vitae' Predicted the Future," Catholic Singles, July 18, 2019, https://www.catholicsingles.com/blog/humanae-vitae-predictions.

12. Kevin Bass PhD MS, (@kevinnbass), "I am a liberal atheist (voted for Biden). . .," Twitter, April 26, 2023, 5:01 p.m., https://twitter.com/ kevinnbass/status/1651330791874478080.

13. Dave Rubin, "Why Ron DeSantis' Disney Fight Matters," Fox News, July 5, 2023, https://www.foxnews.com/opinion/why-ron-desantis -disney-fight-matters.

14. Bronze Age Pervert, *Bronze Age Mindset* (independently published, 2018).

Chapter 1: Come, Let Us Reason Together

1. Donavyn Coffey, "Why Does Christianity Have So Many Denominations?" Live Science, July 29, 2022, https://www.livescience .com/christianity-denominations.html.
2. These quotes are from James Davison Hunter, *To Change the World: The Irony, Tragedy, and Possibility of Christianity in the Late Modern World* (New York: Oxford University Press, 2010), 10–11.
3. Ibid., 16–17, 45.
4. James Q. Wilson, *American Politics: Then and Now* (Washington, D.C.: AEI Press, 2010), quoted in Robert Samuelson, "We've Promised More Than We Can Deliver," *Newsweek*, April 11, 2011.
5. Jim Geraghty, "Everything Is the Culture War Now," *National Review*, April 27, 2023, https://www.nationalreview.com/the-morning -jolt/everything-is-the-culture-war-now.
6. Jay Nordlinger, "Reagan, Zombies, and More," *National Review*, February 7, 2022, https://www.nationalreview.com/2022/02/reagan -zombies-and-more.
7. Quoted in C. Bradley Thompson, "John Adams and the Coming of the French Revolution," *Journal of the Early Republic* 16, no. 3 (Autumn 1996): 361, https://doi.org/10.2307/3124056.

Chapter 2: The Law Is Written on the Heart, Stone, and Parchment

1. Phil Lawler, "How the 'Church Tax' Corrupts German Catholicism," Catholic Culture, November 20, 2015, https://www.catholicculture.org /commentary/how-church-tax-corrupts-german-catholicism.
2. Hadley Arkes, *Mere Natural Law: Originalism and the Anchoring Truths of the Constitution* (Washington, D.C.: Regnery Gateway, 2023).
3. Promiscuity is wrong not because it leads to venereal disease; rather, venereal disease is a natural consequence that can remind us that promiscuity is wrong.
4. Some believe that natural law is just a Catholic idea. That's not true. Rev. Martin Luther King Jr. appealed to it in his "Letter from Birmingham Jail." When he did so, he was tapping into a common Christian inheritance. See, for instance, Stephen J. Grabill, *Rediscovering the Natural Law in Reformed Theological Ethics* (Grand Rapids, Michigan: Eerdmans, 2006), and Greg Forster, *The Contested Public Square* (Downers Grove, Illinois: InterVarsity Press, 2008). While many twentieth-century Protestant theologians, such as Karl Barth, Stanley Hauerwas, and Reinhold Niebuhr, rejected natural law, the early mainstream Reformers, such as John Calvin, did not.

5. J. Budziszewski, *What We Can't Not Know: A Guide* (San Francisco: Ignatius Press, 2011), 227–34.
6. Ibid., 28–50.
7. For a discussion of John Locke's theory of when revolution can be justified, see Greg Forster, *The Contested Public Square* (Downers Grove, Illinois: InterVarsity Press, 2008), 182–201.
8. C. S. Lewis gives examples of common moral themes in different cultures in his book *The Abolition of Man* (San Francisco: Harper One, 2001), first published in 1943. He refers to natural law as the "Tao" in the book, to avoid giving the impression that natural law was exclusively Christian.
9. From *Federalist Papers* No. 51, Bill of Rights Institute, https://billofrightsinstitute.org/primary-sources/federalist-no-51.
10. *Planned Parenthood of Southeastern Pennsylvania v. Casey*, 505 U.S. 833, at 851, June 29, 1992, Oyez, https://www.oyez.org/cases/1991/91-744.
11. *Dobbs v. Jackson Women's Health Association*, 597 U.S. ___, June 21, 2022, Oyez, https://www.oyez.org/cases/2021/19-1392.
12. "Transcript of Dr. Martin Luther King's Speech at SMU on March 17, 1966," Southern Methodist University, January 10, 2014, https://www.smu.edu/News/2014/mlk-at-smu-transcript-17march1966.
13. Greg Forster, "A Political Idea That Won't Go Away: Implications of Moral Law for America's Foundation and Future," Heritage Foundation, March 17, 2009, https://www.heritage.org/political-process/report/political-idea-wont-go-away-implications-moral-law-americas-founding-and.
14. Matthew Spalding, *We Still Hold These Truths* (Wilmington, Delaware: ISI Press, 2009), 137.
15. Samuel Adams Heritage Society, http://www.samuel-adams-heritage.com/quotes/popular.html.
16. Philosopher Peter Kreeft even calls this "Colson's Law." See his discussion in *How to Win the Culture War* (Downers Grove, Illinois: InterVarsity Press, 2002), 46–54.
17. Edmund Burke to a Member of the National Assembly, January 19, 1791, Eighteenth Century Collections Online Text Creations Partnership, 68, https://quod.lib.umich.edu/e/ecco/004804929.0001.000/1:3?rgn=div1;view=fulltext.
18. "On the Right to Rebel against Governors." For this and similar quotations, see Matthew Spalding, *We Still Hold These Truths*, 136–39.

Chapter 3: God in Public

1. Alexandria Ocasio-Cortez (@AOC), "Something tells me Jesus would . . . ," Twitter, February 12, 2023, 10:01 p.m., https://twitter.com/aoc/status /1624967013817884674.

2. John Zmirak, "AOC Warns Us: Ads Like 'He Gets Us' Won't Stop Her from Coming to Get Us," The Stream, February 19, 2023, https:// stream.org/aoc-warns-us-ads-like-he-gets-us-wont-stop-her-from -coming-to-get-us.

3. See, for instance, Andrew L. Seidel, *The Founding Myth: Why Christian Nationalism is Un-American* (New York: Union Square & Co., 2021).

4. Liel Leibovitz, "The Return of Paganism," *Commentary*, May 2023, https://www.commentary.org/articles/liel-leibovitz/paganism-afflicts -america.

5. Jefferson borrowed the idea from Baptist Roger Williams, who had founded Providence, Rhode Island, after being kicked out of Puritan Massachusetts. See discussion in Richard Land, *The Divided States of America* (Nashville, Tennessee: Thomas Nelson, 2011), 116–22. There's a difference between an institutional separation of church and state and the prohibition of religious practice in public. Jefferson supported the former, not the latter. See Daniel L. Dreisbach, *Thomas Jefferson and the Wall of Separation between Church and State* (New York: New York University Press, 2002).

6. All three of Satan's temptations to Jesus describe the presumed powers of a Roman emperor. A key point of the temptation narratives is to show that Jesus rejected a purely political fulfillment of His Messiahship, which was what most Jews at the time were expecting.

7. During Jesus's ministry, Tiberius, the son of Augustus, was emperor. So, Jesus was referring to a denarius with an abbreviated inscription that said: "Tiberius Caesar, Worshipful Son of the God, Augustus." We may miss the theological undertones that His original audience would have grasped.

8. In fact, early on, the Romans called Christians "atheists." See Greg Forster, *The Contested Public Square* (Downers Grove, Illinois: InterVarsity Press, 2008), 20.

9. Almost everything we read is critical of Constantine, so it's nice to see a book by a Presbyterian scholar that corrects the stereotype. See Peter Leithart, *Defending Constantine: The Twilight of an Empire and the Dawn of Christendom* (Downers Grove, Illinois: InterVarsity Press, 2010). Two good books on this subject are H. A. Drake, *Constantine and the Bishops: The Politics of Intolerance* (Baltimore, Maryland: Johns Hopkins University Press, 2002), and Elizabeth DePalma Digeser, *The Making of a Christian Empire: Lactantius and Rome* (Ithaca, New York: Cornell University Press, 1999).

10. "The Virginia Declaration of Rights, First Draft (1776)," Encyclopedia Virginia, https://encyclopediavirginia.org/entries/the-virginia -declaration-of-rights-first-draft-1776.

11. They will cite the many statements by Founders showing their Christian piety or commending the value of Christianity for society. There are, of course, many such quotes. See the examples at the WallBuilders website at: http://www.wallbuilders.com/ LIBissuesArticles.asp?id=78.

12. A great book on this topic is Mark David Hall, *Did America Have a Christian Founding? Separating Modern Myth from Historical Truth* (Nashville, Tennessee: Thomas Nelson, 2019).

13. Almost all were Protestants, though Charles Carroll, who signed the Declaration of Independence, was a Catholic. There were also two Catholics at the Constitutional Convention (1787), both of whom signed the Constitution. See the unbiased list of Founders and their religious affiliations here: http://www.adherents.com/gov/Founding _Fathers_Religion.html.

14. James D. Richardson, *Compilation of Messages and Papers of the Presidents, 1789–1897*, vol. 1 (Washington, D.C.: US Government Printing Office, 1907), 213.

15. Though what they said publicly doesn't always square with their private beliefs.

16. It's fair to call Jefferson a deist, though we think Gregg Frazer's term "theistic rationalist" is more accurate. Gregg L. Frazer, *The Religious Beliefs of America's Founders: Reason, Revelation, and Revolution* (Lawrence, Kansas: The University of Kansas Press, 2012).

17. John Adams, *The Works of John Adams, Second President of the United States*, vol. 9, ed. Charles Francis Adams (Boston: Little, Brown, and Co., 1854), 229. See many other quotes along these lines at: http://www.wallbuilders.com/LIBissuesArticles.asp?id=63.

18. This is from Obama's speech at a Call to Renewal event on June 28, 2006. "Obama's 2006 Speech on Faith and Politics," *New York Times*, June 28, 2006, http://www.nytimes.com/2006/06/28/us/politics /2006obamaspeech.html.

19. Gillian Richards, "Defining Nationalism," *Law & Liberty*, March 29, 2023, https://lawliberty.org/defining-nationalism.

20. Stephen Wolfe, *The Case for Christian Nationalism* (Moscow, Idaho: Canon Press, 2022).

Chapter 4: Bearing the Sword

1. J. Mohan Malik, "Dragon on Terrorism: Assessing China's Tactical Gains and Strategic Losses after 11 September," *Contemporary*

Southeast Asia 24, no. 2 (August 2002): 252–93, http://www.jstor.org/stable/25798597.

2. Jon Brown, "Thousands of Unvaccinated Service Members Could Still Be Booted over Rescinded COVID-19 Policy," Fox News, March 9, 2023, https://www.foxnews.com/politics/congressmen-blast-dod-policy-could-boot-thousands-unvaccinated-service-members-divisive-cruel.

3. John M. Donnelly, "Fight Brews over Pentagon's Push to Counter Extremists," *Roll Call*, July 22, 2022, https://rollcall.com/2022/07/22/fight-brews-over-pentagons-push-to-counter-extremists.

4. Steve Beynon, "Army to Provide Gender Transition Care, Surgeries for Transgender Soldiers," Military.com, June 28, 2021, https://www.military.com/daily-news/2021/06/28/army-provide-gender-transition-care-surgeries-transgender-soldiers.html.

5. Steve Beynon, "Army Expects to Miss Its Recruiting Goal Again This Year," Military.com, May 2, 2023, https://www.military.com/daily-news/2023/05/02/we-are-going-fall-short-army-will-miss-its-recruiting-goal-year.html.

6. The details are complicated. The Hebrew word, *ratsach*, is used elsewhere for a legally permissible form of killing, such as capital punishment for convicted murderers (Numbers 35:30). So, the word doesn't mean "murder" exclusively.

7. Biblical scholars dispute the meaning of these Old Testament commands. While they look straightforward to modern readers—if somebody intentionally blinds you in one eye, you should blind them in one eye—ancient readers may not have interpreted the commands in this way. See, for example, Raymond Westbrook, *A History of Ancient Near Eastern Law* (Boston: Brill Academic Publishers, 2003).

8. Francis J. Beckwith, *Politics for Christians: Statecraft as Soulcraft* (Downers Grove, Illinois: InterVarsity Press, 2010), 56.

9. Quoted in Thomas Sowell, "The Good Are Afraid of the Bad," LewRockwell.com, August 17, 2011, https://www.lewrockwell.com/2011/08/thomas-sowell/the-good-are-afraid-of-the-bad.

10. This is from an informal Facebook discussion between Ben Witherington and Lawson Stone, which Witherington posted on his blog at Beliefnet: "Recently Heard on Facebook: A Conversation between Lawson Stone and Ben Witherington on the Bible, Christians, and Violence," *The Bible and Culture* (blog), December 2, 2010, https://www.beliefnet.com/columnists/bibleandculture/2010/12/recently-heard-on-facebook——a-conversation-between-lawson-stone-and-ben-witherington-on-the-bible.html.

11. For instance, he called for a drawdown of American forces in Afghanistan in September 2012 against the unanimous opposition of military leaders. It seems clear that his decision had nothing to do with

military strategy or wisdom and everything to do with the upcoming 2012 presidential election.

12. In John Howard Yoder, *The Politics of Jesus* (Grand Rapids, Michigan: Eerdmans, 1972), 157, 12, 100. Quoted in James Davison Hunter, *To Change the World* (New York: Oxford University Press, 2010), 162.

13. In Stanley Hauerwas and William H. Willimon, *Resident Aliens: Life in the Christian Colony* (Nashville, Tennessee: Abingdon Press, 1989), 30. Quoted in Hunter, *To Change the World*, 162.

14. Perhaps the most prominent secular just war proponent now is Michael Walzer.

15. Brian Orend, "War," *Stanford Encyclopedia of Philosophy*, May 3, 2016, http://plato.stanford.edu/entries/war.

16. For more discussion, see Jonathan R. Witt and Jay W. Richards, *The Hobbit Party: The Vision of Freedom That Tolkien Got, and the West Forgot* (San Francisco: Ignatius Books, 2014), chapter 6.

17. See the discussion in Niall Ferguson, *Empire: The Rise and Demise of the British World Order and the Lessons for Global Power* (New York: Basic Books, 2001), 303–17.

Chapter 5: Big Government, Bad Government

1. "Government Spending in Historical Context," National Taxpayers Union Foundation, https://www.ntu.org/foundation/tax-page/government-spending-in-historical-context.

2. Sidney M. Milkis, "Progressivism," *Britannica*, April 16, 2023, https://www.britannica.com/topic/progressivism.

3. Steven Hayward, *Mere Environmentalism: A Biblical Perspective on Humans and the Environment* (Washington, D.C.: AEI Press, 2010), 60.

4. "Pennsylvania Assembly: Reply to the Governor, 11 November 1755," National Archives: Founders Online, https://founders.archives.gov/documents/Franklin/01-06-02-0107, originally printed in *Votes and Proceedings of the House of Representatives*, 1755–1756 (Philadelphia, 1756), 19–21.

5. Stéphane Courtois et al., *The Black Book of Communism: Crime, Terror, Repression* (Cambridge: Harvard University Press, 1999).

6. David Bernhardt, "The Deep State Is All Too Real," *Wall Street Journal*, May 9, 2023, https://www.wsj.com/articles/the-deep-state-is-all-too-real-congress-chevron-delegation-civics-hunter-biden-985ed65e.

7. Ibid.

8. Ibid.

9. In the "Foreword: A Promise to America," *Mandate for Leadership: The Conservative Promise*, ed. Paul Dans and Steven Groves

(Washington D.C.: The Heritage Foundation, 2023), https://thf_media
.s3.amazonaws.com/project2025/2025_MandateForLeadership_FULL.
pdf.

10. John H. Durham, "Report on Matters Related to Intelligence Activities
and Investigations Arising out of the 2016 Presidential Campaigns,"
Office of Special Counsel, U.S. Department of Justice, May 12, 2023,
https://www.justice.gov/storage/durhamreport.pdf.

11. James Sherk, "The President Needs the Power to Fire Bureaucrats,"
Wall Street Journal, August 8, 2022, https://www.wsj.com/articles/the-
power-to-fire-insubordinate-bureaucrats-schedule-f-executive-order-
trump-deborah-birx-at-will-civil-service-removal-appeals
-11659989383.

12. David Ditch, "These Seven Charts Show Why Congress Must Get
Spending under Control Immediately," The Daily Signal, July 5, 2022,
https://www.dailysignal.com/2022/07/05/7-charts-show-why-congress
-must-get-spending-under-control-immediately-if-not-sooner.

13. James C. Capretta, "Federal Unfunded Liabilities Are Growing More
Rapidly than Public Debt," Real Clear Policy, November 7, 2022,
https://www.realclearpolicy.com/articles/2022/11/17/federal_unfunded
_liabilities_are_growing_more_rapidly_than_public_debt_865384
.html.

14. "The Ratio of Workers to Social Security Beneficiaries Is at a Low and
Projected to Decline Further," Peter G. Peterson Foundation, August 4,
2022, https://www.pgpf.org/blog/2022/08/the-ratio-of-workers-to
-social-security-beneficiaries-is-at-a-low-and-projected-to-decline
-further.

15. A classic book on the collapse of money in Germany and Austria after
World War I was written in 1975 and rereleased in 2010. Adam
Fergusson, *When Money Dies: The Nightmare of Deficit Spending,
Devaluation, and Hyperinflation in Weimar Germany* (New York:
Public Affairs, 2010).

16. "Little Public Support for Reductions in Federal Spending," Pew
Research Center, April 11, 2019, https://www.pewresearch.org/politics
/2019/04/11/little-public-support-for-reductions-in-federal-spending.

17. Linley Sanders, "How Americans Evaluate Social Security, Medicare,
and Six Other Entitlement Programs," YouGov, February 8, 2023,
https://today.yougov.com/topics/politics/articles-reports/2023/02/08/
americans-evaluate-social-security-medicare-poll.

18. Though these words are widely attributed to Alexander Fraser Tytler,
it's unclear who first wrote them. See Loren Collins, "The Truth about
Tytler," January 25, 2009, at http://www.lorencollins.net/tytler.html.

Chapter 6: Choose Life

1. According to the National Right to Committee, there had been 63,459,781 by the end of 2021. See "The State of Abortion in the United States," January 2022, https://www.nrlc.org/uploads/communications/stateofabortion2022.pdf.

2. Jeff Diamant and Besheer Mohamed, "What the Data Says about Abortion in the U.S.," Pew Research Center, January 11, 2023, https://www.pewresearch.org/short-reads/2023/01/11/what-the-data-says-about-abortion-in-the-u-s-2.

3. Katie Booth, "What I Learned about Disability and Infanticide from Peter Singer," Big Think, January 11, 2018, https://bigthink.com/health/what-i-learned-about-disability-and-infanticide-from-peter-singer.

4. Ezekiel Emanuel et al., "Attitudes and Practices of Euthanasia and Physician-Assisted Suicide in the United States, Canada, and Europe," *Journal of the American Medical Association* 316, no. 1 (2016): 79–90, https://pubmed.ncbi.nlm.nih.gov/27380345.

5. "Didache," Early Christian Writings, https://www.earlychristianwritings.com/text/didache-roberts.html.

6. John Calvin, *Commentaries on the Last Four Books of Moses*, vol. 3, trans. Charles William Bingham (Grand Rapids, Michigan: Eerdmans, 1950), 41–42.

7. A pessary is a device that can be inserted into the uterus to induce an abortion.

8. Randy Sly, "From New President of Episcopal Divinity School: 'Abortion Is a Blessing,'" Catholic Online, April 2, 2009, http://www.catholic.org/national/national_story.php?id=32962.

9. Michelle Ye Hee Lee, "Is the United States One of Seven Countries That 'Allow Elective Abortions after 20 Weeks of Pregnancy?'" *Washington Post*, October 9, 2017, https://www.washingtonpost.com/news/fact-checker/wp/2017/10/09/is-the-united-states-one-of-seven-countries-that-allow-elective-abortions-after-20-weeks-of-pregnancy/.

10. See the latest numbers from Gallup at "Abortion," https://news.gallup.com/poll/1576/abortion.aspx. Even NPR is forced to concede the fact that Americans generally want some restrictions on abortion. Domenico Montanaro, "Poll: Americans Want Abortion Restrictions, but Not as Far as Red States Are Going," NPR, April 26, 2023, https://www.npr.org/2023/04/26/1171863775/poll-americans-want-abortion-restrictions-but-not-as-far-as-red-states-are-going.

11. Oliver Burkeman, "Sunday Miscellany: Obama Fails to Give Concise One-Sentence Answer to Question That Has Baffled Mankind for Millennia," *The Guardian*, August 17, 2008, https://www.theguardian.com/world/oliverburkemanblog/2008/aug/17/sundaymiscellanyobamafails.

12. Conception and fertilization are synonyms, but under pressure from pro-abortion activists, "conception" in some contexts has been redefined to refer to implantation of the zygote in the uterine wall. So, fertilization is now the more precise term. See, for instance, the sample quotes from medical and embryology textbooks at the webpage, "Life Begins at Fertilization," Princteon, http://www.princeton.edu/~prolife/articles/embryoquotes2.html.

13. Ayn Rand, "Introducing Objectivism," Ayn Rand Institute, https://courses.aynrand.org/works/introducing-objectivism/. Rand denied the facts of biology, comparing unborn human beings to skin cells, tonsils, and a ruptured appendix in "The Age of Mediocrity," *The Objectivist Forum*, June 1981.

14. Quoted in "Abortion Not a Gray Area for Catholic Politicians," *Bemidji Pioneer*, December 1, 2009, https://www.bemidjipioneer.com/opinion/abortion-not-a-gray-area-for-catholic-politicians.

15. For an excellent recent defense of the need for prolife laws, see Ryan T. Anderson and Alexandra DeSanctis, *Tearing Us Apart: How Abortion Harms Everything and Solves Nothing* (Washington, D.C.: Regnery Publishing, 2022).

Chapter 7: A Man Shall Cling to His Wife

1. Elizabeth Fox-Genovese, *Marriage: The Dream That Refuses to Die* (Wilmington, Delaware: ISI Books, 2008), 113ff.

2. Gregory S. Baylor, "What You Should Know about the Respect for Marriage Act," Alliance Defending Freedom, updated December 14, 2022, https://adflegal.org/article/what-you-should-know-about-respect-marriage-act.

3. In no-fault divorce, neither party must prove wrongdoing by the other. A husband or a wife can simply declare a desire and grounds for divorce and get out of a marriage, even if the other spouse disagrees.

4. Benjamin Wiker, *Ten Books That Screwed Up the World: And 5 Others That Didn't Help* (Washington, D.C.: Regnery Publishing, 2008).

5. Maggie Gallagher, *The Abolition of Marriage: How We Destroy Lasting Love* (Washington, D.C.: Regnery Publishing, 1996), 150.

6. "Divorce Statistics: Over 115 Studies Facts and Rates for 2022," Wilkinson & Finkbeiner, https://www.wf-lawyers.com/divorce-statistics-and-facts.

7. Belinda Luscombe, "The Divorce Rate Is Dropping: That May Not Actually Be Good News," *TIME*, November 26, 2018, https://time.com/5434949/divorce-rate-children-marriage-benefits.

8. Sabrina Tavernise and Robert Gebeloff, "Once Rare in Rural America, Divorce Is Changing the Face of Its Families," *New York Times*, March 23, 2011, https://www.nytimes.com/2011/03/24/us/24divorce.html.

9. Wendy D. Manning and Lisa Carlson, "Trends in Cohabitation Prior to Marriage," Bowling Green State University, November 4, 2021, https://www.bgsu.edu/ncfmr/resources/data/family-profiles/manning -carlson-trends-cohabitation-marriage-fp-21-04.html.
10. Mike McManus and Harriet McManus, *Living Together: Myths, Risks, and Answers* (New York: Howard Books, 2008). Also, Scott Stanley, "Is Cohabitation Still Linked to Greater Odds of Divorce?," Institute for Family Studies, January 12, 2021, https://ifstudies.org /blog/is-cohabitation-still-linked-to-greater-odds-of-divorce.
11. "The emergence of widespread contraception, especially the emergence of the pill, helped separate sexuality and marriage from childbearing." Glenn Stanton and Bill Maier, *Marriage on Trial* (Downers Grove, Illinois: InterVarsity Press, 2004), 121–22.
12. Ibid., 96, 98.
13. Ibid., 100.
14. Ibid., 100–2.
15. George Gilder, *Men and Marriage* (Gretna, Louisiana: Pelican Books, 1986).
16. See Carle C. Zimmerman, *Family and Civilization*, 2nd abridged edition, ed. James Kurth (Wilmington, Delaware: ISI Books, 2008).
17. Sherif Girgis, Robert P. George, and Ryan Anderson, *What Is Marriage? Man and Woman: A Defense* (New York: Encounter Books, 2020).
18. In women, this includes both the sexual organs and the lactation system in breasts. The lactation system itself is complete, but it requires another human being, a baby, to fulfill its proper end. This strengthens the argument above.
19. Sherif Girgis, Robert P. George, and Ryan Anderson, "What Is Marriage?," *Harvard Journal of Law & Public Policy* 34, no. 1 (December 2010): 255. The best book explaining the nature of marriage is the expanded book version of this essay, by the same authors, op. cit. note 119.
20. "After all, if a certain emotional state . . . were necessary [for marriage], then it would be impossible to commit sincerely to marriage. For this would require promising to keep up feelings, over which you have no direct control, and you can't sincerely promise to secure what you can't control." Sherif Girgis, "Real Marriage," *National Review*, April 5, 2011.
21. Stanton and Maier, *Marriage on Trial*, 43.
22. *What Is a Woman?*, directed by Justin Folk, featuring Matt Walsh (The Daily Wire, 2022), https://www.dailywire.com/videos/what-is -a-woman.
23. Stanton and Maier, *Marriage on Trial*, 42.

24. Mike McManus argues that we could cut the divorce rate in half just by replacing no-fault divorce laws with "mutual consent" laws for marriages with young children. *How to Cut America's Divorce Rate in Half* (Potomac, Maryland: Marriage Savers, 2008).

25. Glenn Stanton, "The Christian Divorce Rate Myth (What You've Heard Is Wrong)," *Baptist Press*, February 15, 2011, https://www.baptistpress.com/resource-library/news/first-person-the-christian-divorce-rate-myth-what-youve-heard-is-wrong.

26. Mercedes Arzú Wilson, "Divorce Rate Comparisons between Couples Using Natural Family Planning & Artificial Birth Control," *Physicians for Life* (March 2001), http://www.physiciansforlife.org/content/view/193/36. The statistical connection between natural family planning and low divorce rates does not, by itself, reveal cause and effect. Perhaps couples who practice NFP tend to be much more religiously committed. Perhaps the complexities of the method bring couples closer together. Or perhaps it's a special blessing from God. Who knows?

Chapter 8: Male and Female He Created Them

1. Caroline Downey, "Male Inmate Sexually Assaulted Female after Transfer to Washington Women's Prison, Former Guard Says," *National Review*, November 22, 2021, https://www.nationalreview.com/news/male-inmate-sexually-assaulted-female-in-washington-womens-prison-former-guard-says.

2. Jared Eckert and Emma Sophia Mull, "Planned Parenthood Profits Big from Getting Kids Hooked on Transgender Hormones through the School-to-Clinic Pipeline," *The Federalist*, May 10, 2022, https://thefederalist.com/2022/05/10/planned-parenthood-profits-big-from-getting-kids-hooked-on-transgender-hormones-through-the-school-to-clinic-pipeline.

3. "Gender Affirming Care and Young People," Office of Population Affairs, U.S. Department of Health and Human Services, https://opa.hhs.gov/sites/default/files/2023-08/gender-affirming-care-young-people.pdf.

4. Chloe Cole (@ChoooCole), "My testimony against SB107 in front of Wiener and the Senate Judiciary Committee," Twitter, September 1, 2022, 11:02 a.m., https://twitter.com/ChoooCole/status/1565356240598810633.

5. According to one recent market analysis, gender surgery is a major growth industry. "U.S. Sex Reassignment Surgery Market Size, Share & Trends Analysis Report by Gender Transition (Male to Female, Female to Male) . . . and Segment Forecasts, 2022 – 2030," Grand View Market Research, https://www.grandviewresearch.com/industry-analysis/us-sex-reassignment-surgery-market.

6. Abigail Shrier, *Irreversible Damage: The Transgender Craze Seducing Our Daughters* (Washington, D.C.: Regnery Publishing, 2020).

7. Kristen Monaco, "Gender-Affirming Chest Surgeries Increase by Nearly 5x in Teens," MedPage Today, October 17, 2022, https://www .medpagetoday.com/pediatrics/generalpediatrics/101252.

8. Lisa L. Littman, "Rapid Onset of Gender Dysphoria in Adolescents and Young Adults: A Descriptive Study," *Journal of Adolescent Health* 60, no. 2, supp. 1 (February 2017): 95–96, https://doi.org/10.1016 /j.jadohealth.2016.10.369.

9. "Gender-Affirming Care and Young People."

10. For an excellent description of the ideas that gave rise to gender theory, see Helen Pluckrose and James Lindsay, *Cynical Theories: How Activist Scholarship Made Everything about Race, Gender, and Identity—and Why This Harms Everybody* (Durham, North Carolina: Pitchstone Publishing, 2020).

11. "Gender Identity and Gender Expression," Ontario Human Rights Commission, https://www.ohrc.on.ca/en/code_grounds/gender _identity.

12. Theresa Thorn and Noah Grigni, *It Feels Good to Be Yourself: A Book about Gender Identity* (New York: Henry Holt and Co., 2019).

13. Nathanael Blake, "Surgeon Castrating 'Gender-Diverse' Eunuchs Manifests the Evil of Transgenderism," *The Federalist*, April 18, 2023, https://thefederalist.com/2023/04/18/surgeon-castrating-gender-diverse -eunuchs-manifests-the-evil-of-transgenderism.

14. Colin Wright, "Are There More than Two Sexes?" *City Journal*, March 2, 2023, https://www.city-journal.org/are-there-more-two -sexes.

15. Activists often cite a higher percentage of 1.7 percent of the population. This is based on a claim by Anne Fausto-Sterling in her book *Sexing the Body: Gender Politics and the Construction of Sexuality* (New York: Basic Books, 2002). She vastly inflated the number by including whole groups of people without a disorder of sexual development into her category of "intersex." Leonard Sax debunked her claim in "How Common Is Intersex? A Response to Anne Fausto-Sterling," *Journal of Sex Research* 39, no. 3 (2002): 174–78, https://www.tandfonline.com/ doi/abs/10.1080/00224490209552139.

16. See the text and references in David H. Thompson, Brian W. Barnes, John D. Ramer, Cooper & Kirk, PLLC, "Why State Legislatures Must Protect Children and Adolescents from Harmful 'Gender Transition' Treatments," Do No Harm (2023), https://donoharmmedicine.org.

17. "Interim Service Specification for Specialist Gender Dysphoria Services for Children and Young People—Public Consultation," NHS England, October 20, 2022, https://www.engage.england.nhs.uk/specialised -commissioning/gender-dysphoria-services.

18. Journalist Jennifer Bilek has done the most to expose these donors. See Jennifer Bilek, "The Billionaire Family Pushing Synthetic Sex Identities (SSI)," Tablet, June 22, 2022, https://www.tabletmag.com/sections/news/articles/billionaire-family-pushing-synthetic-sex-identities-ssi-pritzkers; Jennifer Bilek, "Who Are the Rich, White Men Institutionalizing Transgender Ideology?" The Federalist, February 20, 2018, https://thefederalist.com/2018/02/20/rich-white-men-institutionalizing-transgender-ideology; Jennifer Bilek, "The Billionaires behind the LGBT Movement," *First Things*, January 21, 2020, https://www.firstthings.com/web-exclusives/2020/01/the-billionaires-behind-the-lgbt-movement.

19. Aaron Sibarium, "How a Left-Wing Activist Group Teamed Up with Big Pharma to Push Radical Gender Ideology on American Hospitals," *Washington Free Beacon*, May 15, 2023, https://freebeacon.com/latest-news/how-left-wing-activist-group-teamed-up-with-big-pharma-to-push-radical-gender-ideology-on-american-hospitals.

20. Carl Trueman, *Strange New World: How Thinkers and Activists Redefined Identity and Sparked the Sexual Revolution* (Wheaton, Illinois: Crossway, 2022).

21. Jay Richards, "Why States Must Define Sex Precisely," *Public Discourse*, March 30, 2023, https://www.thepublicdiscourse.com/2023/03/88194.

Chapter 9: Multiply and Fill the Earth

1. Glenn Stanton and Bill Maier, *Marriage on Trial* (Downers Grove, Illinois: InterVarsity Press, 2004), 103.

2. Jane Anderson, "The Impact of Family Structure on the Health of Children; Effects of Divorce," *Linacre Quarterly* 81, no. 4 (November 2014): 378–87, https://www.ncbi.nlm.nih.gov/pmc/articles/PMC4240051.

3. Stanton and Maier, *Marriage on Trial*, 104–5.

4. David Ellwood, *Poor Support: Poverty in the American Family* (New York: Basic Books, 1988), 46, quoted in Stanton and Maier, *Marriage on Trial*, 106.

5. W. Bradford Wilcox, "Marriage Is an Important Tool in the Fight against Poverty," Institute for Family Studies, March 21, 2016, https://ifstudies.org/blog/marriage-is-an-important-tool-in-the-fight-against-poverty. Related statistics: Some 71 percent of poor families in the United States are headed by unmarried parents.

6. Stanton and Maier, *Marriage on Trial*, 108–9.

7. Jeff Johnston, "Kids Need a Mom and a Dad—That's What the Research Shows," Daily Citizen, February 26, 2018, https://dailycitizen

.focusonthefamily.com/kids-need-a-mom-and-a-dad-thats-what-the -research-shows.

8. From an interview with Kathryn Lopez, "30 Rock Knows Best," *National Review*, June 18, 2011, http://www.nationalreview.com/ articles/269942/i30-rocki-knows-best-interview.

9. Stanton and Maier, *Marriage on Trial*, 113–16.

10. Sara McLanahan and Gary Sandefur, *Growing Up with a Single Parent: What Hurts, What Helps* (Cambridge: Harvard University Press, 1994), 38.

11. "The Case for Marriage," *National Review*, September 20, 2010, https://www.nationalreview.com/2010/09/case-marriage-editors.

12. David Popenoe, *Disturbing the Nest: Family Change and Decline in Modern Societies* (Piscataway, New Jersey: Aldine Transactions, 1988); Alan Wolfe, *Whose Keeper? Social Science and Moral Obligation* (Berkeley, California: University of California Press, 1991).

13. Mike Huckabee, *A Simple Government* (New York: Sentinel HC, 2011).

14. Patrick F. Fagan, "The Family GDP: How Marriage and Fertility Drive the Economy," *The Natural Family*, March 13, 2010, https:// thenaturalfamily.org/article/the-family-gdp-how-marriage-and-fertility -drive-the-economy.

15. Ibid.

16. Quoted in ibid.

17. Isabel V. Sawhill, "Families at Risk," in Henry J. Aaron and Robert D. Reischauer, eds., *Setting National Priorities: The 2000 Election and Beyond* (Washington, D.C.: Brookings Institution Press, 1999), 97, 108.

18. Robert Rector, "Marriage: America's No. 1 Weapon against Childhood Poverty," *Heritage Foundation Backgrounder*, no. 2465, September 16, 2010, http://thf_media.s3.amazonaws.com/2010/pdf/ bg2465.pdf.

19. Roger Clegg, "Percentage of Births to Unmarried Women," Center for Equal Opportunity, February 26, 2020, https://www.ceousa.org/2020 /02/26/percentage-of-births-to-unmarried-women.

20. See the references in John R. Lott Jr., *Freedomnomics: Why the Free Market Works and Other Half-Baked Theories Don't* (Washington, D.C.: Regnery Publishing, 2007), 164–65.

21. Nicholas Kerry et al., "Experimental and Cross-Cultural Evidence That Parenthood and Parental Care Motives Increase Social Conservatism," *Proceedings of the Royal Society B* 289, no. 1982 (September 14, 2022), https://doi.org/10.1098/rspb.2022.0978.

22. For more detailed statistics on family trends, see Family Facts at: http:// www.familyfacts.org.

23. Benjamin Paris and Jamie Hall, "How Welfare Programs Discourage Marriage: The Case of Pre-K Education Subsidies," *Heritage Foundation Backgrounder*, no. 3742, January 5, 2023, https://www.heritage.org/sites/default/files/2023-02/BG3742.pdf.

24. Janet Adamy, "Why Americans Are Having Fewer Kids," *Wall Street Journal*, May 26, 2023, https://www.wsj.com/articles/why-americans-are-having-fewer-babies-3be7f6a9.

25. "Fertility Rate, Total (Births per Woman)," The World Bank, 2022, https://data.worldbank.org/indicator/SP.DYN.TFRT.IN.

26. Patrick F. Fagan and Scott Talkington, "Ever Had an Unwed Pregnancy," Marriage, Religion, and the Common Good 101, *Mapping America* (Washington, D.C.: Marriage and Religion Research Institute, 2011), http://www.frc.org/mappingamerica/mapping-america-101-likely-to-have-an-unwed-pregnancy.

27. "More Siblings Means Less Chance of Divorce as Adult," *Ohio State News*, August 12, 2013, https://news.osu.edu/more-siblings-means-less-chance-of-divorce-as-adult.

28. See, for example, Tomas Frejka and Charles F. Westoff, "Religion, Religiousness and Fertility in the U.S. and Europe," *European Journal of Population* 24, no. 1 (March 2008): 5–31, https://www.jstor.org/stable/40271476.

29. "New York Abortion Statistics," (using Alan Guttmacher and CDC data), Abort73.com, https://abort73.com/abortion_facts/states/new_york.

30. Eric Kaufmann, *Shall the Religious Inherit the Earth?* (London: Profile Books, 2011).

31. Jonathan Leake, "Atheists a Dying Breed as Nature 'Favours Faithful,'" *Sunday Times*, January 11, 2011, https://www.thetimes.co.uk/article/atheists-a-dying-breed-as-nature-favours-faithful-sr962szfdfn.

Chapter 10: Train Up a Child

1. "Church Dropouts Have Risen to 64%—but What about Those Who Stay?," Barna, September 4, 2019, https://www.barna.com/research/resilient-disciples.

2. Caryle Murphy, "Half of U.S. Adults Raised Catholic Have Left the Church at Some Point," Pew Research Center, September 15, 2015, https://www.pewresearch.org/fact-tank/2015/09/15/half-of-u-s-adults-raised-catholic-have-left-the-church-at-some-point.

3. Jacob Ausubel, Gregory A. Smith, and Alan Cooperman, "Denominational Switching among U.S. Jews: Reform Judaism Has Gained, Conservative Judaism Has Lost," Pew Research Center, June 22, 2021, https://www.pewresearch.org/fact-tank/2021/06/22/

denominational-switching-among-u-s-jews-reform-judaism-has
-gained-conservative-judaism-has-lost.

4. David Carleton, "Old Deluder Satan Act of 1647 (1647)," *First Amendment Encyclopedia*, Middle Tennessee State University, https://mtsu.edu/first-amendment/article/1032/old-deluder-satan-act-of-1647.

5. For a detailed discussion, see Andrew J. Coulson, *Market Education: The Unknown History* (Piscataway, New Jersey: Transaction Publishers, 1999). For a detailed outline of the history of American education, see "A Brief History of Education in America," https://cblpi.org/wp-content/uploads/2015/10/EdHistory_0.pdf.

6. John R. Lott Jr., *Freedomnomics* (Washington, D.C.: Regnery, 2007), 191.

7. Zachary M. Schrag, *The Fires of Philadelphia: Citizen-Soldiers, Nativists, and the 1844 Riots Over the Soul of a Nation* (New York: Pegasus Book, 2021).

8. Richard Land, *The Divided States of America* (Nashville: Thomas Nelson, 2011), 54–55.

9. Lott, *Freedomnomics*, 190–91. See the references on these pages for Lott's academic publications on American education.

10. Kevin Ryan, "Another Coffin Nail for US Public Education," Mercatornet, July 11, 2011, http://www.mercatornet.com/articles/view/another_coffin_nail_for_us_public_education.

11. Keri D. Ingraham and Arina O. Grossu, "Community Schools' 'Woke' Indoctrination Agenda," *Washington Times*, July 27, 2022, https://www.washingtontimes.com/news/2022/jul/27/community-schools-woke-indoctrination-agenda.

12. "How Many Homeschoolers Are in the U.S.? (2022)," Classical Conversations, October 3, 2022, https://classicalconversations.com/blog/how-many-homeschoolers-in-us-2022.

13. For some horror stories, see the Free Sweden website at: http://freesweden.net/religion_index.html.

14. *Pierce v. Society of Sisters*, 28 U.S. 510 (1925).

15. In 2011, investigative reporting revealed Atlanta Public Schools—teachers, principals, and superintendents—had conspired for a decade to falsify scores on standardized tests used to evaluate their schools. See Heather Vogell, "Investigation into APS Cheating Finds Unethical Behavior across Every Level," *Atlanta Journal Constitution*, July 6, 2011, http://www.ajc.com/news/investigation-into-aps-cheating-1001375.html.

16. James Tooley and Pauline Dixon, *Private Education Is Good for the Poor* (Washington, D.C.: Cato Institute Press, 2005), http://www.cato.org/pubs/wtpapers/tooley.pdf. See also James Tooley, *The Beautiful Tree: A Personal Journey into How the World's Poorest People Are Educating Themselves* (Washington, D.C.: Cato Institute Press, 2009).

17. "Teachers Unions Summary," Open Secrets, https://www.opensecrets
.org/industries/indus.php?ind=l1300.

18. Dominic Rushe, "The US Spends More on Education than Other
Countries. Why Is It Falling Behind?," *The Guardian*, February 7,
2018, https://www.theguardian.com/us-news/2018/sep/07/us
-education-spending-finland-south-korea.

19. Kimberly Amadeo, "U.S. Education Rankings Are Falling behind the
Rest of the World," The Balance, March 26, 2023, https://www
.thebalancemoney.com/the-u-s-is-losing-its-competitive-advantage
-3306225.

20. For poll information and the latest summary and explanations of
school choice in America, see *The ABCs of School Choice*, produced
annually by EdChoice. The 2023 edition is available online at https://
www.edchoice.org/wp-content/uploads/2023/01/2023-ABCs-Ready
-for-Web-01-25-23.pdf.

21. Jason Bedrick and Lindsey Burke, "Florida Sets Shining Example on
School Choice. Here's How," Fox News, March 27, 2023, https://www
.foxnews.com/opinion/florida-sets-shining-example-school-choice
-heres-how.

22. See a response to this and other "school choice myths" at "Funding
Students Not Systems," American Federation for Children, https://
www.federationforchildren.org/school-choice-myths.

23. Jennifer Kabbany, "The Higher Ed Bubble Won't Burst in 2023, but It
Will Definitely Deflate," The College Fix, January 3, 2023, https://
www.thecollegefix.com/the-higher-ed-bubble-wont-burst-in-2023-but
-it-will-definitely-deflate. Federal grant and student loan programs were
meant to help poor students get a college education but have shot
college costs into the stratosphere. Since 1985, costs have gone up four
times faster than the rate of inflation. Gordon H. Wadsworth, "Sky
Rocketing College Costs," InflationData.com, October 15, 2010,
http://www.inflationdata.com/inflation/Inflation_Articles/Education_
Inflation.asp. In 2011, total student loan debt topped a trillion dollars.
Tamar Lewin, "Burden of College Loans on Graduates Grows," *New
York Times*, April 11, 2011, http://www.nytimes.com/2011/04/12/
education/12college.html.

24. Stanley Rothman, Robert Lichter, and Neil Nevitte, "Politics and
Professional Advancement among College Faculty," *The Forum* 3, no.
1 (2005): https://www.researchgate.net/publication/40823273_Politics
_and_Professional_Advancement_Among_College_Faculty.

25. You should do your homework, but here's a list of both public and
private colleges that are considered the most conservative: "2023 Most
Conservative Colleges in America," Niche, https://www.niche.com
/colleges/search/most-conservative-colleges.

26. Christian philosopher Alvin Plantinga mentions these two ideas under the names of "creative anti-realism" and "naturalism" in his famous article, "On Christian Scholarship," http://www.veritas-ucsb.org/library/plantinga/ocs.html. See also his "Advice to Christian Philosophers," *Faith and Philosophy: Journal of the Society of Christian Philosophers* 1 (October 1984), https://www.leaderu.com/truth/1truth10.html.

27. Pete Hegseth and David Goodwin, *The Battle for the American Mind: Uprooting a Century of Miseducation* (New York: Broadside Books, 2022).

28. For more details, read Stacy Manning and Katy Faust, *Raising Conservative Kids in a Woke City* (Brentwood, Tennessee: Post Hill Press, 2023); Hillary Morgan Ferrer, *Mama Bear Apologetics* (Eugene, Oregon: Harvest House Publishers, 2019).

29. Jill Christensen, "Children and Screen Time: How Much Is Too Much?" Mayo Clinic Health System, May 28, 2021, https://www.mayoclinichealthsystem.org/hometown-health/speaking-of-health/children-and-screen-time.

30. We recommend the C. S. Lewis six-pack for high schoolers. These are six little books, often bundled together as Signature Classics, by the great twentieth-century scholar and apologist: *Mere Christianity, The Screwtape Letters, A Grief Observed, The Problem of Pain, Miracles,* and *The Great Divorce*. Don't let your children leave home until they've read them. And while you're at it, get them a copy of J. Budziszewski's *How to Stay Christian in College* (Colorado Springs: NavPress, 2004).

Chapter 11: All Men Are Created Equal

1. Shirley Leung, "Effort to Close Gender and Racial Wage Gap Kicks into High Gear with Soccer Player Samantha Mewis, AIM," *Boston Globe*, May 9, 2023, https://www.bostonglobe.com/2023/05/09/business/effort-close-gender-racial-wage-gap-kicks-into-high-gear-with-soccer-player-samantha-mewis-aim.

2. Lila Guterman, "Statistically Speaking, 2019 Nobel Prize Lineup of 11 Men and One Woman Was Bound to Happen," Science, October 15, 2019, https://www.science.org/content/article/statistically-speaking-2019-nobel-prize-lineup-11-men-and-one-woman-was-bound-happen.

3. James Lindsay, "Equity," New Discourses, https://newdiscourses.com/tftw-equity.

4. Henry Hazlitt, *Economics in One Lesson* (New York: Three Rivers Press, 1979), 136.

5. For years, we heard the standard of a dollar a day per person. The World Bank bumped that to $1.25 in 2005. See Martin Ravallion,

Shaohua Chen, and Prem Sangraula, "Dollar a Day Revisited," *The World Bank Economic Review* 23, no. 2 (2009): 163–84. These income definitions make it easier to make comparisons, but poverty surely has more to do with material needs than with income.

6. "HHS Poverty Guidelines for 2023," U.S. Department of Health and Human Services, January 19, 2023, https://aspe.hhs.gov/topics/poverty -economic-mobility/poverty-guidelines.

7. Brian Goesling, Hande Inanc, and Angela Rachidi, "Success Sequence: A Synthesis of the Literature," *OPRE Report Number* 2020-41, December 2020, https://www.acf.hhs.gov/sites/default/files/documents/ opre/Success_sequence_review_2020_508_0.pdf.

8. "Income of Families and Persons in the United States: 1960," Report Number P60-37, U.S. Census Bureau, January 17, 1962, https://www .census.gov/library/publications/1962/demo/p60-037.html.

9. Rakesh Kochhar and Stella Sechopoulos, "How the American Middle Class Has Changed in the Past Five Decades," Pew Research Center, April 20, 2022, https://www.pewresearch.org/short-reads/2022/04/20/ how-the-american-middle-class-has-changed-in-the-past-five-decades.

10. Katherine Schaeffer, "6 Facts about Economic Inequality in the U.S.," Pew Research Center, February 7, 2020, https://www.pewresearch.org/ short-reads/2020/02/07/6-facts-about-economic-inequality-in-the-u-s.

11. Kochhar and Sechopoulos, "How the American Middle Class Has Changed in the Past Five Decades."

12. Age is one of the main factors that determine one's income and location on the distribution of national incomes. See Santiago Budría Rodríguez et al., "Updated Facts on the U.S. Distributions of Earnings, Income, and Wealth," *Federal Reserve Bank of Minneapolis Quarterly Review* 26, no. 3 (Summer 2002): 3, https://doi.org/10.21034/qr.2631.

13. "Percent of Income Spent on Food in the U.S.," Farm & Food Facts (2006), http://www.ilfb2.org/fff06/51.pdf. The big exceptions to this decline of real prices over time are in housing, college tuition, and health care. They're exceptions because of government meddling with these markets, which was designed to make them more available to more people. Instead, it has caused their prices to go up much faster than inflation for decades.

14. "Food-at-Home Prices Increased 11.4 Percent in 2022 Compared with 2021," USDA Economic Research Service, last updated February 27, 2023, https://www.ers.usda.gov/data-products/chart-gallery/gallery/ chart-detail/?chartId=76961.

Chapter 12: Am I My Brother's Keeper?

1. For detailed documentation, see Amity Shlaes, *The Forgotten Man: A New History of the Great Depression* (New York: HarperCollins, 2007).

2. "Biden's Budget: A Future That's Built on Government Dependence," House Budget Committee, March 15, 2023, https://budget.house.gov/press-release/7582.

3. Michael Tanner, "Replacing Welfare," *Cato Policy Report* 18, no. 6 (November/December 1996): https://www.cato.org/sites/cato.org/files/serials/files/policy-report/1996/11/cpr-18n6-1.pdf.

4. See Robert Rector and Rachel Sheffield, "Setting Priorities for Welfare Reform," *The Heritage Foundation Issue Brief* no. 4520, February 24, 2016, http://thf-reports.s3.amazonaws.com/2016/IB4520.pdf.

5. For detailed analysis through 2014, see Robert Rector and Rachel Sheffield, "The War on Poverty after Fifty Years," *Heritage Foundation Backgrounder*, no. 2955, September 15, 2014, http://report.heritage.org/bg2955.

6. "3.4 Million More Children in Poverty in February 2022 than December 2021," Center on Poverty and Social Policy, Columbia University, March 23, 2022, https://www.povertycenter.columbia.edu/news-internal/monthly-poverty-february-2022#:~:text=Monthly%20poverty%20remained%20elevated%20in,for%20the%20total%20US%20population.

7. The World Bank study and quote are referenced in Dambisa Moyo, *Dead Aid: Why Aid Is Not Working and How There Is a Better Way for Africa* (New York: Farrar, Straus and Giroux, 2009), 39.

8. Ibid., 3–5.

9. Raghuram G. Rajan and Arvind Subramanian, "Aid and Growth: What Does the Cross-Country Evidence Really Show?" *The Review of Economics and Statistics* 90, no. 4 (November 2008): 643–65, http://www.mitpressjournals.org/doi/abs/10.1162/rest.90.4.643.

10. Moyo, *Dead Aid*, 143, 144.

11. Ibid., xix.

12. William Easterly, *The White Man's Burden: Why the West's Efforts to Aid the Rest Have Done So Much Ill and So Little Good* (New York: Penguin Books 2007), 13–14.

13. Read more at "Water for LIFE," Life Outreach International, https://lifetoday.org/outreaches/water-for-life.

14. You can read about VisionTrust at http://www.visiontrust.org.

15. "The World Bank in Haiti," The World Bank, last updated March 31, 2023, https://www.worldbank.org/en/country/haiti/overview.

Chapter 13: A Place to Call Our Own

1. The only successful examples of communal living are outside the political realm. Rodney Stark, *The Victory of Reason: How Christianity Led to Freedom, Capitalism, and Western Success* (New York: Random House, 2005). For a history of socialism that discusses some of voluntary communal experiments, see Joshua Muravchik, *Heaven on Earth: The Rise, Fall, and Afterlife of Socialism* (San Francisco: Encounter Books, 2003).

2. Quoted in Matthew Spalding, *We Still Hold These Truths* (Wilmington: ISI Books, 2009), 70.

3. Richard Pipes, *Communism: A History* (New York: Modern Library Chronicles, 2003), 45.

4. Lenin thought of manufacturing, transportation, the generation of energy, and the like as the "commanding heights" of the economy, so he was able to sell the idea of partial privatization of agricultural land to his party, the Bolsheviks. See Arnold Kling and Nick Shultz, "The New Commanding Heights," *National Affairs* 8 (Summer 2011), http://nationalaffairs.com/publications/detail/the-new-commanding-heights.

5. James D. Gwartney et al., *Common Sense Economics* (New York: St. Martin's Press, 2010), 48.

6. Stéphane Courtois et al., *The Black Book of Communism* (Cambridge, Massachusetts: Harvard University Press, 1999), 463–64.

7. See it online at Leo XIII, *Rerum Novarum*, May 15, 1891, Libreria Editrice Vaticana, http://www.vatican.va/holy_father/leo_xiii/encyclicals/documents/hf_l-xiii_enc_15051891_rerum-novarum_en.html.

8. From *The Politics*.

9. Spalding, *We Still Hold These Truths*, 80.

10. Hernando de Soto, *The Mystery of Capital: Why Capitalism Triumphs in the West and Fails Everywhere Else* (New York: Basic Books, 2000).

11. Ibid., 19.

12. Ibid., 21, 26–27.

13. Ibid., 5–7.

14. Rafael Di Tella, Sebastian Galiani, and Ernesto Schargrodsky, "Property Rights and Beliefs: Evidence from the Allocation of Land Titles to Squatters," *Quarterly Journal of Economics* 122, no. 1 (February 2007): 209–41, https://www.jstor.org/stable/25098841.

15. Riley Walters and David Beleson, "This Chinese Company's Intellectual Property Theft Is No Isolated Incident," Heritage Foundation, February 12, 2018, https://www.heritage.org/asia/commentary/chinese-companys-intellectual-property-theft-no-isolated-incident.

Chapter 14: Free to Prosper

1. In recent years, this term has become a common way to attack defenders of the market economy without making an actual argument. See, for instance, Jim Wallis, "Elizabeth and Goliath," *Sojourners*, February 11, 2010.
2. Adam Smith leads with this idea of valuing things in terms of labor or cost of production in *An Inquiry into the Nature and Causes of the Wealth of Nations*, ed. Edwin Cannan (New York: Modern Library, 1994), lix. Nevertheless, the idea was more central to Marx's thought than to Smith's.
3. Smith, *An Inquiry into the Nature and Causes of the Wealth of Nations*, 485.
4. A mature form of Hayek's argument is in *The Fatal Conceit: The Errors of Socialism* (Chicago: University of Chicago Press, 1989).
5. Thomas Sowell, *Basic Economics* (New York; Basic Books, 2015), 11.
6. James D. Gwartney et al., *Common Sense Economics* (New York: St. Martin's Press, 2010), 8.

Chapter 15: Global Trade, Globalism, and the Threat of Communist China

1. Marian L. Tupy and Gale L. Pooley, *Superabundance: The Story of Population Growth, Innovation, and Human Flourishing on an Infinitely Bountiful Planet* (Washington, D.C.: Cato Institute Press, 2022).
2. Gale Pooley and Marian L. Tupy, "The Simon Abundance Index 2023," Human Progress, April 22, 2023, https://www.humanprogress.org/the-simon-abundance-index-2023.
3. Ryszard Legutko, *The Demon in Democracy: Totalitarian Temptations in Free Societies* (New York: Encounter Books, 2016).
4. See, for instance, Bani Dugal, "Is the Nation State Past Its Sell-by-Date?," World Economic Forum, January 22, 2015, https://www.weforum.org/agenda/2015/01/idea-of-a-nation-state-past-its-sell-by-date.
5. Kerwin Kofi Charles, Erik Hurst, and Mariel Schwartz, "The Transformation of Manufacturing and the Decline in U.S. Employment," *NBER Working Paper 24468*, March 2018, https://www.nber.org/papers/w24468. See also Anne Case and Angus Deaton, *Deaths of Despair and the Future of Capitalism* (Princeton, New Jersey: Princeton University Press, 2021).
6. Scott Lincicome, "Testing the 'China Shock': Was Normalizing Trade with China a Mistake?," *CATO Institute Policy Analysis no. 895*, July 8, 2020, https://www.cato.org/policy-analysis/testing-china-shock-was-normalizing-trade-china-mistake; David Autor, David Dorn, and

Gordon Hanson, "On the Persistence of the China Shock," Brookings Papers on Economic Activity, Fall 2021, https://www.brookings.edu /articles/on-the-persistence-of-the-china-shock; Scott Kennedy and Ilaria Mazzocco, "The China Shock: Reevaluating the Debate," Big Data China, October 14, 2022, https://bigdatachina.csis.org/the-china -shock-reevaluating-the-debate.

7. "Manufacturing by Country 2023," World Population Review, https:// worldpopulationreview.com/country-rankings/manufacturing-by -country.

8. Ashton Cohen, "Why America No Longer Builds Anything," GenBiz, March 28, 2023, https://genbiz.com/why-america-no-longer-builds -anything.

9. This does not mean there will be fewer total jobs in the future. See Jay W. Richards, *The Human Advantage: The Future of American Work in the Age of Smart Machines* (New York: Forum Books, 2018).

10. Adam Smith, *Wealth of Nations*, ed. Charles Jesse Bullock (New York: Cosimo Classics, 2007), 353.

11. See the animated graphs on worldwide economic growth at Gapminder, http://www.gapminder.org/world.

12. See the latest ranking of countries on the 2023 Index of Economic Freedom, http://www.heritage.org/Index.

13. This is through its parent company ByteDance.

14. Dov S. Zakheim, "Time to Shut Down All Confucius Institutes— Whatever They Might Be Called," *The Hill*, November 11, 2022, https://thehill.com/opinion/national-security/3729453-time-to-shut -down-all-confucius-institutes-whatever-they-might-be-called.

15. Ivan Watson and Ben Westcott, "Watched, Judged, Detained: Leaked Chinese Government Records Reveal Detailed Surveillance Reports on Uyghur Families and Beijing's Justification for Mass Detentions," CNN, February 2020, https://www.cnn.com/interactive/2020/02/asia/ xinjiang-china-karakax-document-intl-hnk.

16. Kevin Roberts, "Foreword," in James J. Carafano, Michael Pillsbury, Jeff M. Smith, and Andrew J. Harding, eds., "Winning the New Cold War: A Plan for Countering China," *Heritage Foundation Special Report* no. 270, March 28, 2023, https://www.heritage.org/sites/ default/files/2023-03/SR270_0.pdf.

17. "Semiconductor Manufacturing by Country 2023," World Population Review, https://worldpopulationreview.com/country-rankings/ semiconductor-manufacturing-by-country.

18. Chris Miller, *Chip War: The Fight for the World's Most Critical Technology* (New York: Scribner, 2022).

Chapter 16: Peace in Our Borders

1. The rhetoric of both the Catholic bishops and the NAE has moderated in recent years, away from straight amnesty. But they still call (if somewhat vaguely) for installment-plan amnesty. See, for instance, Mario Dorsonville, Walter Kim, and Ed Litton, "We Represent Diverse Christian Denominations, but We Agree on Immigration Reform," *Newsweek*, March 9, 2022, https://www.newsweek.com/we-represent -diverse-christian-denominations-we-agree-immigration-reform-opinion -1685722.

2. Mark Morgan and Mike Howell, "How Feds Use Charities to Hide the True Cost of the US Border Crisis," *New York Post*, December 21, 2022, https://nypost.com/2022/12/21/how-feds-use-charities-to-hide -the-true-cost-of-the-us-border-crisis.

3. Mark Steyn attributes the quote to James C. Bennett. Allahpundit, "Steyn on Multiculturalism," Hot Air, August 25, 2006, https://hotair .com/allahpundit/2006/08/25/steyn-on-multiculturalism-n143776.

4. Andy J. Semotiuk, "U.S. Immigration – 2022 Year in Review," *Forbes*, December 22, 2022, https://www.forbes.com/sites/andyjsemotiuk /2022/12/30/us-immigration-2022-year-in-review/?sh=71867f721da3.

5. Mark Krikorian, "Creating Facts on the Ground," *National Review*, May 26, 2011, https://www.nationalreview.com/corner/creating-facts -ground-mark-krikorian-2/.

6. Tristan Justice, "Left-Wing Martha's Vineyard Elites Deport Illegal Immigrants after Just 24 Hours," The Federalist, September 16, 2022, https://thefederalist.com/2022/09/16/left-wing-marthas-vineyard-elites -deport-illegal-immigrants-after-just-24-hours.

7. "How Many Illegal Aliens Are in the United States? A 2023 Update," Federation for American Immigration Reform, June 22, 2023, https:// www.fairus.org/issue/illegal-immigration/how-many-illegal-aliens-are -united-states-2023-update#:~:text=FINDINGS,population %20estimate%20of%2015.5%20million.

8. Steven Camarota et al., "Mapping the Impact of Immigration on Public Schools," Center for Immigration Studies, June 20, 2023, https://cis.org/PanelTranscripts/panel-mapping-impact-immigration -schools.

9. Virginia Allen, "Cartels, not US Government, Are Choosing 'Who Enters This Country,' Sen. Sinema Says," The Daily Signal, April 6, 2023, https://www.dailysignal.com/2023/04/06/cartels-not-us -government-are-choosing-who-enters-this-county-sen-sinema-says.

10. "Migrants in Mexico Fall Victim to Rampant Scams on Their Way to the US," Associated Press, June 28, 2023, https://apnews.com/article/ migrants-misinformation-999462e93876c4181a9759974d10ff18.

11. Lora Ries, "Biden's Misleading New Asylum Rule Is a Gimmick atop a Shell Game," The Daily Signal, February 24, 2023, https://www

.dailysignal.com/2023/02/24/bidens-misleading-new-asylum-rule-is
-a-gimmick-atop-a-shell-game.

12. We're not saying we should forbid the use of other languages or outlaw
road signs written in Spanish. We would all do well to learn other
languages.

13. James Jay Carafano, John G. Malcolm, and Jack Spencer, "An Agenda
for American Immigration Reform," *Heritage Foundation Special
Report* No. 210, February 20, 2019, https://www.heritage.org/sites/
default/files/2019-02/SR210_0.pdf.

Chapter 17: Be Fruitful

1. The generic word "man" in Hebrew is *adam*, which is related to the
word "ground," *adamah*.

2. See the helpful interactive charts: Max Roser, "Employment in
Agriculture," Our World in Data, https://ourworldindata.org/
employment-in-agriculture.

3. "Fast Facts about Agriculture & Food," American Farm Bureau
Federation, https://www.fb.org/newsroom/fast-facts.

4. Michael Novak, *The Spirit of Democratic Capitalism*, rev. ed.
(Lanham, Maryland: Madison Books, 2000).

5. Peter Drucker, *Post-Capitalist Society* (Oxford: Butterworth-
Heinemann, 2013), 18.

6. "Timeline of Invention," Academic Kids, https://www.academickids
.com/encyclopedia/index.php/Timeline_of_invention.

7. Richard L. Stroup, *Eco-nomics: What Everyone Should Know about
Economics and the Environment* (Washington, D.C.: Cato Institute
Press, 2003), 10.

8. *The Call of the Entrepreneur*, directed by Simon Scionka (Grand
Rapids, Michigan: Acton Media, 2007).

9. George Gilder, *Wealth & Poverty* (Washington, D.C.: Regnery
Gateway, 2012), 47.

Chapter 18: Have Dominion

1. Lynn White Jr., "The Historical Roots of Our Ecologic Crisis," *Science*
155, no. 3767 (March 10, 1967): 1203–7, doi.org/10.1126/science.155
.3767.1203.

2. Peter Gwynne, "The Cooling World," *Newsweek*, April 28, 1975,
https://iseethics.files.wordpress.com/2012/06/the-cooling-world
-newsweek-april-28-1975.pdf.

3. "Carbon Dioxide Now More than 50% Higher than Pre-Industrial
Levels," National Oceanic and Atmospheric Administration, June 3,
2022, https://www.noaa.gov/news-release/carbon-dioxide-now-more
-than-50-higher-than-pre-industrial-levels.

4. Christopher Monckton et al., "Why Models Run Hot: Results from an Irreducibly Simple Climate Model," *Science Bulletin* 60, no. 1 (January 2015): 122–35, doi.org/10.1007/s11434-014-0699-2.

5. Roy Spencer, *The Great Global Warming Blunder: How Mother Nature Fooled the World's Top Climate Scientists* (New York: Encounter Books, 2010); Johannes Mülmenstädt et al., "An Underestimated Negative Cloud Feedback from Cloud Lifetime Changes," *Nature Climate Change* 11 (June 3, 2021): 508–13, doi.org /10.1038/s41558-021-01038-1. The best we can say now is that most models overpredict warming and so don't accurately model the real climate. But we don't know why.

6. In *An Inconvenient Truth*, Al Gore grossly misrepresented this. He shifted the placement of the records on his display to make it look like warming took place after carbon dioxide increased.

7. Guillermo Gonzalez and Jay W. Richards, *The Privileged Planet* (Washington, D.C.: Regnery Publishing, 2004), 21–43.

8. See Lawrence Solomon, "Science Getting Settled," *Financial Post*, August 26, 2011, https://financialpost.com/opinion/lawrence-solomon -science-now-settled.

9. For a report of this, see Kate Ravilious, "Mars Melt Hints at Solar, Not Human, Cause for Warming, Scientist Says," *National Geographic News*, February 28, 2007. Ironically, this story does report the facts but tries to dismiss their obvious meaning.

10. Dennis Avery and S. Fred Singer, *Unstoppable Global Warming: Every 1,500 Years* (Lanham, Maryland: Rowman & Littlefield, 2007).

11. Steven E. Koonin, *Unsettled: What Climate Science Tells Us, What It Doesn't, and Why It Matters* (New York: BenBella Books, 2021).

12. Bjørn Lomborg, *Cool It* (New York: Knopf, 2007), 40–3. See also Lomborg's more recent book *False Alarm: How Climate Change Panic Costs Us Trillions, Hurts the Poor, and Fails to Fix the Planet* (New York: Basic Books, 2020).

13. Indur M. Goklany, "Fossil Fuels Are the Greenest Energy Sources," CO_2 Coalition, August 30, 2022, https://co2coalition.org/publications/ fossil-fuels-are-the-greenest-energy-sources.

14. William Cline, "The Challenge of Global Warming," Copenhagen Consensus, March 2004, https://copenhagenconsensus.com/sites /default/files/imported/cp-globalwarmingfinished.pdf.

15. Bjørn Lomborg, "Impact of Current Climate Proposals," *Global Policy* 7, no. 1 (February 2016): 109–18, doi.org/10.1111/1758-5899.12295.

16. Michael Shellenberger explains the details well in *Apocalypse Never: Why Environmental Alarmism Harms Us All* (New York: Harper, 2020).

17. Alex Epstein, *Fossil Future: Why Global Human Flourishing Requires More Oil, Coal, and Natural Gas—Not Less* (New York: Portfolio, 2022).

18. See discussion at the Copenhagen Consensus Center, www.copenhagenconsensus.com. See also the compilation *Global Crises, Global Solution*, edited by Bjørn Lomborg (Cambridge: Cambridge University Press, 2004).

19. Julia Simon, "China Is Building Six Times More New Coal Plants than Other Countries, Report Finds," NPR, March 2, 2023, https://www.npr.org/2023/03/02/1160441919/china-is-building-six-times-more-new-coal-plants-than-other-countries-report-fin.

20. Anna Yukhananov and Valerie Volcovici, "World Bank to Limit Financing of Coal-Fired Plants," Reuters, July 16, 2013, https://www.reuters.com/article/us-worldbank-climate-coal/world-bank-to-limit-financing-of-coal-fired-plants-idUSBRE96F19U20130716.

21. Bjørn Lomborg, *The Skeptical Environmentalist* (Cambridge: Cambridge University Press, 2001), 3–33.

22. Steven F. Hayward, *Index of Leading Environmental Indicators*, 14th edition (San Francisco: Pacific Research Institute and Washington, D.C.: American Enterprise Institute, 2009).

23. Lomborg, The Skeptical Environmentalist, 33. For more recent information, see Indur M. Goklany, "Have Increases in Population, Affluence and Technology Worsened Human and Environmental Well-Being?" *Electronic Journal of Sustainable Development* 1, no. 3 (2009): https://www.researchgate.net/publication/253464732_Have_increases_in_population_affluence_and_technology_worsened_human_and_environmental_well-being.

24. There is, of course, a lot of debate about the details, but the EKC seems to be holding up well for pollutants such as sulfur dioxide. Steven F. Hayward, "The China Syndrome and the Environmental Kuznets Curve," American Enterprise Institute, December 21, 2005, https://www.aei.org/research-products/report/the-china-syndrome-and-the-environmental-kuznets-curve. See also Indur M. Goklany, *The Improving State of the World: Why We're Living Longer, Healthier, More Comfortable Lives on a Clean Planet* (Washington, D.C.: Cato Institute, 2007).

25. Quoted in CFACT's *Special Report from Washington* 5, no. 2 (January 2011).

26. One Christian organization that we find helpful is the Cornwall Alliance for the Stewardship of Creation, http://www.cornwallalliance.org.

27. The Property and Environment Research Center specializes in finding market solutions to environmental problems; learn more at http://www.perc.org.

Chapter 19: Till It and Keep It

1. Tracy McVeigh, "Beckhams a 'Bad Example' for Families," *The Guardian*, July 16, 2011, http://www.guardian.co.uk/lifeandstyle/2011/jul/17/population-control-beckham-family.
2. David Graber, "Mother Nature as a Hothouse Flower," *Los Angeles Times*, October 22, 1989; quoted in Steven F. Hayward, *Mere Environmentalism* (Washington, D.C:. AEI Press, 2010), 18. This brief volume describes the biblical perspective on humans and the natural world.
3. Paul Ehrlich, *The Population Bomb* (New York: Ballantine Books, 1968), xi.
4. Thomas L. Friedman, "The Earth Is Full," *New York Times*, June 8, 2011, http://www.nytimes.com/2011/06/08/opinion/08friedman.html.
5. We're not saying that this is good or bad. We're just reporting the demographic facts. People in some cultures will start having lots of babies in 2045. But there is no trend suggesting that right now, and the move toward lower fertility rates at high levels of industrialization holds, to some degree, in every culture. See "World Population to 2300," by the UN's Department of Economic & Social Affairs (New York: United Nations, 2004), https://www.un.org/development/desa/pd/sites/www.un.org.development.desa.pd/files/files/documents/2020/Jan/un_2002_world_population_to_2300.pdf.
6. Thomas Sowell, *Basic Economics* (New York: Basic Books, 2004), 205.
7. Ibid., 207. For examples of historical prices of resources, see Julian Simon, *The Ultimate Resource* 2 (Princeton, New Jersey: Princeton University Press, 1996), 23–52. Simon discusses his famous bet with Ehrlich on pp. 32–3. See also Bjørn Lomborg, *The Skeptical Environmentalist* (Cambridge: Cambridge University Press, 2001), 118–48.
8. From the NRPE page on "environmental justice": "Faith and Creation," National Religious Partnership for the Environment, http://www.nrpe.org/perspectives—resources.html.
9. Quoted in Lomborg, *The Skeptical Environmentalist*, 120. This quote has been attributed to different people, including Sheik Yamani, Saudi Arabian oil minister and founder of OPEC.

Conclusion

1. For some practical advice on how to do this, see Arthur C. Brooks, *Love Your Enemies: How Decent People Can Save America from the Culture of Contempt* (New York: Broadside Books, 2019).
2. Excerpted from a longer quote reprinted as the Meditation of the Day for August 9, 2011, in *Magnificat*.